THE CIVIL DIVISIONS OF THE COUNTY OF DOI DIGESTED AND ARRANGED, COMPRISING LIST MINISTERIAL OFFICERS, MAGISTRATES, AND SUBORDINATE OFFICERS • EDWARD BOSWELL

-:c- -:c- -:c- -:c- -:c- -:c- -:c- -:c-

SVCIVIL DIVISION OP THE ©ountg of Dorset. 7/ METHODICALLY DIGESTED AND ARRANGED. COMPRIZING LISTS OP THE CIVIL MINISTERIAL OFFICERS. MAGISTRATES, AND SUBORDINATE OFFICERS: WITH A COMPLETE NOMINA VILLARUM, IN FOUR PARTS; A LIST OF THE COUNTY AND OTHER BRIDGES; TOGETHER WITH THE ANNUAL VALUE OF REAL PROPERTY; AMOUNT OF THE LAND-TAX; OF THE POOR'S-RATE, AND COUNTY RATE; THE POPULATION; AND THE RULES AND ORDERS FOR REGULATION OF THE PRACTICE OF THE QUARTER SESSIONS; , AND OTHER MATTERS: WITH REMARKS AND OBSERVATIONS THEREON. K AN APPENDIX " CONTAINING 1 '» ABSTRACTS Off RJITURNSOF CHARITA-BLE DONATIONS, 'J t CORRECTED TO THE PRESENT TIME. *Vfot* Seionti IjWtfon: CORRECTED, AUGMENTED, AND IMPB-OVED. BY EDWARD BOS WELL. Borrfjester: PRINTED AND PUBLISHED BY WESTON, SIMONDS, AND SYDENHAM.

1916 SUBSCRIPTION OF 1913 TO

The Right Hon. EDWARD EARL Of DIGBY, VISCOUNT COLESHILL, BARON DIGBY IN ENGLAND, AND LORD DIGBY, BARON OF GEASHILL, IN IRELAND, LORD LIEUTENANT, AND CUSTOS ROTULO-RUM, D.C.L., &c. &c. &c. AND TO THE HIGH SHERIFF, AND MAG-ISTRATES OF THE COUNTY OF DORSET, THIS WORK IS DEDICATED, BY THEIR MUCH OBLIGED AND OBEDIENT SERVANT, THE AUTHOR. pre-fare *IN presenting to the Public, at the Solicitations of many of the Magistrates and others, a New Edition of " The Civil Division of the County of Dorset," the Editor begs to state, that in conse-quence of the many Alterations which have taken place since the Publication of the first Edition, it became necessary for the whole to be re-written, which has been done, and other Matters in-troduced throughout. The same method has however been pursued in the pre-sent, as in the former Edition: and in or-der to render the Work more generally useful and easy to be consulted, in ad-dition to the Indexes, he has prefixed a Table of the Contents. It would be su-perfluous for the Editor to enlarge up-on the probable Advantages of a Work of this kind as a Book of reference; but he may be permitted to hope that it will be found useful, not only to the Mag-istrates, whose attention to the good of the Community requires that they should have all the Information and As-sistance which can be afforded them, but also to every Public Officer, Parish Officer, Land Owner, and principal In-habitant of the County. Dorchester, June, 1833.*

Eittrotmrttom

The Shire, or County of Dorset, is a maritime County, situated in the South West of England, between 50. 30'. and

51. 6'. North Lat. and 1. 58'. and 30. 11'. West Long. bounded on the North by Somersetshire and Wiltshire, on the West by Devonshire and part of Somersetshire, on the East by Hampshire, and Southward 'tis all Sea Coast; is in length from North to South about 35m. and in breadth from East to West 55m. and is nearly 160m. in circumference, according to the latest authorities: it appears to be 1005 square *statute* miles, or 043,200 acres; wherefore the number of inhabitants in each square mile, containing 640 acres, according to the last population returns (1831) averages 158 persons.

The County is divided into 9 Divisions; 35 Hundreds; 22 Liberties, and 8 Boroughs *(see p. 27)*; also into 241 Parishes; 41 parochial Chapelries; 5 extra-parochial Places, and 3 Tithings and Hamlets, which maintain their own poor; and it contains 20 Towns; 404 Tithings; 253 Vills; 244 Hamlets, and 617 Farms and Lands.

The Names of the principal *Civil Ministerial Officers,* and Magistrates, having jurisdiction and authority within the County, and the subordinate Officers under them, with their salaries, fees, and allowances, are given, and Lists thereof digested and arranged, according to the method adopted by Mr. Justice Blackstone, commencing from different periods, and continued to the present time, under separate heads; These three Places belong to the Parishes of Canford Magna anil lieer Regis. with the dates and every other matter relative to these appointments.

The 9 Divisions, above mentioned, were newly arranged at Midsummer Sessions, 1830, and this arrangement was carried into effect the 1st of September following, stats. 9 G. 4, c. 43, and 10 G. 4, c. 46. The *number* of the Divisions is the same as in the year 1740, (see *p.* 108), but the *names* are more agreeable to modern usage. These Divisions have been formed by a junction of the small Tithings and Places, and by a partition of the large Hundreds and Liberties, from one Division to another, as seemed most convenient and proper to be altered or changed; regard

having been had to the distances of each Tithing and Place, in every Division, from the Town where special Sessions are held. Part II. contains the *Tithings only* in each Hundred, Liberty, and Division; and Part IV. contains the *Parishes* and *Places* which maintain their own Poor in each of the New Divisions.

The 35 Hundreds, or some of them, have, for the convenience of the public, been severed; and such Hundreds are situate in two or more Divisions: therefore, in order to shew the extent of such alterations, and the number of Tithings, Parishes, and Places in each Division, a *Synopsis* is given, shewing all the Divisions, and the whoie number of Tithings, Parishes, and Places, originally in the Old Divisions, and how the same are now disposed of in the New Divisions mentioned in Parts II. and IV. pp. 108 and 109.

The 22 Liber Ties, or some of them, have been severed in the same manner as the Hundreds, and by the like authority; and the Synopsis shows the extent of the alterations, and where the Tithings, &c., are now placed—*see* Part II. p. 106.

It has been remarked that to reform ancient customs which have been long associated with the occurrences of common life, is however, an inconvenient task. An instance of this occurs in Wales *temp* Hen. 8,1535, for the ancient Cantresses and Commots were altered into *Hundreds* by commission under the Great Seal; the alteration met however with much difficulty, and, although extended periods were allowed for its taking effect, yet the new Counties and Hundreds exhibit more instances of distinct boundary, i. e. of Parishes, and Townships, not contuminous with the County or Hundred than do the ancient Counties: while the remembrance of the abolished Cantresses and Commots still occasionally creatts some confusion.— See *Prelim. Ola. to Pop. Abst,* 1811. The 8 Boroughs have been placed in he same manneras the Hundreds, &c, and (he Synopsis shews the alterations, and where these Boroughs now are.

The 241 Parishes are numbered and

placed alphabetically, Part I. col. 2. These Parishes contain the precincts of the parochial Parish Church, and are *primaries Ecclesice,* or Mother Church; originally the Kingdom, with reference to *Civil* Matters, was divided into Towns and Vills; and Parishes were a Division in reference to Ecclesiastical affairs only; the Common Law took no notice of Parishes, but as Vills, for all Parishes have, or had originally, Vills, though there are Parishes in this County where the Vill which retains the name of the Parish, is depopulated and the Church destroyed: these are noted where they occur. However in 1530, (22 Hen. 8, c. 12,) Parishes became Divisions, and are taken notice of in (*ivil* matters. — H*Hlliams's Justice,* 1. p. 587.—*Freeman's Hep.* This mixture of the Civil and Ecclesiastical Divisions has created great confusion; and Mr. Justice Blackstone observes, that "wbere the *statute* law have not the foundation of the *common law* to build on, what miserable shifts and lame expedients have from time to time been adopted, in order to patch up the flaws occasioned by this neglect."—*Comm.* 1, vol. p. 365

The 41 Parochial Chapelries are also numbered, Fart I. col. 3, and placed under the Parishes to which they belong. These Chapelries have the Liberties of Baptism and Sepulture, and have Chapel wardens; but they are not exempted from the visitation of the ordinary, nor are the Parishioners who resort thither, from the repairs of the *Mother* Church, especially if they bury there; for those Chapels generally belong to, and are as it were part of the Mother Church, and the Parishioners are *obliged* to go to the Mother Church, but not to the Chapel.— *Rolls Abri.* 289. The *Chapels,* not numbered, are Chapels of ease.

Extraparochial *Places* are such as are out of any Parish, and are priviledged and exempt from the

B duties of a Parish: heretofore there were lands in various parts of the Kingdom in the hands, probably, of irreligious and careless owners, situate in Forests and desert Places, and which for unsearchable reasons wore never united to any Parish, and therefore continue to this day Extraparochial—*Black. Comm.* vol.1, p. 113; and, it has been said, that these Places are usually found to have been the site of *religious houses* or of *ancient castles,* whose owners may have been supposed, in rude times, to have resisted any interference with their authority within the limits of their residence.—*Pop. Abstracts,* 1811. The 5 Places in Part 1, col. 2, claiming to be Extraparochial, are numbered, viz:—114, *Hanford* which anciently belonged to *Tarrant Abbey,* and the Glebe and Tithes of the *Parish* were possessed by that Abbey, and having passed through various hands is now in possession of the present owner.

No. 119.—*Heringslone* belonged to Farringdon Winterbome Parish, until the Vill of Farringdon 'became depopulated and the Church destroyed; and then a Chapel was built in Herringstoue House, and consecrated, for divine service to be performed there.

No. 144.—*Leiveston* belonged to Longburton Parish, which was in *Sherborne Abbey.* It now pays the Rates to Lillington Parish and the Land Tax to Holnest Chapelry.

No. 219.—*Steepleton Preston* (more properly Steepleton Iwerne,) was anciently a distinct Parish, and maintained its own poor, but now the Vill is depopulated, and but one house remaining.

No. 279.—*Woodyates West*—formerly the Parsonage belonged to *Tarrant Abbey,* it is now united, and pays to Pentridge Parish; therefore every one of these places seem, very anciently, to have been distinct *Parishes,* or united as above mentioned. There are 3 other Places which maintain their own

"Why and when this Parish had the addition of *Preston* the Editor has not beenable to discover, except from *Priest-town,* which is synonimous with *Steeple-town.* He has kept to the names and spelling found in the ancient records, otherwise he is apprehensive, much contusion might arise to make any alteration in the present day.

jioor, viz:—Longfieet, a Tithing and Hamlet, and Parkstone a Hamlet, both in CanfordMagna Parish, and Milborne Stileham Tithing, in Beer Regis Parish.

TriR 20 Towns enumerated and distinguished by stars, in Part 1., have, or had, the same signification in Law as Vills, and include *Boroughs* and *Common Towns.* The Borough Towns which send Members to Parliament are now, by the Reform Act, 2 W. 4, c. 45, seven, (including Poole), and by a subsequent Act, 2 & 3 vv. 4, c. 64, Sch. O, the *Boundaries* thereof are described,—p. 187. The other Boroughs are Blandford Forum and Corfe Castle, which formerly sent Members to Parliament; other Towns there are, viz., Beaminster, Cerne Abbas, Cranborne, Sherborne, Sturminster Newton. Stalbridge, and Wimborne Minster, which have privileges of Markets *and Fairs* and the remainder, Abbotsbury, Beer Regis, Evershot, Frampton, and Milton Abbas, had those privileges, but they arc fallen into disuse and not kept, but all are equally *Towns* in Law.

The 404 Tithings enumerated and distinguished by stars, Part I. col. 5; also in Part II. p. 110, are the same as anciently paid to the Land Tax; there are many other Tithings, where Tithingmen are appointed at the Court Leet, but the uniting of these took place very early.—*See Observations,* pp. 2i), 36; Part I. p. 69 to 104; Part II. pp. 110 to 118; Part 111. pp. 120 to 130. These Tithings appear to have had the same signification in Law as Parishes, *Towns,* and Vills, for each had but one Parish, Town, Vill, or *Tithing;* and us they increased the Tithing seems to have been the *Manor* of the present day, for the Chief was the Tithiugmau, and his Court the tribunal of the Manor; but now, by the increase of inhabitants, the Towns are divided into several Parishes, and the Parishes into several Tithings: thus it frequently happens that some of the Tithings extend into two or more Parishes, maintaining their own Poor, and contain several Hamlets, Farms, and Lands within the same. This will appear in There are 2/ other l'laces where Faiis are kept.

Part III. p. 120, where the Parishes are given alphabetically, and the Tithings within the same; and because the *Land Tax* has always been collected in Tithings, *eo nomine* (not in Parishes), and the *County Rate* hath always been collected in Parishes, this List has been arranged so as to shew the Proportions of the two Taxations; and it will be perceived that there are several Tithings and Places which pay to the Land Tax aud County Rate, though they do not belong to the Parish or Tithing under which they are placed, but are put there to shew the sums of money originally paid in aid to that particular Parish or Tithing, (distinguished in *italic letter.*) This intermixture of Parishes and Tithings one with another, and the seeming contradictious are noted, and this List is preserved merely to shew the sums paid in *Tithings* to the Land Tax (for no mention is made of it elsewhere), and the proportions originally paid, when the County Rate was settled in the year 1740.

The 253 Vills or Villages enumerated in Part I. col. G, are distinguished by *stars;* though there are some of the Villages depopulated, and have no Parish Officers, or Poor, these are noted where they occur.

Th E 244 Hamlets enumerated in Part I. col. 7, are distinguished in like manner. As the people increased in numbers, they spread themselves and inhabited other places within the precincts of the *Tithings,* and which, by beiug inhabited, became known, and took its name from two Saxon words *Ham,* Home, Hame, *(Scotch,)* which signified a dwelling, and *Let* signified to assign. They did not compose separate Societies in Civil or Ecclesiastical affairs, but remained Members of the Tithings, *Manors,* or Parishes, to which they originally belonged.—*Finch b.* 2, c. 1; *St. Amand,* p. 69. *Hamlets* are very early taken notice of, for in the *Stat, of Exeter* 256, 14 Edw. 1, (1285), mention is made of *intire Vills, demi Vills,* and *Hamlets;* and the Sheriff was conimauded from the List or Roll to be made to him by the Bailiffs of Hundreds, &c, to summon the Jurois accordingly, viz., 8 from the intire Vill; 6 from the demi Vill; and 4 from the Hamlet; out of which were to be selected, 6 from the eight; 4 from the six; and 2 from the four; and in this proportion throughout his county.—*See App. to Statutes p.* 14, *Cotton MS., Claudius D.* 2.

The617 Farms and Lands, enumerated in Part I. col. 8, are distinguished in like manner. The original names of these farms have been sometimes changed by the owners; but the number of such will be found to be very few. According to the present arrangement of Part I. although the Civil and Ecclesiastical Divisions are placed together in one List, yet by the method adopted they are easily seen and distinguished, and in the enumeration of the Places, by marking such Places with *stars,* and bringing the whole into one point of view, the errors (if any) may be readily corrected with the pen. Upon the whole, this part mil show the extent of the Parish, and every Chapelry, Town, Tithing, Vill, Hamlet, and Farm, within the same.

The List, Part IV. p. 131, contains the New Divisions delineated on the Map or Plan of the County, prefixed hereto, and all the Parishes, Chapelries, and Places, maintaining their own poor are alphabetically arranged and numbered in each Division, and referred to by the numbers on the said map or plan, and this List shows at one view in four columns, viz.:— 1st. The estimated value of real Property made in 1815; 2d. The amount of the Poor Rates raised in the same year; 3d. The amount of the present County Rate; and 4th. The population in 1831, in every Parish, Place, and Division.

The 1st and 2d are taken from the Official Returns published by order of the House of Commons, on the 3d March, 1818, and the 1st October, 1831.

The List, Part V. contains the New Divisions, and the Parishes and Places, as in List Part IV., with the names of the Bri Dges, inalphabetical order, within the same, and by whom such Bridges are to be repaired: distinguishing the County Bridges, and when first ordered to be repaired. This Listgis as perfect as it could be made from the information received from the Constables, and others.

The Extracts of particular Rules and Orders made at the Quarter Sessions, from the year 1664, are given in alphabetical order, and are preserved to be referred to, as occasion may require. The Rules and Orders for the regulation of the practice of the Court of General Quarter Sessions of the Peace, for the use and information of the Profession of the Law attending at such Sessions, made and settled Michaelmas Sessions, 1830, is given p. 173, and is preceded by a Table of its Contents.

The Polling Districts settled by the Justices in Quarter Sessions, assembled 16th October, 1832, in pursuance of the Act 2 and 3 W. 4, c. 64, s. 35, for the Election of *Knights of the Shire,* are given p. 181, and also the Boundaries of the Seven Boroughs for the Election of *Burgesses, sect.* 35 of the said Act, p. 187.

In the Appendix is contained an Abstract of the Returns made to Parliament, in the year 1786, in pursuance of the Act 26 G. 3, c. 58. The Parishes in this County are arranged alphabetically, and the Heads of the Answers made to the Enquiries are extracted as fully as the size of the Book would admit of; and though several *additions* are made from the information since received, yet the account is still imperfect and far from being complete. The annual produce, in money is *£844* 10s. Id.; and the produce in land £4,066 5s. loJd.; making together £4,910 15s. lljd. The amount thereof from the Returns made to Parliament, viz., in money £386 6s.; and in land £4,474 19s. 8d.; making together 4,861 5s. 8d.; so that it appears there is a difference of £59 5s. 3d. per annum *more* than returned to Parliament. To assist this Enquiry an Index is made to the names of the Donors; and in the Index 28 Donors unknown are referred to.

A'ote.—The donations given formerly to the poor Prisoners confined in the Gaol, appear not to have been returned.

& Ut'gt of Subscribers.

A. I

Ashley, the Lord, M. P.

Atden, George, attorney, Weymouth

Arden, Christopher, esq. Dorchester

Arnold, Dr., Ilsington, 2 copies

Abbott, T. attorney, Dorchester

Andrews, Mr. R. W. Ditto

B.

Banket, H.esq. Kingston Hall, 10 co.

Browne, F. J. esq. Frampton,20 cop.

Browne, J. H. esq. Weymouth

Bartlett, Tho. esq. Wareham. 2 cop.

Bond, John, esq. Grange

Best, Hon. and Rev. S. Blandford St. Mary

Bowles, C. esq. Shaftesbury, 3 cop.

Brouncker. Rd. esq. Boveridge

Bastard, Rev. John, West Lodge

Billett, I'. esq. Sutton Pointz

Baker, Mr. Mark. Dorchester

Boswell, Win. attorney, Ditto

Bastard, T. H. esq. Charlton

Bond, Wm. esq. Uynehavn

Batson and Warry, attorneys, Sherborne

Bower T. Bowyer, esq. Iweme Minster

Blennerhassett, Rev. J. Ryme In trinseca Bishop, Wm. Dorchester Bower, James, esq. Weymouth Buckland, C. E. attorney, Shaftesbury

Bartlett, C. O. attorney, Wareham

C

Castleman, Wm. attorney, Wimborne

Crosse. Rev. Robert, M.

Cox, Samuel, esq. Beaminster

Chitty, G. attorney, Shaston

Calcraft. J. H. esq. M. P. Rempston Hall

Colson, Rev. J. M. Piddlehinton

Coombs, T. attorney, Dorchester

Colson, Rev. J. M. Ditto

Carpenter, T. C, M.D. Lyme

Clarke, T. E. attorney, Chard

Clarke, Geo. bookseller, Dorchester.

Churchill, Rev. W. R. H. Colliton

D.

Digby, Earl of, 50 copies

Digby, Sir Henry, Minteme

Drax, J. S. W. S. Erie. esq. 4 copies

Dashwood, T. attorney, Sturminster Newton

Dale, James, esq. Glanvilles Wootton

Darner, Hon. H. D. Milton Abbey

Dowland, Rev. J. J-G. Broadwinsor

E.

England. Rev. W., D.D., Stafford

Eliot, Wm. esq., Weymouth

F.

Farquharson, J. . esq. Langton

Frampton, J.esq. Morelon, ficopies
Frampton, H. esq. Ditto, 2 copies
Fyler, J.C. esq. Heffeldon, 2 copies
Freeman, Mr. W. Wimborne
Fooks, T. esq. Sherborne
Filliter, G, attorney, Wareham, 2 cop
Foster, A. esq. Warmwell
Frampton J. attorney, Cerne
Fisher, T. esq. Dorchester

G.

Glyn. Sir R. C. Bart., Gaunt's House
3 copies
Goforth. Rev. F. Whitechurch Cann'
Guodford, John, esq. Yeovil

H.

Hoare, Sir R. C. Bart. Stowerhead
Hanham, Rev. Sir J. Bart. Dean's
Ci urt, 2 copies Hanham, W. esq.
High Hall Herbert,Mr. H. Wimborne
Henning, J. attorney, Weymouth Henning, G. esq. Fordington Hardwicke, T.
B. esq., Lyme Regis, 2 copies Hussey,
John, Esq., Ditto Harvey, R. R. attorney
Sturminster
Newton Hardy, Mr. J. Piddletown
Hoskins, W., N. Perrott, Somerset
Hawkins. J. Adair, esq. Lewell
Henley, the Lord
Harrison, John, attorney, Blandford
Henning, C. B. attorney, Dorchester

I.

Ilchester Earl of, Melhury, 10 copies
Jennings, J. attorney, Evershot
Jennings, J. C. attorney, Somerton
Jacob, Messrs. stationers, Dorchester
Jennings, Wm. esq. Evershot
Johns, H. W. attorney, Blandford
Jacob, G. T. esq., Shillingston

K.

Keddle. Sherring attorney. Bridport
King, J. T. attorney, Blandford

L.

Legg, Wm. attorney, W«ymouth
Lambert. J. J. esq, Dorchester l.ofius, G.
C. esq. Woolland House Lester, B. L.
esq. M P., Poole

M.

Meyrick, Rev. Wm. Bath
Alanfield, Wm. attorney, Dorchester
Mallock, K. attorney. Ax minster
Marshall, Rev. W. Chickerill
Melmoth, J. P. attorney, Sherborne
Messiter, Rev. R. Stourton Caundle
Alichel, John, esq. Dewlish

N

Nepean, Sir M. H. Bart. Loders
Nicholetts. E. attorney, Bridport

O.

Okeden, D O. P. esq. Cri chell 2 cop

P.

Portman, E. B. esq. 10 copies
Pitt, W. M. esq. 2 copies
Phillips, R. C. attorney, Weymouth
Penn, Governor, Portland, 6 copies
Peach, N. W. esq. 4 copies
Pickard, Rev. G. Warm well, 2 copies
Pickard, Rev. G, Jun. Bloxworth
Pickard, H. W. esq. Warmwell
Pretor, S. esq. Sherborne, 2 copies
Pattison R. esq. Wrackleford

R.

Rivers, Lord
Rowden, H. att. Wimborne 2 copies
Read, T. G attorney, Dorchester Rudge,
J., D.D., Hawkchurch

S.

Shaftesbury, Earl of. St Giles 10 cop.
Smith, Sir J. W. Bart 4 copies
Smith, J. J. esq.. T he Down House.
Steward, Colonel, Nottington, 2 cop.
Strangways, Hon.and Rev. C. 2 cop.
Strangways. Kev. H. Rew near Exeter, 2 copies
Smith, G. attorney, town clerk, Lyme
Stone, J. attorney, Dorchester
Strong, R. esq. (bilcombe
Smith. S. attorney Blandford
Sturt, H. C. esq. 10 copies
Steward, G. T. esq. Candover, near
Basingstoke

T.

Templer. J. attorney, Bridport
Tucker, W. esq. Coryton
'l izard, H. H. attorney, Weymouth
Templeman, J. esq. Lyme Regis
Tregonwell, St. Barbe. esq. Bourne
Templer, Rev. J. A. Piddletown
Tucker, B. C. attorney. Chard
Tomlyns., esq. Western Circuit

U.

Underhill, Air. Cups Hotel, Lyme

W.

Wollaston. C. B esq. 20 copies
Weld, H. esq. Chideock
Weston, S. C esq. 2 copies
Willis, John. esq. Dorchester
Williams, R. esq. AI.P. 2 copies
Whittle, Air. John, Toller Fratrum

Y.

Yeatman. Rev. H. F. 4 copies

The Civil Division of the County of Dorset was, from the time of our Saxon Ancestors, in Hundreds and Tithings, and Officers, called the *Hundredary* and *Tithingman,* were elected and chosen to preside over each, and were the *Civil* Magistrates thereof. Out of these Hundreds certain Franchises, called *Liberties* and *Boroughs* have since been granted by the Crown to particular Persons, and to Bodies Corporate, and when the whole Hundred (which was frequently the case) has been granted, it has been sometimes called a *Liberty.* A certain Number of Tithings compose each Hundred and Liberty, and the Hundreds and Liberties (or Parts thereof) and Boroughs are placed into nine Divisions--, which now make up the County or Shire; the Civil Government and Administration of which are intrusted to certain Ministerial Officers and Masristrates, with other Persons having jurisdiction by substitution, delegation, or authority under them: such as the Clerk of the Peace, Under-Sheriff, County Clerk, Gaoler, Governor or Keeper of the House of Correction, and others, and are disposed in the following order:— These Hundreds and Tithings are mentioned in the *Inquis. GheldianA Rot' Hund'orum,* and to whom granted.— *See fasten wider Chief Constables,* VI., and *under Tithingmen,* VII.

t These Divisions were formed in pursuance of the Acts of 9 G. 4, c. 43 and 10 G. 4, c. 46, at *Midsummer* Sessions, 1830, and carried into effect 1st September following.

I.—CUSTOS ROTULORUM. II.—SHERIFF. III. CORONERS. IV. —JUSTICES of the Peace.
V.—TREASURER.
VI.—CONSTABLES.
VII.—TITHINGMEN.
VIII.—SURVEYORS of Bridges.
IX. ————— of Highways.
X. —OVERSEERS of the Poor.

I.—The Custos Rotulorum or *Keeper* of the *Bolls* or *Records* of the Sessions of the Peace, and of the Commission of the Peace for the County, appears to have been first appointed in 1390 (14 Rich. 2, c. 11) by the Lord Chancellor, for by reference to the stat. 3 Edw. 6, c. 1, mention is made that the nomination of the Custos Rotulorum (being a special Justice of the Peace) had of long-time before belonged to the Office of Chancellor, until in the year 1545, (37 Hen. 8. c. 1) it was taken away, though in five years afterwards, the nomination thereof is restored, by the above statute of 3 Edw. 6, to the Lord Chancellor. This special Officer, so denominated, is usually a Person of Quality, is always a Justice of the Quorum, and the principal *Civil* Officer of the County. His appointment is by the King's Sign Manual, and to him the appointment of the Clerk of the Peace belongs. 37 Hen. 8, c. 1, s. 2, and 1 W. & M. stat. 1, c. 21, s. 4.—1 *Black' Com',* 349, *and 4, p.* 273.

The following are the Noblemen appointed for the County since the year 1680, the Clerks of the Peace and their Deputies:— *Custodes Rutulorum. Clerks of the Peace. Deputies.* 1680. John Earl of Bristol 1680. Edw. Atwell (06.1698) 1694. R. Constable 1699. Charles Duke of Bolton (ofi. 1722) 1703. Thos. Coward (06. 1726) This was the *tni* Duke who was appointed Lord Lieutenant of Ireland, and on 6th July, 1715, Denis Bond was appointed Custos Rotulorum *during pleasure.—* fee *Records of the Sessions,* 1715, *Mid' S. Custodies Rotulorum. Clerks of the Peace. Deputies.* 1715. Bryan Combe 1726. Bryan Combe.

1727. Charles Duke of Bolton... 1727. W. Templeman *(ob. 1754) (ob. 1754)* 1733. Anthony E. of Shaftesbury 1749. Robert Smith *(ob.* 21st *April,* 1771) 1750. R. Lambert 1754. John Wallis *(ob. 1792)* 1761. John Way. 1792.E. Boswell. 1771. Henry, Lord, (afterwards
Earl of) Digby *(ob.* 1793) 1792. Wm. Burnet 1793. Geo. Ld. Rivera (oM803) (od.1828) 1803. George Earl of Dorchester *(ob.* 1808) 1803. Edw. Earl of Digby 1820. Thos. Fox.
1826. Thos. Fooks

The Clerk of the Peace is the *Deputy* of the Custos Rotulorum, for by 1W. &M, stat. 1, c. 21, s. 5, the Custos Rotulorum or other Person to whom it belongs to appoint, shall, where the Office shall be void, nominate a sufficient Person residing in the County, to exercise the same by himself, or sufficient Deputy, (so that the Deputy be admitted by the Custos Rotulorum, 37 H. 8, c. 1, s. 3) and to take and receive the Fees, Profits, and Perquisites thereof, for so long time *only* as he shall well demean himself in his office. By the Act 2 G. 2, c. 46, s. 14, no Clerk of the Peace, nor his Deputy, shall act as Solicitor, Attorney, or Agent at the Sessions where he shall execute the Office.

For the *Fees* taken by the Clerk of the Peace, Clerk of Arraigns, and Clerk of Indictments, see Sch. A.—Crier's Fees, see Sch. B.

II.—The Sheriff.—At the first division of this kingdom into Counties, the custody of the Shire is said to have been committed by the King, to the Earl or *Comes:* but the Earls, in process of time, by reason of their high employment and attendance on the King's person, not being able to transact the business of the County, were delivered of that burthen *(Dalt.* c. 1), reserving to themselves the honour, but the labour was laid on the Sheriff; and though the Sheriff be still called the *Vice-Comes,* (deputy to the Earl), yet he is entirely independent of, and not subject to him, the King, by his Letters Patent, committing *Custodiam Comitates* to the Sheriff, and him alone. He is considered in our books as *Bailiff* to the Crown, and his County, of which he hath the care, and in which he is to execute the King's writs, is called his *Bailiwick, 7 Co'* 33. The Sheriffs were originally chosen by the people in their *Folkmote* or *County Court— Selden's Tit' of Hon'* 610. Lord Coke says they were chosen, the same as the Coroner, by all the Freeholders, 2 *Inst'* 174, 558. In confirmation of this ancient usage in the year 1300 it was ordained by 28 Edw. 1, stat. 3, c. 8, "The King hath granted unto his People, "that they shall have election of their Sheriff in "every Shire, (where the Sbrivalty is not of Fee) "if they list;" and, in c. 13, "Forasmuch as the King "hath granted the Election of Sheriffs to the Commons "of the Shire; The King will that they shall chuse "such Sheriffs that shall not charge them, and that "they shall not put any Officer in authority for Rewards "or Bribes. And such as shall not lodge too oft in "one place, nor with poor persons, or men of religion." But this election seems not to have been vested *absolutely* in the People, for it required the royal approbation. Shortly after, in the year 1316, these popular elections growing tumultuous, were put an end to by an Act of the Legislature, *(9 Edw. 2, stat.* 2, c. *1,)* and the Sheriffs were to be assigned by the Chancellor, Treasurer, Barons of the Exchequer,

Judges, and other Officers of the King: and that none should be Sheriff unless he had sufficient Land within the County, of which he was Sheriff, to answer to the King and his People: and thus this Office continued for upwards of four hundred and thirty years; subject to several regulations enacted by divers *statutes* concerning the appointments and nominating and chusing the Sheriffs until the year 1751, when by the Act 24 6. 2, c. 48, s. 12, for the abbreviation of *Michaelmas* Term, all the Judges, together with the other great officers, were to meet in the Exchequer Chamber on the morrow of *St. Martin* yearly, instead of the morrow of *All Souls,* and then and there propose three Persons to the King, who afterwards (if approved of) appoints one of them to be Sheriff, by marking each Name with the prick of a Pin; and for that reason this

particular Election is generally termed pricking for Sheriffs.—1 *Black' Com,'* 341, *n.* 4.— *Impey's Sheriff, p.* 8.

The following is the present mode of nominating Sheriffs in the Exchequer, on the morrow of Saint Martin:—

The Chancellor, Chancellor of the Exchequer, the Judges, and several of the Privy Council assemble, and an Officer of the Court administers an Oath to them in old French, that they will nominate no one from favour, partiality, or any improper motive: this done, the same Officer having the list of the Counties in alphabetical order, and of those who were nominated the year preceding, reads over the three Names, and the last of the three he pronounces to be the present Sheriff. If any of the Ministry or Judges have an objection to any Person named in the List, he then mention! it, and another Gentleman is nominated in his room; if no objection be made, some one rises and says, " to the two "Gentlemen I know no objection, and I recommend A. B. "Esq. in the room of the present Sheriff."

Another Officer has a Paper with a number of names given him by the Clerk of *A* ssize for each County, which paper generally contains the names of the Gentlemen upon the former List, and also of Gentlemen who are likely to be nominated, and whilst the three are nominated, he prefixes 1, 2, or 3 to their names, according to the order in which they are placed; which, for greater certainty, he afterwards reads over twice. Several objections are made to Gentlemen; some, perhaps, at their own request; such as, that they are abroad, that their Estates are small and incumbered, that they have no Equipage, that they are practising Barristers, or Officers in the Militia, &c.

The new Sheriff is generally appointed about the end of the following *Hilary* Term; this extension of the time was probably in consequence of the 17th Edw. 4, c. 7, which enables the old Sheriff to hold his office over Michaelmas and H ilary Terms.

The counties of *Dorset* and *Somerset* bad but one Sheriff until the 1st Nov. 1567, when, by and under the authority

of the stat. 8 Eliz. c. 16, a Sheriff was appointed for each county.

The Officers appointed by (he Sheriff are—1. UnderSheriff. 2. County Clerk. 3. Bailiffs, and 4. Gaoler. The following is a List of Sheriffs from the year 1760, their Under-Sbcriffs, and County Clerks.

Sheriffs. Under Sheriffs.
Robert Willis.,
Ditto
Ditto, *County Clerks.* Samuel Slade...
....
Ditto
Ditto 1760. Ralph Willett 1761. William Pitt 1762. Edm. Morton Fleydell *Sheriffs. Under Sheriffs. County Clerks.* 1763. Wm.Richards, jiin Robert Willis.. ..Samuri Slade.... 1764. JohnPinney, *of Dorchester.*.Ditto Ditto 1765. John Pinney, *of Blarkdown.* ..*Vitto* Ditto 1766. Thomas Robinson Ditto Harry Foot 1767. Wm. Churchill, *of Colleton...*Ditto Ditto 1768. James Gollop Ditto Ditto 1769. Wm.Thorpe Holder Ditto William Old.... 1770. James Dale Ditto Ditto 1771. John Newton Ditto Ditto 1772. John Smith (afterwards *Sir* John Smith, Burt.) Ditto Ditto 1773. Henry Cornish Henley Ditto Ditto 1774. Harvey Ekins Ditto Robt. Willis, *jum.* 1775. George Gould Ditto Ditto 1776. William Tavnton Ditto Ditto 1777. George Snow Ditto Ditto 1778. Wllliam Trenchard Ditto Ditto 1779. Robert Goodden Ditto Ditto 1780. Peter Beckford Ditto Ditto 1731. L. D. G. Tregonwell Robert Willis, jun..John Bowie 1782. Wm. Churchill, *of Uenbury,* Ditto Ditto 1783. Prancis John Browne llobert Stickland..J. C. Mantield 1784. Isaac Sage.......Ditto.....Ditto 1785. *Hon.* Lionel Damer Ditto Ditto 1786. Henry William Portman..Thomas Waters..Ditto 1787. Peter William Baker Walter Whitaker Ditto 1788. Anthony Chapman Robert Stickland.. Ditto 1789. Fred. T. Wentworth Ditto Ditto 1790. Henry William Fitch Ditto Ditto 1791. Sir Stephen Nash, *Knt* Ditto Ditto 1792. Mark Davis Ditto Ditto 1793. James Frampton Thos. Gould Read..Ditto 1794. Edward Buckley Batson....Robert Lambert..Ditto 1795. Edward Grealhed

Robert Stickland..Ditto 1796. Thomas Bowyer Bower....John T. King....Ditto 1797. Edw.Berkeley Portman....John Ridout Ditto 1798. William Clavell Thomas Bartlett..Ditto 1799. Henry Seymer John Ridout Ditto 1800. Rich. Erie Drax Grosvenor..John Treg. King. .Ditto 1801. Thomas Rose Drewe Thomas Fox Ditto 1802. Edmund Morton Pleydell..Thos. GouldRead..Ditto 1803. Josiah Wedgwood John Treg. King..George Stickland 1804. Robert Williams Robert Williams..George Score....

1805. John Gould Ditto George Stickland 1806. Edward Williams..........Ditto Ditto *Sheriffs. Under Sheriffs. County Clerks.* 1807. Arthur Cosens Giles Runell George Stickland. 1808. Nicholas Charles Daniel.... Thos. W. Browne Ditto 1809. James John Farquharson..Septimus Smith..Ditto 1810. Henry Seymer.......Ditto Ditto 1811. Edward Oreathed Win. Castleman..Ditto 1812. Thomas Horlock Bastard....SeptimusSmith....Ditto IBI3. Robert Radclyffe John T. King....Ditto 1814. *Sir John W.Smith, Bait*.....George Moore... .Thomas Coombs., 1815. George Smith Septimus Smith..Ditto 1816. John Herbert Browne Thomas Fox Ditto 1817. .Sir Wm. Oglander, *Hart* Ditto Ditto 1818. John Disney Ditto Ditto 1819. George Purling Thomas G. Bead.. William Spencer.. 1820. Thomas Billett... ....Thomas Fox......Thomas Coombs. . 1821. John White Thomas Coombs. .Joseph Stone...... 1822. *lit. Hon.* Sir Evan Nepcan Thomas Fox Ditto 1823. Henry Charles Sturt Thomas Parr...... Ditto 1824. George Garland William Parr Ditto 1825. Christopher Spurrier Ditto Ditto 1826. Charles Buxton........ ....John Henning....Cha. Burt Henning. 1827. John Bingley Garland Robert H. Parr....Joseph Stone 1828. William Gill Paxton......Edward Castleman Ditto 1829. William Boucher Ph.Matt. Chitty. .Ditto 1830. John Bond George Filliter Ditto 1831. *Hon.* Heory Dawson Damer Thomas Fox Ditto 1832. *Sir Edw. B. Baker, Dart...* Septimus Smith....Ditto Died in this Year, and Andrew Bain was appointed his successor. 1.—The Under Sheriff usually performs all the duties

of the Office, a very few only excepted, where the *personal* presence of the High Sheriff is necessary; but no Under Sheriff shall abide in his Office above one Year, *Dalt.* c. 9; and if he does, by an Act passed in 1444, (23 Hen. 6, c. 7,) he forfeits £200, a large sum in those days: and no Under Sheriff or Sheriff's Officer shall practise as an Attorney during his continuance in such Office: 1 Hen. 5, c. 4. *Black. Com.* 1. p. 344. In the year 1416, all Sheriffs were to have Allowance upon their Accounts, by their Oaths, o/" *things casual,* 4 Hen. 5, c. 2. Afterwards, in 1548, they were to have such *Talliesf of Reward* as they then afore had, and they were to be discharged in the Exchequer of such sums of Money which they *could not levy.* They were also to have an Allowance for the Charges and Expenses which they should sustain by the diet of the Justices of Assize, *and by other means:* 2 & 3 Edw. 6, c. 4. Likewise for the Wages of Justices of the Peace at their Quarter Sessions, 12 Rich. 2, c. 10—14 Rich. 2, c. 11. *Dallov's Justice,* c. 120. The Clerk of the Peace, after *Michaelmas Sessions* in every Year, returns to the UnderSheriffa List, containing the Names of all the Justices who have attended the several Sessions; and whatever the Number may have been, the Sum of £48 is always allowed to the Sheriff at the Exchequer, and is paid by him to the Cleik of the Peace, who accounts for the same to the Justices towards a Fund which is appropriated at their discretion. When the counties of Dorset and Somerset, as before observed, were separated in 1567, the Sheriff of this County was to pay only half Charges and Pees, and the Charges and Rewards from thenceforth have been divided. Stat. 8 Eliz. c. 16, and 13 Eliz. c. 22. *Note.*—The yearly sum of £4000 is set apart at the Exchequer for paying allowances. 3 G. 1, c. 16. s. 1. The share of this County is £101. 6s. Among these Casuals *Two Shillings and Shpence* a Week is allowed for each *Convict* in the Gaol, *after* Conviction, and until removed to his or her destination, to be paid to the Gaoler by the Sheriff. t What these Tallies are *see*

Cowel, word Tailes.

By an Act passed 12th May, 1815, (55 Geo. 3, c. 50. s. 10.) The Sheriff or Under Sheriff is to be paid his *customary fee* for every *Liberate* granted to any Debtor on his discharge, out of the County Stock, by order of the Justices in Sessions; subject, however, to the approbation of the Judges of Assize. See a list of Under Sheriff's Fees in Schedule C.

2. —The County Clerk is appointed by the High Sheriff, as his Officer in the County Court, where all causes of 40s. value and under, are heard and determined; which is to be held once every month upon a *Wednesday,* the month being computed according to eight and twenty days in the month, and not according to the Calendar. *(Mag. Charta, c.* 35. 9 H. 3, c. 35. 2 Edw. 6, c. 25.)— see a List of his Fees "Schedule D." 3. —The Bailiffs or Sheriff's Officers are usually bound with sureties to the Sheriff, in an obligation for the due execution of their Office, and these are called " *Bound* Bailiffs."f *Special* Bailiffs are nominated by the Plaintiff, or his Attorney, and appointed by the Sheriff, *pro hac vice, Tidd.* 214. *Dalt.* 185,187. See a List of their Fees, Sch. E. The Names of the Bound Bailiffs in this County (1832), are

George White, of Dorchester.

Wm. Sherring, jun., of Beaminster.

James Major, of Bridport.

John Hall, of the same Place.

Walter Pride, of Sherborne.

William Burge.of Stalbridge.

George Highman, of Shaftesbury.

George Best, of Wareham.

J. M. Long, of Wincanton, *Somerset.*

John Justins, of Sherborne.

By virtue of a Writ of *Justicies,* the Court may hold Plea of any Sura above 40s.—4 lmt. 266.

t The Bailiffs of Hundreds and Liberties are appointed at the Court Leeu See No. IV. *Postea*—See 1 *Black. Com.,* p. 345. 4.—The Gaoler is appointed by the Sheriff, and he must be responsible for his conduct, 14 Edw. 3, c. 10. His business is to keep safely-all persons committed to him by lawful Warrant, and if he suffer any such to escape, the Sheriff shall answer it to the King, if it be a *criminal* matter, or, in a *civil* case, to the party injured, 4 *Rep.* 34, 2 *Inst.* 592. Every County hath two sorts of Gaols, one for the Prisoners by the Sheriff taken for Debt, and the other for Breach of the Peace and matter of the Crown, which is the County Gaol, *Latch* 16, 1 *And.* 345. As the Gaoler is but the Sheriff's Servant, therefore he may discharge him at pleasure, and if he refuses to surrender up or quit possession of the Gaol, the Sheriff may turn him out by force, as he may any private person: and each are under the Regulation of the Court of King's Bench. Reg. 29, *Impey's Sheriff, p.* 51. On the 1st October, 1815, all Fees payable by any Prisoner, either *civil or criminal*, to the Gaoler or his Servants, were abolished, and an allowance is made in lieu thereof by way of salary, under Stat. 55 G. 3, c. 50 — 56 G. 3, c. 116, s. 3. By the Act (4 Geo. 4, c. 64) which passed 20th July, 1823, the several Statutes and Acts, and parts of Statutes and Acts, then existing relative to the Building, Repairing, and Regulating of Gaols and Houses of Correction in *England* and *Wales* are repealed; and certain general Rules and Regulations are thereby established, which are directed to be carried into effect in all Gaols and Houses of Correction in every County, so far as they may be applicable to the particular description or Class of Prisoners confined therein: such Rules to be binding on the Sheriff, and all other Persons, provided they do not interfere with the right or duty of the Sheriff to appoint or remove Ibe Keeper of the *County Gaol.* The 12th s. ofthe Statute also gives further Authority to the J usti ces in Sessions to make additional Rules and Regulations for the Government of Prisons within their Jurisdiction, subject to the Approbation of the Justices of *Gaol Delivery* at the *Assizes.* In pursuance of this Act the Justices assembled at fhe *Midsummer* Quarter Sessions, 1824, proceeded to make the Rules and Reflations to be observed in the County Gaol and House of Correction at Dorchester and by these Rules and Regulations, the duties of the several Officers appointed, viz.: The

Gaoler—Chaplain— Surgeon—Matron—Clerk—Turnkeys. and Waidsmen and Wardswomen, are particularly mentioned and expressed. The Persons who have held the Office of Gaoler from the year 1680, are 1B80. Thomas Knapton.

1714. Ren. Knapton.
1722. Edw.Chaffey.
1728. James Chaffer.
1732. Batt Chaffey. 1786. Geo. Andrews. 1808. Robert W. Andhiws.

By the 25th sec. of the above-mentioned Statute, (4 G. 4, c. 64), the Justices in Session have power to appoint such *Keepers,* Matrons, and other Officers, as to them may seem expedient, for every Prison within their Jurisdiction, except the Keeper of the *Common Gaol,* so that the Keeper of the Prison at Dorchester, which contains the County Gaol, and also the House of Correction, has a double Appointment, one annually from the Sheriff, and the other from the Justices in Session, who have also a power to remove such Officers as occasion may require. By sec. 26 of the same The Rules and Regulations for the government of the Gaol and House of Correction, at Dorchester, were published in 1824. Printed by G.Clark, Dorchester. Octavo. Price 2s. pp. 60.

Statute, they are also empowered to fix Salaries and Air lowances for the Keeper and other Officers, and to alter them from time to time; such Salaries and A Uowances to be paid out of the County Rate. The Salaries now paid to him and his Assistants are as follow:— Gaoler and Keeper £260; three Turnkeys, one at 17s. per Week, the others at 14s. per Week each, £117:— Matron, £43; —Clerk, £30, making together the Sum of £450 per Ann. 5. The Chaplain or Ordinary was first appointed at Michaelmas Sessions, 1773, (13 G. 3, c. 58) to officiate and perform Divine Service in the Gaol, according to the rites of the Church of England, which Act was repealed in 1823, by the 4 G. 4, c. 64, and he is now appointed under the authoiity of the last-mentioned statute; his Duties are specified in clauses 30 and 34 of that Act, and by the said Rules and Regulations of the

Prison, sec. IV, p. 28. His Salary has been fixed at £200 per Annum, payable quarterly out of the County Rate. The following are the Names of the Clergymen who have been appointed, viz.:— 1773. Richard Daubeny, i 1821. Evan Davies.

1786. Thomas Bryer. I 1823. *George Wood.* 1802. John Palmer. I 182S. Dacbe Clemetson.

A Chaplain formerly officiated, and did Doff on Sundays and Wednesdays only. 6. The Surgeon and Apothecary was first appointed at Midsummer Sessions, 1774, (14 G. 3, c. 59), to attend at the Gaol, and House of Correction, which Act was repealed in 1823, by the 4 G. 4, c. 64, and under the authority of that statute he has been appointed to visit the Prison, and his Duties are specified in the 33d Clause of the said Act, and in the said Rules and Regulations, Sec. V, p. 31. His Salary has been fixed at £50 per Annum, payable quarterly out of the County Rate, exclusive of Medicines, and other Articles for the Sick. The following are the Names of the Surgeons appointed, viz.:— 1774. John Kenn. I 1789. Christopher Arden. 1784. James Nooth. I 1812. Christ. Arden. Jun.

A Surgeon formerly attended at the Gaol, without Salary, but made a Bill. III.—Coroners are of equal antiquity with the Sheriff, and were ordained with them to keep the Peace when the Earls gave up the *Wardship* of the County. *Mirr'* c. 1. s. 3.. Coroners for the County are chosen by the Freeholders by virtue of the King's Writ *de coronatore eligendo,* directed to the Sheriff, in which it is expressly commanded "that he do cause such one to be chosen as of the best informed and most willing and able to hold that office:" and in order to effect this more surely, in 1354 it was enacted by the st. 28 Ed. 3, c. 6. "That all Coroners of the *Counties* shall be "chosen in the full Counties by the Commons of the "same Counties, of the most meet and most lawful "people that shall be found in the said Counties, to "execute the said office, saved always to the King "and other Lords which ought to make such Coro"ners their Seigniories and Franchises." His office is to make enquiry concerning the death of the King's subjects, and certain Revenues of the Crown; and also, in particular cases, to supply the office of Sheriff. The Coroners for this county appear never to have been more than *three.* Their Names, from the year 1760 are as follow:— 1760—William Filliter, of Wareham.

Stafford Moore, of Sturminster Newton.

Thomas Jones, of Bridport.

1762—Samuel Slade, of Dorchester, *vice* Jones. 1765—Ambrose Penny, of Sturminster Newton, *vice* Moore, dee. 1774—Richard Moore, of the same, *vice* Penny, dec.

— James Daniel, of Beaminster, *vice* filliter, dec.

1776—Nathaniel Stickland, of Dorchester, *vice* Slade, dec.

1786—George Andrews, of Dorchester, *vice* Stickland, dec.

1797—Joseph Johns, of Weymouth, vice Daniel, dec.

1802— Robert Williams Andrews, of Dorchester, *vice* his Father. 1803—Edw. Charles Buckland, of Shaftesbury, *vice* Moore, res. 1804— Samuel Mitchell Andrews, of Blandford, *vice* Buckland, dec. 1807—Charles Hansen, of Shaftesbury, rice S.M.Andrews, res. 1809—John Wallis, of Dorchester, *vice* R. W. Andrews, res. 1817—Robert Fowler Pitfield, of Bridport, uice Johns, dec. 1824—John Tucker, of Bridport, *vice* Pitfield, res.

A'ofe—The Names in small Capitals are the present Coroners.

The Coroners within *Franchises* have an exempt jurisdiction within the Precinct of the *Hundred, Liberty,* or *Borough,* over which they are appointed by the Lords of such Franchises, with which the Coroners of the County cannot intermeddle; as the Coroners of these Franchises may not intermeddle within the County out of such Franchises. *Hawkins' P. C.* The Names of the present Coroners (1832) within these Franchises are— *Hundreds. Lords. Coroners.*

Cogdea"? Henry Bankes' Usq:...William Castleman, of Wimborne. nrnpeme Marluis of Salisbury. Charles Harbin, of Ringwood, *Hants.*

YrtmmTter "' j Earlof Digby Thomas Fooks, of Sherborne.

Liberty.

Gillingham Marq. of Westminster...P. M.Chitty, of Shaftesbury.

Boroughs.

Blandford The Bailiff The Bailiff.

Bridport The Bailiffs Ditto.

Corfe Castle The Mayor The Mayor.

Dorchester Ditto Ditto.

Lyme Regis Ditto Ditto.

Shaftesbu ry Ditto Ditto.

Wareham and"»

Isles of Pur-fDitt Dilto.

beck and (Brownsea ...J

Mgt"0 m«

See a List of their Fees, *Schedule O.* tV.-«-JUstices Of The Peace were first created artd assigned Keepers and Conservators of the Peace in the years 1327,1328, and 1344, by statutes 1 Edw 3, C.16; 4 Edw. 3, c. 2; and 18 Edw. 3, c. 2, by the King's Commission, and in this manner was the election of the Conservators of the Peace taken from the People and given to the King; but still they were only Conservators, Wardens, or Keepers, till 1360, by the st. 34 Edw. 3, c. 1, which gave them the power of trying Felonies, and then they acquired the more honourable appellation of Justices. *Black' Com'* 1, *p.* 351; and afterwards, in the year 1444, by the stat. 2 Hen. 5, c. 1, the constituting Justices of the Peace became inherent and inseparable from the Crown, and their appointment is by commission in the King's name made, of common course, under the *Great Seal* of *England,* by the direction of the Lord Chancellor, according to the before-mentioned statute of Henry 5.

A *List of the* Justices *of the* Peace, *named in the Commission of tht Peace for this County, that passed the Seals the 8th day of Deeember,*—1st W. IV., 1830.

Ernest Augustas, Duke of Cumberland.

Augustus, Duke of Sussex.

Adolphus, Duke of Cambridge.

William Frederick, Duke of Gloucester,

Leopold, Prince of Saxe Cobourg.

William, Archbishop of Canterbury,

Primate and Metropolitan of all England.

Henry Lord Brougham and Vaux, *Lord Hinh Chancellor.*

Edward Venables, Archbishop of York, *Primate and Metropolitan of England.*

Henry, Marquis of Lansdown.

John, Lord Durham, *Keeper of the Privy Seal.*

William Spencer, Duke of Devonshire, *Chamberlain of the Household.*

Richard, Duke of Buckingham and Chandos, *Steward of the Household.*

Bernard Edward, Duke of Norfolk.

Charles, Duke of Richmond.

George William Frederick, Duke of Deeds.

John, Duke of Bedford.

Alexander, Duke of Hamilton and Brandon.

George, Duke of Gordon.

James, Duke of Montrose.

William Henry, Duke of Portland.

Charles, Duke of Dorset.

Hugh, Duke of Northumberland.

Arthur, Duke of Wellington.

Charles Ingoldsby, Marquis of Winchester, *Groom of the Hole.*

George Granville Deveson, Marquis of Stafford.

Francis Charles, Marquisof Hertford.

Richard, Marquis Wellesley.

John Jeffreys, Marquis Camden.

Henry William, Marquis of Anglesey.

George James Horatio, Marquis of Cholmondeley.

Charles William, Marquis of Don--donderry.

Henry, Marquis Conyngham.

Ulick, Marquis of Clanricarde,

James, Marquis of Graham.

Edward, Karl of Derby.

John, Earl of Westmoreland.

George, Earl of Carlisle.

1790—Cropley Ashley, Earl of Shaftesbury.

George, Earl of Jersey.

Thomas, Earl of Haddington.

James, Earl of Lauderdale.

Thomas, Earl of Elgin and Kincardine.

George, Earl of Aberdeen.

Charles Augustus, Earl of

Tankerville.

George, Earl of Macclesfield.

William, Earl Fitzwilliam.

Philip, Earl of Hardwicke.

Henry Stephen, Earl of llchester.

George John, Earl Spencer.

John, Earl of Chatham.

Henry, Earl Bathurst.

John, Earl of Clarendon.

Charles, Earl Talbot.

Robert, Earl Grosvenor, now Marquis of Westminster.

Richard, Earl of Mount Edgcumbe.

1803. Edward, Earl of Digby.

James George, Earl of Courtown.

Robert, Earl of Roden.

John, Earl of Carysfort.

John, Earl of Clare.

James, Earl of Rosslyn.

Charles, Earl of Romney.

Richard, Earl of Clancarty.

Edward, Earl of Powis.

Charles, Earl Grey.

Dudley, Earl of Harrowby.

Henry, Earl of Mulgrave.

William, Earl Cathcart.

John, Earl of Eldoh.

William Pitt, Earl Amherst.

John William, Earl of Dudley.

Karl of Belfast.

Earl of Uxbridge.

Lord Charles Henry Somerset.

Lord John Russell.

Lord Robert Spencer.

Lord William Henry Cavendish Bentinck.

Lord William Charles Cavendish Bentinck.

Henry Viscount Hereford.

Percy Clinton Sydney, Viscount Strangford.

Henry John, Viscount Palmerston, *Secretary of State.*

William Viscount Melbourne, *Secretary of State.*

Robert, Viscount Melville.

Henry, Viscount Sidmouth.

Thomas William, Viscount Anson.

Granville Leveson, Vis. Granville.

William Carr, Viscount Beresford.

Frederick John, Viscount Goderich, *Secretary of State.* Lord Burghersh.

Viscount Althorp, *Chanetltir of ihe Exchequer.* 1831—Lord Ashley. Viscount Lowther. Viscount Marsham.

Viscount Encombe. Lord Francis Leveson Gower. Lord John Townshend. *mta* John Thynne. Lord George Thomas Bereforri. Charles James, Lord вUhou of

London.

Peter Robert, Lord Willoug b. I)e Eresby.

Henry Richard, Lord Holland.

Horace, Lord Rivers.

George, Lord Carteret.

William Wyndham, Lord Grenville.

John, Lord Rolle.

George, Lord Auckland.

Charles George, Lord Arden.

Alleyne, Lord Saint Helen's.

John, Lord Teignmouth.

Frederick Morton, Lord Henley.

Edward, Lord Ellenborough.

Thomas, Lord Manners.

Rowland, Lord Hill.

William, Lord Maryborough.

William, Lord Stowell.

Nicholas, Lord Bexley.

Benjamin, Lord BloomfJeld.

Charles, Lord Faraborough.

John Singleton, Lord Lyndhurst.

Charles Lord Tenterden, *Chief Justice of K. B.*

William Lord Plunket.

Henry, Lord Cowley.

Charles, Lord Stuart De Rothesay.

William, Lord Heytesbury.

Thomas, Lord Wallace.

William Draper, Lord Wynford.

Charles Manners Sutton, *Speaker of the House of Commons.*

Edward Stanley.

WilliamThomas Horner Fox Strang, ways.

Charles Redlynch Fox Strangways. Stephen Digby Fox Strangways. Giles Digby Fox Strangways. John George Charles Fox Strangways. *Sir* Arthur Paget, G. C. B. Robert Grosvenor. William Henry John Scott. *Sir* John Leach, Knt., *Master of the Sails.*

Sir Lancelot Shad well, Knt., *Vice Chancellor. Sir* Nicolas Conyngham Tindal, Knt.

CAief *Justice of Common Fleas. Sir* William Alexander, Knt., *Chief Baron of Exchequer. Sir* George Fitzgerald

Hill, *Bart. Sir* John Sinclair, *bart. Sir* John Newport, *bart. Sir* William Grant. Sir John Nicholl.

Thomas Grenville.

William Dundas.

Charles Philip Yorke.

Charles Bathurst.

William Wickham.

"Nathaniel Bond.

Sir William Drummond.

Charles Arbuthnot.

John Hnokham Frere.

Reginald Pole Carew.

John Sullivan.

Henry Pierrepont.

Richard Ryder.

Sir Robert Liston, G. C. B.

William Vesey Fitzgerald.

Hugh Elliott.

William Sturges Bourne.

Sir Robert Peel, *bart.*

William Adam.

Sir Charles Bagot. G. C. B. *Sir* Edward Thornton. *Sir* John Beckett, tart. *Sir* George Henry Rose, *bai l. Sir* Samuel Shepherd. *Sir* Henry Russell, fturf. Charles Grant.

Henry Goulburn.

Charles Watkin Williams Wynn.

Sir v illiam H enry Fremantle, *Sir* George Wairender, *bai t.* Charles Hope.

David Boyle.

Sir Stratford Canning, G. C. B. *Sir* Gore Ouseley, *bart.* Augustus John Foster.

S.r Frederick James Lamb, G. C. B. Charles Vaughan.

Sir George Cockburn, *bart. Sir* Samuel Hulse.

Stephen Rumbold Lushington.

"Sir Anthony Hart.

John Charles Herries.

Sir James M'Intosh. *Sir* William Keppel. *Sir* Christopher Robinson. *Sir* Henry Hardinge.

Thomas Peregrine Courtenay.

John Wilson Croker.

Lieut—General Sir George Murray. "John Calcraft.

Henry Hobhouse.

Thomas Franklin Lewis.

Robert Adair.

Sir Brook Taylor, G. C. H. *Sir* William Rae, *bart. Sir* William Johnstone Hope.

Robert Grant.

George James Welbore Agar Ellis.

Sir James Graham, *bai t.*

George Robert Dawson.

Charles Poulett Thomson.

Sir John Bayley, Knt. *Sir* James Allan Park, Knt. *Sir* William Garrow, Knt. Air Joseph Littledale, Knt.

Sir Stephen Gaselee, Knt. *Sir* John Vaughan, Knt. *Sir* James Parke, Knt. *Sir* William Bolland, Knt. *Sir* James Bernard Bosanquet, Knt. *Sir* William Elias Taunton, Knt. *Sir* Edward Hall Alderson, Knt. *Sir* John Patteson, Knt. *And the Judges of the King's Bench, the Judges of the Common Pleas, and the Barons of the Court of Eichequer for the time being.*

William Francis Spencer Ponsonby.

George Pitt, now Lord Rivers.

Horace Pitt.

George Lionel Dawson Damer.

Henry Dawson Damer.

1831 — William Samuel Best.

1831—Samuel Best, *Clerk.*

1807— *Sir* William Oglander, dart.

1805—*Sir* James Hanham, *bart.*

1792-Air John Wyldbore Smith,&arr.

1794—*Sir* Richard Colt Hoare,6arf.

Sir Charles Chad, *hart.* 1817—*Sir* Richard Carr Glyn, *bart.* 1823—*Sir* Edward Synge, *bart.* 1823—*Sir* Molyneux Hyde Nepean-, *bart. Sir* Edward Baker Baker, *bart.* 5'ir Francis Hartwell, *bart. Sir* William Coles Medly cott, *bart. Sir* Colquhoun Grant, K.C.B. Air Henry Fane. 1823— *Sir* George Ridout Bingham, K C B

Sir il enry Fane, K.C.B.

Sir Thomas Denman, *Kt., Attorney-General.*

Sir William Horne, *Knt., Solicitor-General.* 1808— William England, D. D., *Archdeacon of Dorset.* William Page Richards, D.D. Thomas Wyndham, D.D. 1831—John Fisher, D. D., *Arch. deacon of Berks.* 1831—William Palmer, D.D.

James Henry Arnold, LL.D.

George Trenchard, LL.D.

John Trenchard Pickard, LL.D.

"Richard Bingham, *jun.*

1809— Henry Bankes.

William John Bankes.

1824— John Bond, *jun.* 1783—Francis John Browne. 1795—John Herbert Browne.

Edward Pery Buckley. 1819—Thomas Bowyer Bower.

Thomas Bowyer Bower, *jun.* John Bragge.

"William Horace Beckford. 1314—Thomas Horlock Bastard.

William Bragge.

Henry Baring.

Henry Tregonwell Bower.

Edward Bower.

William John Bethel. 1831—Richard Brouncker.

William Bond. 1831—Nathaniel Bond. 1831—William Boucher.

George Bankes. 1831—Charles Bowles.

James Bennett.

William Churchill.

John Calcraft. 1825—John Hales Calcraft.

Alexander Cunningham. 1827—Samuel Cox.

—Henry Combe Compton. 1831—James Benjamin Coles.

Robert Colmer. 1812—Admiral Henry Digby, now Sir Henry, K. C. B.

Mark Davis.

1815— John Disney.

Edward St. Vincent Digby.

Kenelm Henry Digby.

Charles Wriothesley Digby. Somerville Digby. 1831—Edward *Ticliborne* Doughty. 1794—James Frampton. 1831—Henry Frampton. 1818—James John Farquharson.

James John Farquharson, jun.

John Floyer. 1831—James Chamness Fyler.

William Charlton *t* rampton.

Thomas Grove.

Thomas Grove, *jun.* 1831—Wyndham Goodden. 1831—John Goodden.

1810—Robert Gordon.

1816— John Goodferd.

1824—John Bingley Garland.

Richard Plumtre Glyn.

Thomas Christopher Glyn.

Robert Thomas John Glyn.

Hugh Chudleigh Haines.

John Greathed Harris.

John Adair Hawkins.

Walter Parry Hodges.

William Hallett. 1831—John Hussey, *of Lyme* fteijis. 1831—John Hussey, *of Marnhull.* 1831—Thomas Brown Hardwicke. 1831—William Hanham. 1824—George Thomson Jacob.

John Kneller Kneller. 1805—Lawrence Edward St. Lo. 1816—Benjamin Lester Lester. 1831—George Colby Loftus.

John Michel.

Charles Michel.

W illiam Coles Medlycott, jun.

Abel Moysey.

1824— Hector Bower Munro. John Michel.

Evan Nepean.

John Oglander. 1823—David Okeden Parry Okeden.

William Parry Okeden.

Henry Oglander.

William Oglander. 1784—William Morton Pitt

I.chimin! Morton Pleydell.

1806— John Penn. 1807— William Pitt. 1816— John Phelipn.

William Gill Paxton.

1823—Edward Berkeley Portman.

George Purling.

Henry Portman.

John Frederick Pinney.

William Pinney.

Henry Portman.

Wyndham Portman.

1825— Henry Charles Sturt.

1814—Henry Ker Seymcr.

1825—John James Smith.

1831-Gabriel Tucker Steward.

Henry Ker Seymer, *jun.*

Richard Tucker Steward.

John Stein,

Charles Fox Strangways.

Thomas Pox Strangways. 1794 Lrwis 1). G. Tregonwell. 1805—William Tucker.

George Nesbit Thompson.

St. Barbe Tregonwell.

John Tregonwell.

Edward Williams.

1819—Charlton Byam Wollaston.

Robert Williams, *of lihodt Hill.*

1817— Robert Williams.

Joseph Weld.

1831—Humphry Weld.

James Weld. 1823—'John White.

John Willis.

Josiah Wedgwood.

George Digby Wingfield.

Richard Baker Wingfield.

Harry Farr V cat man.

E$quirtrm 1801—Richard Blackmore.

Edward Bradford.

William Bond.

Thomas Bond.

William J as. Brookland. 1819—John Bastard.

Edward Bullock.

Edward Bankes.

John Bragge.

Champness Pleydell Bragge. 1823-»William Alleyne Barker. Henry Bower.

Thou. Wickham Bircb. 1793-John Clavel. 1831—Wm. Rush Hallet-tChurchill. 1807—lohn.Morton Olson.

John Cohner.

Hinckley Cooper.

Horace GeorgeCholmondeley.

William Digby, *Canon of Worcester.* 1816—Charles Dighy, *Canon of* 11 hidsor. 181(1—John Davis. 1807-John Dampier. 1831—John James Golden Dowland.

William England, *jun*

Edward Mar wood Elton.

Robert Frome.

Geo. Clutterbuck Frome.

Thomas Lane Fox. 1816—William Frederick Grove.

George Gould. 1816—Francis Goforth. 1831—Wyndham Jeane Goodden.

Carr Glyn. 1831—lohn Hampden. 1831—Matthew Irving. now D.D. 1824—William MossKing. of *Loner Critchell.*

James Michel.

John Munden.

Giles Meech.

1824-Edward Murray.

William Meyrick. 1795—Charles Phelips. 1824— William Phelips.

George Pickard. 1808—George Saxby Penfold. now

D. D. 1814—John Parsons.

Geo. Trenchard Pickard. 1823—George Pickard, *jun.*

Edward Peacock.

Charles Russell.

Gregory Raymond.

Samuel Serrel.

George Augustus Seymer. 1823—Henry Fox Strangways. 1827—Robert Salkeld.

Andrew Tucker.

Nathaniel Templeman. 1831—James Acland Templer. 1831—George Henry Templer. 1814—James Venables.

John Williams.

John Wills. 1816—Ed»ard Walter West.

David Williams.

John Watts.

John Digby Wingfield.

John Heathcote Wyndham, and 1813-HarryFarrYeatman. *Clerks. Note.*—The year is mentioned when the acting Justices took out their *dedimus potestatem;* and those with a Star (») prefixed, have died since the Commission passed.

The Mayors and Bailiffs of Boroughs, in this County, are constituted by their Charters of Incorporation, to exercise the office of *Justices* within their Jurisdictions, with almost equal powers as the Justices of the County at large. See a List of the present *Mayors, Bailiffs,* and their *Town Clerks,* under the head of Constables within Franchises, *postea,* sect. VI.

1. The Names of the Clerks to the Justices of the Peace, acting within the several Divisions of this County, (1832,) and their Residence, are— *Divisions. Names. Residence.*

Doicbester Thomas Coombs Dorchester.

Br id port Thomas Fox Beaminster.

Divisions.

Oerne

Names. lltsidences.

.ThomasCockeram,jun....Cerne Abba«.

.Charles O. Bartlett Wareham. .J. T. King and Son Blandford. . Henry Rowden Wimborne.

Charlet E. Buckland Shaftesbury.

.James F. Melmotfa Sherborne.

Wareham.,

Blandford..

Wimborne..

Shaftesbury

Sherborne..

Sturm inster

Robert R. Harvey Sturminster Newton.

See a List of their Fees, *Schedule* H.

2. The Master or Governor of the House of CorRection was first directed to be appointed in 1573, by the stat. 18 Eliz. c. 3. with a Salary to be paid him quarterly by the Treasurer of the County; but no one appears to have been regularly appointed until 1610, stat. 7 Jac. 1, c. 4. The Names of the Persons appointed to the House of Correction at *Sherborne,* which seems to have been the only one in this County, are— 1610-16.—James Gascoigne. 1708—Nathaniel Thornton, *vice* Gascoigne, dec. 1718 Francis Derbie, *vice* Thornton, dis. 1722—Francis Derbie, *vice* his Father, dec.

1730—Robert Ring, *vice* Derbie, res.

1754—John Bown, *vice* Ring, res.

1772—John Gerrard, *vice* Bown, dec.

1793—Isaac Gerrard, *vice* his Father, dec.

The House of Correction was removed from *Sherborne* to Dorchester, in the year 1793, and united with the County Gaol, and there has been no other in the County since that time. The Gaoler is now appointed the Keeper of the said House of Correction, by the Justices in Sessions, under the Regulations of the stat. 4 G. 4, c. 64. His Salary extends to both offices.—See Sec. II, No. 4, Gaol.

V.—The Treasurer of the County keeps the County Stock. He is appointed in pursuance of the stat. 12 G. II, c. 29, s. 11, by the Justices in Sessions, who have power to continue or remove him at their pleasure. At the *Michaelmas* Sessions, 1739, soon after the passing the above-mentioned Act, two Treasurers were appointed, one for the Western, and the other for the Eastern Districts of the said County, the Act allowing the appointment of more than one Treasurer, and these appointments were continued until the *Midsummer* Sessions, 1820, when the offices were united, and the two persons who then held the separate offices were appointed to the single office of Treasurer for the whole County. The Treasurers appointed for the two separate Districts since the year 1739, have been as follow:—

WESTERN DISTRICT. EASTERN DISTRICT.

1739—Nicholas Stickland. *Mich. S.*

1739—Robert Loder. *Mich. S.* 1769—Robert Lambert. *Epivh.S.* 1751—Walter Erie. *Easter S.* 1802—John C. Manfield. *Mich. S.* 1775—George Hayward. *Mich. S.* 1808—Kdwaibboswiii. *Mich. S.* 1780—Thos. Waters, jun. *Mids. S.* 1787—J. T. KlJTG. *Easter S.*

The office is now held by Edward Boswell and John Tregonwell King, with a Salary of *£60* per annum, payable cut of the County Rate, under the authority of the statutes 12 G. 2, c. 29, s. 11, and 55 G. 8, c. 51, s. 17.

The before mentioned statute, 12 G. 2, c. 29, directed the mode of levying and paying the County Rates, and a new Rate was then made (1740), which has subsisted ever since. The various payments chargeable on the County Rate, are specified by several statutes: and no charge but such as is authorised by statute can be legally paid out of the County Rate without the special direction of the Justices in Session.

Before the passing of the Act, 12 G. 2, c. 29, the various expenses borne by the county appear to have been discharged by what was termed a *Bridge Rate,* which varied as to the amount. The following Rate (which is at £250) was collected in the year 1672 by the High Constables of the several Hundreds, Liberties, and Boroughs, in theatre Divisions of this County, as hereinafter mentioned, viz.—

The amount of the Money expended by Treasurers from the year 1740 to the year 1823 inclusive, specified under the respective heads, to which the Public Stock of the County is applicable *by* Law: and likewise the Money raised by Rates, or otherwise received by Treasurers, making the County Stock, within the same period to meet such Expenditure, is hereafter given in an Abstract Schedule I.

Bailiffs of *Hundreds* and *Liberties* are appointed at the Courts Leet, held at *Michaelmas* yearly, or in default thereof by the Justices in Sessions, and frequently, if none are appointed, the Chief Constables do the duty. These officers execute the Precepts of the Justices within their Franchises, Hundreds, or Liberties; attend the Assizes or Quarter Sessions, collect Fines, summon Juries, &c., though of late years, for want of regular appointments to this office, the latter is done by the *bound* Bailiffs.

VI.—Constables of *Hundreds* and *Liberties* were officers ordained by the Common Law in the Saxon age, for when *Hundreds* were derived out of Counties, in every Hundred High Constables were appointed, and in process of time, in most of the large Towns and Boroughs, Petty Constables, or *Headboroughs,* besides the *Tithingman,* were also chosen, who, by virtue of their offices, were, as well as the High Constables, Conservators of the Peace within their respective Jurisdictions.—*Fineux, Lord C. J. of K. B. temp. H. 7.—Dalt' Jusf* c. 16.—*Salk' Rep'* 3, *p.* 98. All these officers were appointed in the Sheriff's Tourn, and afterwards in the Courts Leet, which This Court was originally derived out of the Tourn—*Co. Inst. e.* 54; as Hundreds were derived out of the County Court, 12 Hen. 7, e. 15.—Bract. were derived out of it, and which seem to have been parcel of, and appendant to the Hundred, granted out by the Crown to the ancient *Thanes,* and others of great rank. On the decline of the Saxon Jurisprudence, in after times, *Manors* were, in like manner, parcelled out and granted to the *Barons;* and as these High and Petty Constables are recognised by the Common Law, it cannot be true, as it is said, that the former were fiTst created in 1285, by the stat. of Winchester, 13 Edw. 1, stat. 2, c. 6, for these appear to have been *specially* chosen and appointed. By this statute every man was obliged, according to his estate and degree, to provide a determinate quantity of such arms as were then in use, in order to keep the peace, and it was enacted " That view of Armour "be made every year, two times, and in every Hun"dred and Franchise two Constables shall be chosen "to make the view of Armour, &c.;" therefore it should seem that the Constables, chosen under the authority of this statute, were, in addition to those before appointed at the Courts Leet, and seems to furnish evidence of the previous existence of such officers. *Salk' Rep* 1, *p.* 175.—2 *Hawk' c.* 10, s. S3.

As the speedy and effectual execution of the Law depends much upon the ability, discretion, and activity of the Constables, it was thought advisable to call the attention of those who have the appointment sect. 24. It is remarkable that the word "Iieet" is not to be found in any of our ancient Law Writers, nor in any statute prior to the 27th Edw. 3, c. 28, (1354); nor again until 4 Edw. 4, c. 1, and 12 Edw. 4, c. 10. though this Court was known to have existed in the time of the Saxons, and frequently occurs in Domesday Book.

These Weapons were changed in 1577, Ph. and M., c. 2,) into others of more modern service; but both this and the former provisions were repealed in 1603, (1 Jac' 1, c. 25). *Black' Com'* 1, ji. 410. of such officers, to the selection of proper persons, and particularly to the *residence* of the Constables in the Hundreds'and Liberties for which they are appointed, during the continuance of their office. With that view the following recommendation was made, *Mid' Ses',* 1792.

"Whereas a material part of the duty of High "Constables of the several and respective Hundreds, "and Liberties, within this County, consists in executing "the Justices' Precepts for the County at large; and in "collecting the Rates of the said County, and in making "returns thereof: And Whereas great inconveniences have "arisen from a want of proper and responsible persons "being appointed to that office:—It is therefore earnestly "recommended to the *Under Sheriff,* and *Stewards* "of the several Courts within this County, where "such High Constables are elected, to prevent, as far "as lies in their power, the appointment of persons who "are improper, and not responsible, to execute the said "office: and also that they, and the acting Magistrates of "this County, will reject all such persons who are improper, "and not responsible, who shall be offered as Deputies: "And it is requested, that the Under Sheriff, and "Stewards aforesaid will, within a few days after the "election of such Constables or Deputies, at the Courts "aforesaid, transmit the *names* and *places of abode* of such "as shall have been so elected, to the Clerk of the Peace "of the said County.

By the Court, WALLIS."

Note.—A Copy of this Recommendation was transmitted generally to the Officers above mentioned.

The allowing Costs to Constables in the execution of their office, in certain cases, is provided for by divers statutes, and a Table of such allowances is given hereafter, Schedule K.

The following are the Names of all the Hundreds, Liberties, and Boroughs, in this County, in alphabetical Order, within which High Constables are elected and chosen, at the Courts Leet held at *Michaelmas* yearly; with the Names of the Lords, Stewards, and Town Clerks, by whom they are appointed, or, in default, by the Justices at their Quarter Sessions; and such Constables are removable by the same authority that appoints them.—I *Salk' Rep'* 150.— *Black' Com* 1, *p.* 355.

Hundreds. Ltrdi. Sttwards.

Badbury Henry Bankes, Esq Wm. Castleman.

Beaminster John Bridge, Esq Peter Cox.

Beaminster Forum & Redhone.

Bere Regis J. S. *W.* S. Erie Drax, Esq. Thomas Shettle.

Brownshall

Buckland Newton Henry Charles Sturt, Esq. R. Henning Parr.

Cerne, Totcombe, & Modbury John Stein, Esq Thomas Fox.

Cogdean Henry Bankes, Esq Wru. Castleman.

Coombs Ditch *li.* 1. G. Tregonwell, Esq. J. T. King & Son.

Cranbome Marquis of Salisbury Charles Harbin.

Culliford Tree Joseph Weld, Esq T. Bartlett & Son.

Eggerton

Godderthorne

George

Hasilor Henry Bankes, Esq Wm Castleman.

Hundredsbarrow SirW.W.Yea, Bart. &o'rs.George Filliter.

Knowlton Earl of Shaftesbury T. G.

Read.

i/oosebarrow SirW.W.Yea, Bart. &o'rs. George Filliter.

Monkton-up-Wimborne

Piddletown Earl of Orford T. Bartlett & Son.

Pimpeme Marquis of Salisbury Charles Harbin.

Redlane

Rowbarrow Henry Bankes, Esq Wm. Castleman.

Rushmore Jas. J. F'arquharson, Esq. J. T. King & Son.

Sixpenny and Sir K. Carr Glyn, Bart. ...P. M. Chitty.

Handley Marquis of Anglesea Wm. Castleman.

Sherborne Earl of Digby Thomas Fooks.

Sturminster Newton Castle...Lord Rivers Robt. R. Harvey.

Hundreds. Lords. Stewards.

Tollerford Earl of Uchester Wm. Jennings:

Uggscombe

Winfrith Joseph Weld, Esq T. Bartlett & Sod,

Wimborne St. Giles Earl of Shaftesbury T. G. Read.

Whiteway The King-Under Sheriff.

Whitchurch Canonicorum...John Bullen, Esq J. Bullen.

Yetminster Earl of Digby T. Fooks.

Liberties.

Alcester John Perring, Esq

Alton Pancras Winchester College Edward Rolfe.

Bindon Joseph Weld, Esq T. Bartlett & Son.

Broadwindsor John Pinney, Esq James Parsons.

Dewlish Earl of Uchester Wm. Jennings.

Forthington Prince of Wales T. Coombs, *Dep.*

Frampton Francis John Browne, Esq. Peter Cox.

Gillingham Marquis of Westminster.. .P. M. Chitty.

Halstock Sir James Scarlett Thomas Fox.

Lothcrs and BothenhamptonSir M. HydeNepean, Bart.Ditto.

Owermoigne John Cree, Esq Francis Ingram.

Piddlehinton Eton College Ditto.

Piddletrenthide Winchester College Edward Rolfe.

Poorstock Marq. of Cleveland *Sc.* o'rs Farwell.

Portland The King H. H.Tizard, *Dep.*

JRyme Intrinseca Prince of Wales T. Coombs, *Dep.*

Stower Provost King's Coll. Cambridge...William Hughes.

Stoborough Lord Rivers Robt. R. Harvey.

Sutton Points Joseph Weld, Esq T. Bartlett & Son.

Sydling St. Nicholas Winchester College Edward Rolfe.

Wabyhouss *Rev.* George Gould Francis Ingram.

Wyke Regis and Elwell Earl of Uchester Edward Bos well.

Boroughs. Lords. Town Clerks.

Dorchester Mayor Joseph Stone.

Bridport Bailiffs Edwin Nicholetts.

Blandford Bailiff Septimus Smith.

Corfe Castle Mayor Wm. Castleman.

Lyme Regis Ditto George Smith.

Shafton Ditto Chas. E. Buckland.

Wareham Ditto Chas. O. Bartlett.

Weymouth & MelcombeRegisDitto H. H. Tizard.

Note.—Within the *Hundreds* marked with a Star () no Courts have been held for a long time past; therefore the High Constables, &c. of these Hundreds are appointed at the Quarter Sessions.

If any Constable appointed as aforesaid shall die, or go out of the Parish or Place, any two Justices may make and swear a new one, until the Lord of the Manor shall hold a Court Leet; and if any Officer shall continue above a year in his office, the Justices in Quarter Sessions may discharge him and put another in his place, until the Lord of the Manor shall hold a Court as aforesaid. —13 $ 14 *Car.* 2, c. 12, s. 15.

VII. —Tithingmen.—These Officers are unquestionably very ancient, and the Borsholder, (Burgh Elder), Headborough, and Tithingman were synonimous, and are also, as well as Constables, elected and chosen at the *Court Leet,* and where no Court Leet is held, by the Justices in Sessions, as before observed. In this County, and in all the

Western Counties of the Kingdom, this officer has been always called the *Tithingman,* and his office is the same as that of the Petty Constable, and both are in aid of the High Constable. In some of the large Parishes in the County, two Tithingmen are appointed, and they take the East or West, North or South parts of the Parish respectively. For the number of these Tithingmen, (see Part II), and for the Allowances to be made to them in the Execution of their Office. (See Sch. K.) VIII. —Surveyors Op Bridges.—By the common law Counties were chargeable with the Repairs of Public Bridges, unless some Persons, by reason of the Tenure of their Lands or Tenements, or others by prescription only, were bound to repair: but that no Town or Freeman shall be distrained to make Bridges, nor Banks, but such as of old time of right have been accustomed, (9 Hen. 3, c. 15); and none can be compelled to make *new* Bridges where never any were before, but by Act of Parliament—*Co. 2 Inst.* 701. From the year 1530, by the stat. 22 Hen. 8, c. 5, the Justices (four of them at the least) shall have power and authority to appoint *two Surveyors* to see all decayed Bridges repaired and amended from time to time, *as often as need shall require,* (s. 4), with such Costs and Charges as by their discretion shall be thought convenient, (s. 5,) and such part and portion of the Highways at the ends of such Bridges to be repaired and amended in like manner, (s, 9.) And the Quarter Sessions may appoint annually *two Justices* in each Division, to give directions for the Repairs of such decayed Bridges, and to issue a written order for that purpose, provided such expenses shall not exceed £20—Stat. 53 G. 3, c. 110, s. 1. Mr. William Evans, of Wimborne Minster, is appointed the Surveyor for this County, at a Salary of £200 per Annum. For an Account of all the Stone Bridges within this County see Part V. IX.—Surveyors Of Highways were first constituted in 1555, by the stat. 2 & 3 Ph. & M. c. 8, and directed to be appointed by the Constable and Churchwarden in every Parish and Place. Before this statute every Parish

Ot Place was bound, of common right to keep the Highways in sufficient Repair, unless by reason of the Tenure of Lands, or otherwise, this Care was consigned to some particular private Person.—*Black. Com'* 1, *p.* 357. Now, by stat. 13, G. 3, c. 78, (1773,) Surveyors are to be appointed after *Michaelmas* annually, by the Justices, out of such *Inhabitants* or others as are described in the said statute, to remove Annoyances in, and to direct the reparation of the Public Highways. For the number of these Officers, see Part IV.
X.—Overseers of the Poor were first ordained in the year 1601, stat. 43 Eliz. c. 2, and are nominated and appointed in every *Parish* or *Place,* on 25th March, or within 14 Days after (though a subsequent nomination will be valid) by two Justices dwelling near the Parish. They must be substantial Householders, and expressed so to be in the appointment of the Justices. The care of the Poor is intrusted to them, in conjunction with the *Churchwardens,* where there are any. They are required to meet at least once a month, in the Church, on *Sunday,* after Divine Service in the Afternoon, under a Penalty. The more prominent part of their duties are—1. *To make a Rate in order to raise a Fund for the maintenance of the Poor. 2.* To ascertain what Poor the Parish or Place for which they are appointed, are bound to maintain. 3. To remove such Persons as it is not liable to support, as soon as they become *actually* chargeable. 4. To inspect the economy, and administer to the wants of the Poor. 5th, and lastly, upon going out of office to make up and pass their accounts, and deliver over any balance in their hands to their successors, together with the property and documents of the Parish.—*Nolan,* 41, 52, 53.
    In the year 1776, Parliament first instituted an enquiry into the state of the Poor, and Overseers of the several Parishes and Places within that part of Great Britain called *England,* were required to make Returns, on Oath, to certain Questions specified in the Act (16 G. 3, c. 40), relative to their Relief and Maintenance; and again in the years 1787, 1803, and 1815, similar Returns

were directed to be made by the Acts 26 G. 3, c. 56,-43 G. 3, c. 144, and 55 G. 3, c. 47.
    The Questions in the last mentioned Statute (Sch. A,) were as follow:— 1. What was the Amount of Money raised by the Poor's Rate, or any other Rate or Rates, in each Year, ending the 25th March?
2. What was the Amount of Money expended in each Year, ending as aforesaid, for the Relief and Maintenance of the Poor? 3. What was the Amount of Money expended in each Year, ending as aforesaid, in Suits of Law, Removal of Paupers, and Expenses of Overseers, or other Officers employed? 4. What was the Amount of Money expended in each Year, ending as aforesaid, for Militia Purposes; distinguishing the Maintenance of the Wives and Children of Militiamen, from any other Militia Charges? 5. What was the Amount of Money expended in each Year, ending as aforesaid, for all other Purposes, (except the two last Questions, 3 and 4), including County Rate, Church Rate, Highway Rate, Rent of Workhouses, Setting the Poor on Work, &c. &c. &c. 6. What was the Total Amount of Money expended in each Year, ending as aforesaid? 7. What was the number of Persons relieved from the Poor's Rate, permanently, throughout the Year: distinguishing Persons so relieved *out* of any Workhouse, and Persons so relieved *in* the House: but not including any Children, whose Parents have been permanently relieved *out* of the House? 8. What was the number of Parishioners relieved occasionally within each Year? 9. W hat is the number of Members of Friendly Societies, &c? 10. What is the average annual Amount or Produce of Charitable Donations, (whether arising out of Land or Money) which have been given by Deed or Will for the Benefit of Poor Persons; and which are distributed by the Minister, Churchwardens, and Overseers, or any of them, distinguishing such Donations as are applicable to the Maintenance of Parish Schools? 11. Is there any Hospital or Almshouse, School, or other permanent Charitable Foundation, which is not under the

management and control of the Minister, Churchwarden, or Overseer, or any of them? AN ABSTRACT

Of the Returns made by Overseers of the Poor of every Parish and Place within this County, in Answer to the Questions before-mentioned, relative to the Expense in Relief and Maintenance of the Poor, in each Year, ending 25th March.

Note.—The above three Years, (1783, 1784, 1785,) contain the *medium* of Expenses, but the number of Poor who received constant or occasional Relief is not returned. For the purpose of compressing this Abstract in the *Octavo* sise, the fractional Parts of a Pound have been omitted. *Column* 1.—These Receipts include the amount of Charitable Donations distributed by the Minister and Parish Officers, Fines, and other Sums received, which make " the Parish Stock." *Column* 2.—The actual Expense in each Year, (except the Years 1783, 1784,1785, being the medium or average of those Years.) *Column* 3 The Expenses of Law Business, Orders of Removal, Examinations, and other Proceedings Expenses of Entertainments at Meetings,

Expenses in Journeys, and Attendance on Magistrates.

Column 4 These Charges must have been included in Column 5, for the first five Years. *Column* 6.—These Charges (except the Money paid to the County Rate, the Money paid for Rent of Workhouses, and for setting the Poor on Work) ought not to have been included in the Parish Stock Account. *Column* 6.—This is the actual Expense, except in the three Years above mentioned.

In the Year 1815 the number of Select Vestries was 34, and the number of Assistant Overseers, 48.

The Total of the Money raised in the Years 1813, 1814, and 1815, appears to have averaged the Sum of *£109,890,* which is at the rate of £0 3s. 2d. in the Pound, according to the Sums assessed to the Property Tax, in the year 1815.

AN ABSTRACT

Of the Returns made by Overseers of every Parish and Place in this County, in Answer to the Questions above mentioned, relative to the State of the Poor. (a) This does not include any Children whose Parents have been relieved out of the House. (b) Thirty-nine Parishes and Places in this County maintain the greater part of their Poor in Workhouses. (c) The number of Persons relieved from the Kate, according to the Population Returns in 1811, appears to have been about a *seventh* part of the Population.

The evidence afforded by the above Abstracts shows that from the first enquiry in 1776 to 1813, (a Period of thirty-seven years), the Money expended in the last year was more than four times the amount in 1776: and that in the last five years the Expenditure has amounted, on an average of those years, to the enormous sum of £108,272 for this County. There appears to have been a diminution in 1815, but it increased again to the above average sum in the years 1827 and 1830, when his Majesty's Government,, and not Parliament, directed Returns to be made. This gradual increase which has taken place, both in the Assessment for the Relief, Support, and Maintenance of the Poor, and in the number of Paupers relieved, must have arisen from Causes inherent in the System itself; as it does not appear to have depended entirely upon any temporary or local circumstances. Scarcity of Provisions and a diminished demand for particular Manufactures have frequently occasioned, and consequently increased, the pressure in particular Parishes or Places: but in this County the largest proportion of the Population is employed in *Agriculture,* and yet there is the same progressive augmentation in the Expenditure as is to be found in the *manufacturing* Counties.

In addition to the *Civil Officers* before mentioned, a *special* Officer was appointed to receive the Public permanent Taxes of the County, namely "The Receiver General," from the Year 1692, (4 W. & M. c. 1.) The following Persons were appointed.

This Office is now transferred to the *Inspector* of Taxes, Mr. Prior, of Bath.

The *Land Tax,* was imposed very early, for ever since the year 1692 it has continued in the form it now stands more than half that time, at 4s. in the Pound; sometimes at 3s., sometimes at 2s., and in the Years 1732 and 1733, at Is., but without any total intermission. The medium has been 3s. 4d. in the Pound. The present Rate is at 4s., but it is, in fact, on an average throughout the County, certainly less than 2s., and is collected on *Tithings* (not on Parishes) *eo nomine,* and a certain number of these Tithings make up the Division, though there are Places denominated Tithings within the same Division, Hundred, or Liberty, and there are others that make part of and pay into *Parishes* which do not belong to the Division, Hundred, or Liberty, and from immemorial custom, or other reasons which cannot now be ascertained, were never separately collected or altered. The Sums assessed on each *Tithing* throughout the County, to this Tax, are particularly mentioned in Part 111, and amount to £32,751 15s. 10Jd., but about one-eighth of this Tax is redeemed.

2ndly—The *Assessed Taxes* were first imposed in 1696, on Houses and Windows; in 1777 on Male

Servants; in 1782 on Carriages; in 1784 on Horses for Riding, &c. Horse Dealers, and on Game Licenses; in 1795 on Hair Powder; in 1796 on Dogs; in 1798 on Armorial Bearings; and in 1808 on Husbandry Horses, &c. These were assessed annually, and in the year 1810, amounted in this County to about £58,000, but since that time, there has been a gradual decrease.

3dly—The *Property Tax* was first imposed in 1798, in order to furnish the means of defraying the enor moust cost of the War. It was at first proposed to triple the Amount of the Assessed Taxes, but this Plan however did not answer, and a Tax on *Income* was substituted in its stead: the Rate of Duty increased in a variety of gradations from £60 to £200 or upwards, and then it amounted to *one-tenth* part, which was its utmost limit; there were several deductions granted on account of Children, &c. This Tax was repealed in 1802, after the Peace. In 1803 it was again revived, under the Name of *Prop-*

erty Tax at 5 per Cent., or Is. in the pound, to this an Addition was made in 1805, and in 1808 it was increased to 10 per Cent., at which it remained till the year 1816, when this Tax was finally repealed. The Assessment on *real* Froperty (Schedule A.) amounted, in the last year (1815) to £69,839, viz. 2s. ia the pound on £698,395 10s. CJd. the estimated annual Value of such *real* Property, the amount of which, in each Parish and Place, is mentioned hereafter, Part IV.

The Names of the Knights and Burgesses who have represented this County in Parliament from the accession of King George the Third; with the times when the *Knights* and *Burgesses* were first sent to Parliament, and the dates of the *Charters* respectively.

KNIGHTS.—18 Edw. 1. 1290. 1760— George Pitt Humphry Sturt. 1768—Ditto ditto. 1774—Ditto ditto. 1776—*Hon. George Pitt, vice his Father, created a Peer.* 1780—Humphry Sturt *Hon.* George Pitt. 1784— *Hon.* George Pitt Francis John Browne. 179ft—Francis John Browne William Morton Pitt. 1796—Ditto ditto. 1802—Ditto ditto. 1806— William Morton Pitt Edward Berkeley Portman. 1807— Ditto ditto. 1812—Ditto ditto. 1818—Ditto ditto. 1820—Ditto ditto. 1323—Edward Berkeley Portman, *vice his Father, dec.* 18J6—Henry Bankes, *vice* Pitt, *vac.* Edward Berkeley Portman...Henry Bankes. 1830— Ditto ditto. 1831— Ditto *Right Hon.* John Calcraft. *Right Hon.* Lord Ashley, *vice* Calcraft, *dec.*

Not more than six Elections appear to have been contested for the Count y. The first began in 1726, in the Sheriffalty of John Hawles Johnson, on the death of Thomas Strangways, Esq. when George Pitt and Thomas Horner, Esqrs. were the Candidates. The numbers were—for Mr. Pitt, 1251—Mr. Horner, 1063; when Mr. Pitt was declared duly elected. In 1727. in the same Sheriffalty, at the General Election, Richard Brodrippi Edmund Morton Pleydell, and George Chafin, Esqrs. were CandidatesThe numbers were—for Mr. Brodripp, 1081—Mr. Pleydell, 1467, and Mr Chafin, 1502; when the two latter

were declared duly elected. In 1806, in the Sheriffalty of Edward Williams, at the General Election. Wm. Morton Pitt, Edw. Berkeley Portman, and Henry Bankes, Esqrs. were Candidates. The numbers were—for Mr. Pitt, 1722—Mr. Portman, 1049-and Mr.Bankes, 827; when the two former were declared duly elected. In 1807, in the Sheriffalty of Arthur Cosens, William Morton Pitt, Edward Berkeley Portman, and Henry Bankes, Esqrs. were Candidates. The numbers were—for Mr. Pitt, 1526—Mr. Portman, 1183-and Mr. Bankes, 1130; when the two former were declared duly elected. In 1831, in the Sheriffalty of the *Hon.* Henry Dawson Damer, at the General Election, Edw. Berkeley Portman, Henry Bankes, Esqrs. and the *Right Hon.* John Calcraft, were Candidates. The Numbers were—for Mr. Portman, 1699—Mr. Bankes, 1176—and Mr. Calcraft, 1452; when Mr. Portman and Mr. Calcraft were declared duly elected. And in the same year, on the death of Mr. Calcraft, the *Right Hon.* the *Lord* Ashley, and the *Hon.* Mr. Ponsonby were Candidates. The Numbers were— for *Lord* Ashley, 1847, and for Mr. Ponsonby, 1811; when the former was declared duly elected.

BURGESSES.

Bridpoet. 23 Edw. 1 *Charter* 19 *Car. II.* 1667.

1760—*Sir* Gerard Napier, *Bart.* ... Thomas Coventry. 1768—Thomas Coventry Sambrooke Freeman. 1774— Ditto. *Hon.* Lucius F. Gary. 1780— Thomas Scott Richard Beckford. 1784—Ditto Charles Sturt. 1790— Charles Sturt James Watson, xx. *D. SjSergt.at Law.* 1795— George Barclay, *nice* Watson, *vac, created a Judge in Bengal.* 1796— Charles Sturt George Barclay. 1802—George Barclay *Sir* Evan Nepean, *Bart.* 1806— Ditto ditto. 1807— *Sir* Evan Nepean, *Bart.* ...*Sir* S. Hood, *K. B.* 1812—William Draper Best Horace David Cholwell St. Paul. 1817— Henry Charles Sturt, *vice* Best, *app. a Welch Judge.* 1818— *Sir a. V.* C, St. Paul, Bort....Henry Charles Sturt. 1820 *Sir* Horace D.C.St.Paul, *Bart.* James Scott. 1826 Ditto Henry Warburton. 1830— Ditto ditto. 1831— Ditto

Ditto.

Cokfe Castie. 14 Eliz.—*Charter* 31 *Car. II.* 1679.

1760 George Viscount Malpas...Henry Bankes. 1762—John Campbell, *vice* Bankes, *vac.* 1764—John Bond, *vice* Viscount Malpas, *dec.* 1768—John Bond John Jenkinson. 1774—Ditto ditto. 1780 Ditto Henry Bankes. 1784— Ditto ditto. 1790—Ditto ditto. 1796— Ditto ditto. 1801— Nathaniel Bond, *vice* John Bond, *vac.* Nathaniel Bond, *app. a Lord of the Treasury.* 1802— Henry Bankes Nathaniel Bond. 1806— Nathaniel Bond, *app. Judge Advocate General.* 1806—Henry Bankes *Right Hon.* Nathaniel Bond. 1807 Ditto Peter William Baker. 1812—Ditto ditto. 1818 Ditto George Bankes. 1820—Ditto ditto. 1823—John Bond, *vice* George Bankes, *vac.*

1826—George Bankes, *vice* Henry Bankes, *vac.* John Bond George Bankes.

1828— Nathaniel William Peach, *vice* Bond, *vac.* 1829— Philip John Miles, *vice* Peach, *vac.*

George Bankes having *vac.* his Seat, re-elected.

1830 George Bankes, *app. a Lord of the Treasury.*

Ditto Philip John Miles.

1831—Ditto Ditto.

Dorchester. 23 Edw. I *Charter* 5 Car. 1. 1630.

1761— Joseph Lord Milton Thomas Foster. 1762— John Damer, vice Lord Milton, an *English Peer.* 1765—William Ewer, *vice* Foster, *dec.* 1768— John Damer William Ewer. 1774—Ditto ditto. 1780— *Hon.* George Damer ditto. 1784—Ditto ditto. 1789— Thomas Ewer, *vice* William Ewer, *dec.* 1790— Hon. Cropley Ashley, *vice* Thomas Ewer, *dec.* Ditto Francis Fane. 1796—Ditto ditto. 1802—Ditto ditto. 1806— Ditto ditto. 1807— Ditto Robert Williams. 1811— C. H. Bouverie, *vice Hon.* C. Ashley, *a Peer.* 1812— Ditto Robert Williams, *Jun.* 1813— William A'Court, *vice* Bouverie, *vac.* 1814— Sir Samuel Shepherd, *KnU, vice* A'Court, *vac.* 1817— Ditto, *app. Attorney-General.* 1818— Robert Williams *Sir* Samuel Shepherd, *KnU* 1819— Charles

Warren, nice Shepherd, *vac.* 1820—Robert Williams Charles Warren. 1826—Ditto *Hon.* William Ashley Cooper. 1830— Henry Charles Sturt, *vice* Cooper, *vac.* Robert Williams Lord Ashley. 1831— Ditto Ditto.

— —*Hon.* A. Henry Ashley Cooped, *vice* Lord Ashley, *vae.*

Lyme Regis. 23 Edw. I.—*Charter.* 10 Car. I. 1634, 1760—Thomas Fane Henry Fane.

1/G8—Lord Burgheish ditto. 1774— Henry Fane *Hon.* Henry Fane. 178!)— *Hon.* Henry Fane David Robert Michel. Ditto *Hon.* Thomai Fane.

1790—Ditto ditto. 1796—Ditto ditto. 1802—*Hon.* Thomas Fane Henry Fane. 180G—Lord Burghersh, *vice* Thomas Fane, *vac.*

Henry Fane Lord Burghersh. 1807—Ditto ditto. 1812—Ditto ditto. 1816—John Thomas Fane, *vice* Lord Burghersh, *vac.* 1818—Ditto Vere Fane. 1820—Ditto ditto. 1826—Ditto *Hon.* Henry Sutton Fane. 1830— Ditto ditto. 1831— Ditto,... Ditto.

Shafton. 23 Edw. I.—CAarter. 17 Car. II. 1665.

1760—*Sir* Gilbert Heathcote, *Knt.* ...Samuel Touchet. 1768—William Chafin Grove...Ralph Payne. 1773— Francis Sykes, *vice* Payne, *vac.* 1774— Ditto Hans Wintrop Mortimer. 1776—George Rous, *vice* Sykes. 1780—Ditto Francis Sykes. 1784—George Rous A. Drummond.

— —J. Drummond, vice A. Drummond, dec.

1790—Charles Duncombe, *Jun.* ...William Grant.

1793—Paul Benfield, *vice* Grant, *vac.*

1796—Ditto Walter Boyd.

1802—Edward Loveden Loveden... Robert Hurst. 1806—Ditto *Sir* Home Popham.

'1807—Ditto *Right Hon.* Thomas Wallace.

1812—Charles Wetherell Edward Kerrison. 1818—J. B. S. Morrit...Edward John Shepherd. 1820 *Hon.* Edward Harbord...Abraham Moore. 1821— Ralph Leycester, *vice* Harbord, *a Peer.* 1822— Hon. Robert Grosvenor, *vice* Moore, *vac.* 1826—Ralph Leycester Edward D. Davenport. 1830— Edward Penrhyn W.

S. Dugdale. 1831— William L. Maberly, *vice* Dugdale, *vac.*

Edward Penrhyn William L. Maberly.

Wareham. 30 Edw. I.—*Charter.* 2 Anne. 1703.

176fl_John Pitt Thomas Erie Drax. 1768—Ralph Burton Robert Palk.

— _Whitshed Keene, vice Burton, *dec.* 1774—William Gerard Hamilton... Christopher D'Oyley.

1780—Thomas Farrer John Boyd. 1784—Ditto Charles Lefevre. 1786— John Calcraft, *vice* Lefevre, *vac.* 1790—*Lord* Robert Spencer Richard Smith. 1796-Ditto Charles Ellis. *Sir* Godfrey Vassall, *Bart. vice* Ellis, Doc. 1799— Joseph Chaplin Hankey, *vice* Spencer, *vac.* 1800— John Calcraft, nice Vassall, *dec.* 1802—Ditto Andrew Strahan. 1806— Ditto, opp. *Clerk of the Ordnance.*

Andrew Strahan Jonathan Raine.

1807— *Sir* Granby Thos. Calcraft, *Knt. Hon.* John William Ward. 1808— *Sir* Samuel Romilly, *Knt. vice* Calcraft, *vac.* 1812—Robert Gordon Theodore Henry Broadhead. 1818—John Calcraft Thomas Denman. 1820—Ditto John Hales Calcraft. 1826—Ditto Charles Baring Wall. 1828—*Right Hon.* John Calcraft, opp. *Vaymasler-General to the forces.* 1830— Ditto James Ewing. 1831— Charles Wood Granby Hales Calcraft.

Weymouth And Jmelcombe Regis.— Weymouth, 12 Edw. II.— Melcombe Regis, 8 Edw. II. *Charter.* 44 Geo. 3. 1804.

1760—John Olmius—Richard Glover— *Sir* JFras. Dashwood—John Tucker. — —Charles Walcot, *vice* Dashwood, *a Peer.* 1762—Richard Jackson, *vice* Olmius, *dec.* 1768—Villars, Lord Waltham—John Tucker—*Sir* C. Davies, *Bart.*— Jer. Dyson. 1774— *Right Hon.* Welbore Ellis—Wm. C. Grove—John Purling—John Tucker. 1780— Ditto. —Ditto. —Ditto.—War. Lisle. Gabriel Steward, *vice* Lisle, *vac.* 1781— W. R. Rumbold, *vice* Grove, *vac.* 1784—*Right Hon.* Welbore Ellis— John Purling—Gabriel Steward—*Sir* T. Rumbold, *Bart.* 1786—George Jackson, *vice* Steward, *vac.* 1788—Gabriel Steward, *vice* Jackson, *vac.* 1790— *Sir*

James Murray—Richard Johnstone van den Bempde—Andrew

Stuart—Thomas Jones.

1791— *Sir* James Johnstone, *vice* Jones, *dec.* 1796—Sir James Pulteney, Bart.—Andrew Stuart—Gabriel Tucker Steward

—William Garthshore. 1801—William Garthshore, *app. a Lord of the Admiralty.* Charles Adams, *vice* Stuart, *dec.* 1802 *Sir* James Pulteney, *Bart.*Gab. Tucker Steward—William Garth. shore—Charles Adams. 1806— Richard Tucker Steward, *vice* Garthshore, *dec. Sir* James Pulteney, *Bart* Gabriel Tucker Steward—Chas. Adams

Richard Tucker Steward.

1807— Sir James Pulteney, *Bart., app. Secretary at War.*

— —*Sir* James Pulteney, *Bart* Gabriel Tucker Steward—Chas. Adams

Richard Tucker Steward.

1810— *Sir* John Lowther Johnstone, *Bart., vice* G. T. Steward, toe. 1811— *Sir* John Murray, Barf., *vice* Pulteney, *dec.* 1812— Sir John Murray, *Bart.*— *Lord* Cranborne—Masterton Ure— Chris topher Idle. 1817— Adolphus John Dalrymple, *vice* Cranborne, *vac.* 1818— *Right Hon.* Thomas Wallace— Masterton Ure—William Williams— 1 nomas Powell Buxton.

1820—Ditto. —Ditto. —Ditto. Ditto.

1824—*Right Hon.* Thomas Wallace, *app. Master of the Mint.*

1826—Ditto.—Masterton Ure— Thomas Powell Buxton—John Gordon.

1828— Edward Burtenshaw Sugden, *vice* Wallace, *created a Peer.* 1829— Sir Edward B. Sugden, *KnU, app. Solicitor-General.* 1830— Masterton Ure— Thomas P. Buxton—John Gordon—*Sir* Edward B.

Sugden, *Knt.* 1831— Masterton Ure— Thomas P. Buxton—John Gordon—

Richard Weyland.

Charles Baring Wall, *vice* Weyland, *elected for County of Oxford.* SCHEDULE A.

57 *G.* III. c. 91.

A TABLE OF FEES,

To be taken by the CLERK OF THE PEACE of the County of Dorset, submitted to his Majesty's Justices of the

Peace, assembled at the Easter Quarter Session, held at DORCHESTER, the 4th day of April, 1826.

Appeals. £. s. d. For entering every Appeal to an Order of Removal 0 6 8 For every Order for Adjournment 0 6 8 For entering the same of Record 0 6 8 For Copy thereof for the Appellant's Attorney to serve on the respondent Parish 0 6 3 For entering every adjourned Appeal for the subsequent Session whether the Appeal be abandoned or not 0 6 8 t For Copy of Order, with the adjudication of the Court, each Party 0 6 8 *X* For entering the same of Record 0 6 8 For Copy of every Order, whether Order be confirmed or quashed, each Party 0 6 8 For entering every Appeal against Poors' Rate or Overseers' Accounts, each *A* ppellant 0 6 8 For every Order for Adjournment 06 8 For entering the same of Record 0 6 8 For Copy thereof for the Appellant's A ttorney to serve on the

Respondents 0 6 8 For entering every adjourned Appeal against Poors' Rate or Over seers' Accounts for the subsequent Session, whether the Appeal be abandoned or not 0 6 8 For Copy of Order, with the Adjudication of the Court, each

Party 0 6 8 For entering the same of Record 0 6 8 *t* For Taxing Costs in any Appeal, each Party 0 6 8 t For every special Case granted, and Copy 0 13 4 t For Copy thereof to the Party not applying for the Case... 0 6 8

For Reading every Order, Notice, Exhibit, or other Document... 0 10 *Highways.*

Enrolling Order for Diverting, Turning, or Stopping up a Highway, &c., including Exhibits, Swearing Witnesses, Entry, &c. 110 The Fees thus marked are paid by the Applicant, Appellant, or Prosecutor.

t Ditto thus marked by the Respondent or Defendant.

J Ditto ditto by both Parties.

§ Ditto ditto by the County.

"Filing and recording every Writ of *ad quod damnum*, 8d. per Sheet.

"For Copy of the same, 4d. per Sheet.
£. i. d. For taking Instructions, and drawing and ingrossing every In dict-

ment, or Presentment of a Highway, Bridge, &c. out of repair 0 13 4 For every *Venire Facias, Capias,* Attachment, or other Mesne

Process 0 4 0 For Service thereof on each Defendant, and bringing him before a Magistrate, to appear at the next Session under a Recognizance, after Presentment made or Indictment found 0 5 0

Fees payable by Defendants, on pleading Guilty. t For filing and entering every Recognizance 0 1 0 *t* For recording and entering Defendant's Appearance 0 4 0 t For entering and recording Plea of Guilty to any

Presentment or Indictment at the first Session... 0 6 8 t For recording and filing every Certificate of repair of a Highway or Bridge 0 7 6 *t* For discharging every Presentment or Indictment at the first Session 113 6 t For Certificate of Discharge 0 6 8 2 19 4 *Fees payable by Defendants, mi pleading Not Guilty.* t For filing and entering every Recognizance 0 10 t For recording and entering Defendant's Appearance... 0 4 0 t For recording Plea of Not Guilty 0 2 4 t For calling and swearing the Jury, each Defendant 0 3 0 t For the Appearance, Copy, Plea, &c. Trial *instanter* 0 18 8 t For making up Record and Trial, Fees thereon... 1 14 8 t For reading Record, and entering and recording

Verdict, each Defendant 0 7 8 3 II 4 t For respiting every Recognizance from Session to Session, on

Motion of Counsel 15 4 *t* For drawing and ingrossing every Special Plea, or Demurrer, 6s. 8d. or 8d. per Folio. t For Copy thereof, 3s. 4d, or 4d. per Folio. t For every *Distringas* 0 12 0 t For *Levari*, Is. in the £.—Bailiff's Fee for levying, 6d. in the £. *Assaults and Misdemeanors.—Fees payable by Prosecutors. £. s. d.*

For every common Indictment for Assault 0 3 6 For every special Indictment, 6s. 8d., or if more than two Counts 3s. 4d. each Count.

Fees payable by Defendants, on Bail, and pleading Guilty. t For filing and entering every Recognizance 0 10 t For recording and entering Defendant's Appearance 0 4 0 t For entering and

recording Flea of Guilty at the first Session 0 6 8 t For reading, filing, and recording every General Re.

lease for each Defendant 0 7 6 t For discharging every Indictment at the first Session 113 6 t For Certificate of Discharge 0 6 8 2 19 4 *Fees payable by Defendants on Bail, and pleading Not Guilty.* t For filing and entering every Recognizance... 0 1 0 t For recording and entering Defendant's Appearance 0 4 0 t For entering and recording Plea of Not Guilty... 0 2 4 t For calling and swearing the Jury, each Defendant 0 3 0 t For the Appearance, Copy, Plea, &c. Trial *inttanter* 0 18 8 t For making up the Record and Trial Fees thereon, on Verdict of Guilty 114 8 t For reading Record, and entering and recording

Fine, each Defendant 0 7 8 3 n 4 t The like Fees on the Verdict of *Not Guilty* and *Acquittal,* discharging Indictment, and Defendant's Recognizance 3 11 4 *Fees payable by Defendants, on Bail, and Bill returned Ignoramus.* t For filing and entering every Recognizance 0 10 t For calling Defendant, on his Recognizance, entering and recording his Appearance and Discharge... 1 4 4 1 5 4 feet *payable by Defendants, on Bail, and no Indictment preferred against them. £. J. i.* t For filing every Recognizance 0 10 t For calling every Defendant on his Recognizance, and also the Prosecutor, and if no Indictment preferred, entering and recording Defendant's Discharge for want of Prosecution... 144 1 4 *Felony.—Fees payable by Prosecutors.* $For every common Indictment 0 2 0

§ For every special Indictment, 6s. ltd., or if more than two Counts, 3s. 4d. each Count. $ For Order on the Treasurer for the payment of the Expenses of

Witnesses, &c. and entering the same of Kecord 0 5 0 *Fees payable by Prisoners, or for them, in Felony. §* For calling and swearing the Jury, reading the Indictment, recording Plea, and entering Verdict of Acquittal 2 18 *i* For every Prisoner discharged by reason of Bill returned Ignoramus 118 *§* For every Prisoner discharged by Proclamation, for want of

Prosecution 0 13 4

§ For the Conviction of a Felon 0 17 4 $ For discharging every Recognizance, in Felony 0 13 4 *Fees payable by Prisoners, or for them, in Misdemeanors.* § For calling and swearing the Jury, reading the Indictment, and recording Plea 14 4 § For entering Verdict of Acquittal 0 17 4 5 For the discharge of every Prisoner by reason of a Bill returned

Ignoramus 1 1 8

§ For the discharge of every Prisoner, by Proclamation, for want of Prosecution 0 13 4

§ For the conviction of every Prisoner for a Misdemeanor, entering and recording Fine, &c 0 17 4

§ For discharging every Recognizance for a Misdemeanor... 0 13 4 § For the Conviction and Order of every Prisoner sentenced to

Transportation, and Copy to send to the Secretary of State... 1 1 0 For administering the Oaths of Allegiance to Constables and common Persons... 0 2 0 For every Certificate thereof, if required 0 3 6

For administering the Oaths of Allegiance to Clergymen qualifying for a Living, or School, or other Person qualifying for an Office 0 10 6 For every Certificate thereof, if required 0 3 S

Orders. $ For drawing and fair Copy of every Order on the Treasurer for payment of any Bill, or demand, or for other purposes, and entering the same of Record 0 6 8 4 For drawing and fair Copy of every special Order of Court, and entering the same of Record 0 13 4 *Miscellaneous.* For the Allowance of a Writ of *Certiorari,* reading the same, and procuring a Magistrate's Signature thereto 16 8

'For making up the Record, drawing and ingrossing the same... 0 13 4 Returning the same 0 6 8 Copy of Order of Removal or Indictment to file on returning

Writ of *Certiorari* 0 6 8 For reading, recording, and filing every Letter of Attorney to plead to any Indictment or Presentment, 0 7 4 For drawing and reading Articles of the Peace exhibited on

Oath in Court 0 13 4 For a Licence

for a Theatre 1 1 0 For Orders of allowance of Duties on Goods destroyed by Fire or otherwise 1 1 0 For the Petition and Appointment of every Constable, filing and recording the same 0 4 6 t For the discharge of a Hundred Constable 0 2 0 For entering and recording every Certificate of a Place for Religious Worship, and Certificate thereof, *by ttatute* 0 2 6 For recording and filing every Alehouse Licence, *by statute* ... 0 2 0 For enrolling any Deed by request, not provided for *by statute,* 8d. per folio.

For enrolling every appointment of a Gamekeeper 0 1 0 For Certificate thereof 0 2 6 For registering and recording Roman Catholic Estates, according to the length. t For filing and recording all Convictions for Deer Stealing, and all other Convictions and Informations whatsoever, where no OS-*The above written Table of Fees was finally confirmed at an Adjournment of the Midsummer Sessions,* 1827.

C. B. WOLLASTON, Chairman.

Midsummer *Assizes,* 1827—*The above written Table of Fees was allowed and eon firmed by us,*

W. D. BEST.

J. BURROUGH.

The Fee marked thus () is paid by the Sheriff.—12 Kich. II, c. 10.

SCHEDULE B.

A LIST of FEES taken by the CRIER of the COURT of Quarter Sessions.

£, s. d.

For every Recognizance and Traverse to try the Issues on Indictment found, of each Defendant 0 2 0

For every Recognizance discharged, for each Defendant 0 1 0

For swearing every Witness on any Indictment, &c 0 0 6

For swearing every Witness in Court (except on Behalf of the

King) 0 0 6

For the Removal of every Indictment by *Certiorari* 0 2 0

For every Highway Rate confirmed 0 1 0

For the Discharge of every Indictment, &c 0 2 0

For calling and swearing Jury, and discharge thereon 0 3 0

For Ditto in Felony 0 4 0

For the discharge of every Prisoner on the Calendar 0 1 0

For respiting every Recognizance 0 1 0

For every new Recognizance entered into and recorded for Appearance, &c. 0 2 0 SCHEDULE C

A LIST of FEES taken by the UNDER SHERIFF.

£,. d.

For a Bail Bond on *Ne exeat Regno* 1 1 0

For Return of *Habeas Corpus,* or *Distringas,* one Writ 0 12 0

For every other Action... 0 3 4

For Execution 0 4 10

If Execution returned, only 0 12 0

For levying Execution Is. in the pound under,£100, and 6d. for every 20s. beyond £100, per stat. 29 Eliz. c. 4. For summoning or distraining a Parish, Hundred, or County, on Process, after an Indictment found, so that they be and appear at the Assizes, &c. 0 4 0

For returning every *Venire* 0 2 6

For Ditto on the Crown Side 0 12 0

For returning a *Tales* 0 2 0

For summoning every Person on Process after an Indictment found, or for taking them on the *Capias,* so that they be and appear at the Assizes, &c. 0 2 0

For every liberate or discharge of a Prisoner for Debt 0 3 6 77i!S *Fee is now paid by the County Treasurer.*—55 6. Ill. c. 50, s. 10.

Note.—There are several other Fees taken by Under Sheriffs, which could not be ascertained—*Query.*—Ought they not to be settled by Statute, so far as he is subservient to Justices of the Peace.

SCHEDULE D.

A LIST of FEES taken by the COUNTY CLERK,

See Stat. 11 Hen. VII, c. 15.

IN COMMON ACTIONS.

For entering every Plaint 0 1 0

For every Summons 0 1 0

For filing every Certificate of Service 0 1.0

For searching for Appearance, Plea, &c 0 0 4

For every Attachment 0 1 4

For every Liberate 0 1 0

For Notice of Appearance 0 0 4

For every Rule or Order of Court 0 1 0

For filing every Declaration 0 10

For Copy of every Declaration 010

For filing every Plea 0 14

For Copy of every Plea 0 14 In Replevin, all Fees as above *double*.

For calling and returning every Proclamation and Exigent on an

Outlawry 0 6 8

For allowing and returning every *Re. fa. lo.* 10 0 SCHEDULE E. A LIST of FEES taken by the BOUND BAILIFFS.

Settled *Epiph. Sess.* 1729. Stat. 2 Geo. IL c. 22. 32 G. II. c. 28,

The Bailiff or Officer of the Sheriff of this County, legally arresting or detaining any Person, may take and receive from any such Perton, viz. for the first night's Lodging in a good

Bed 6 10

For every other Night, per Night 0 0 6

For Diet, three Meals a day, and small Beer 0 10 ¥3-The like Fees to be taken by the Bailiff of the Liberty of Sherborne and Castle there, and his Under-Bailiffs and Officers.

Note.—There are several other Fees taken by bound Bailiffs; but it has been determined that Justices in Sessions have no authority to fix Bailiffs' Fees for Arrests in *Civil* Suits; nor will the Court of B. R. allow more than the usual fee of one Guinea, though a larger sum has been in fact paid, under the sanction of a Table of Fees settled by the Sessions, and acted upon in practice for many years.—*Mich. Term,* 30, G. *III.—Term Reports, vol.* 3 *p.* 427—Bailiffs are therefore guilty of extortion, if they exact more than is allowed *colore officii.*
SCHEDULE F.

A LEST of FEES taken by the GAOLER or KEEPER of the Sheriff's Ward, at Dorchester. 03-These Fees were abolished by the Statutes 55 G. III. c. 50—and 56 G. III.c. 116, s. 3.
SCHEDULE G.

A LIST of FEES taken by CORONERS. Stat. 25 G. II. c. 29.

£. t. d.

For returning every *Venire Facias* 0 2 6

For returning every Habeas Corpus or Distringass 0 12 0

For returning a *Tales* when the Sheriff is related to either Party, or interested in the Suit 0 2 0

For every Inquisition (not taken upon view of a Body dying in

Gaol) which shall be duly taken, (s. 1.) 10 0

For travelling Charge, at per Mile 0 0 9

For every Inquisition taken upon view of a Body dying in Gaol, such Sum as the Justices iu Session shall think fit to allow, not exceeding (s. 2) 1 0 0

For every Inquisition taken upon view of a Body *slain* or *murdered,* of the Goods and Chattels of the Slayer or Murderer, or of the Amercements of the Town, &c. if he escape, in addition to the above Allowances, the Sum of (s. 3.) 0 13 4 See Order of the Quarter Sessions—" That to prevent any dispute which "for the future may arise on account of taking any Inquisition on any "person dying in the County Gaol— Ordered, That the Sum of 5s. shall "be allowed the Coroner for every Inquisition, and no more."—*Mich. Sess.* 1761.
SCHEDULE H.

Stat. 26 G. II. c. 14.

A TABLE of FEES to be taken by CLERKS to

JUSTICES of the PEACE,

Acting in and for the said County of Dorset, as settled by a Committee of Magistrates, December 22d, 1825, *and approved by the Court of General Quarter Session of the Peace, held at Dorchester, on* Tuesday the *lOtn day of* January, 1826.

Affidavit.

Every Oath in Writing, or Copy, (except for pensions and half.

pay), taken before one or more Justices 0 10 *Ale Licenses.*

Filling up License, and taking and returning Recognizance... 0 5 0

Fee to the Clerk of the Peace filing the same 0 3 0

Allowance of the transfer of a License 0 S 0 *Apprentice.*

Examination of Indenture previous to binding—Allowance of and registering the same, and Certificate under 56 Geo. 111. c. 139, for each pair 0 5 0

Allowance of the Assignment and registering 0 3 6

Discharge of an Apprentice and Duplicate 0 2 6 *Bastardy.*

Examination before Birth 0 1 0

Warrant to apprehend 010

Recognizance and Notice 0 3 6

Commitment 0 10

Discharge 0 10

Certificate to suspend or discharge Recognizance 0 3

Examination after Birth, to obtain an order of Filiation and Oath 0 2 0

Warrant or Summons to the Father and Mother 0 1 0

Duplicate to prove, if ordered by the Justices 0 10

Adjudication and order of Filiation and Oath, and for each Duplicate thereof 0 16

Information for disobedience of Orders and Oath 0 10

Warrant thereon 0 10

Commitment 0 2 0

Discharge,,,,,....... 0 1 0 *Conttable. £. u A.*

Swearing every Peace Officer into office, and Certificate 8 10

Order on the County Treasurer 0 10 *Commitment.*

Every Commitment not otherwise provided for in this Table, whether before one or more Justices 0 1 0 *Conviction.*

For every Conviction drawn out in Writing, where the form is given by statute, and where the Penalty does not exceed 40s. 0 2 6

Where the form is given by statute, and the Penalty exceeds 40s., or being under 40s. the Evidence is set out 0 S 0

Where the Penalty is above 40s. and the Evidence is specially set out 0 7 6

Additional for every Common Law Sheet exceeding Ten... 9 1 0 *Deserted Premises.*

Complaint and affixing Notice where Rent does not exceed *50...* 0 3 6

Where the same exceeds,£60 0 5 t

Delivery of Possession, Rent not exceeding £50 0 3 6

Where the same exceeds £50 0 S 0 *Discharge.*

Liberate, Supersedeas, and every other Discharge (except Felony) 0 10 *Highways.*

Appointment of each Surveyor with Bond 0 16

For each Abstract delivered to Surveyors 0 0 6

Allowance of old Surveyors' Accounts and Oath 0 10

Every Adjournment of Allowance of Accounts 0 10

Application for an extra Bate and Oath 0 1 0

Order for Ditto 0 2 0

Every Information or Complaint not before charged by or against any Surveyor of Highways, respecting any Act belonging to his Office 0 10 *£. i. i.*

Oath on Ditto 6 10

Order on Ditto 0 2 0

Certificate of Repair of Road indicted 02 6

Magistrates signature to an Order for turning or stopping up a

Highway 63 0

For every additional Highway included in the same Order... 0 1 0

Each Consent to Ditto 0 10 *Information.*

Every Information in Writing under the Excise Laws 0 3 6

Ditto under the Game Laws, or relative to Tithes and Friendly

Societies 0 2 0

Every other Information in Writing, (except Felony), not ex ceeding two folios, or a Copy thereof 0 10

Every additional Folio 0 10 *Jury List.*

Every Notice to Constables or Overseers to return Lists, and attend at the Petty Sessions, with service thereof. 0 2 6

Examining and allowing List, indorsing the same, and Oath... 0 1 0 *Order.*

For every Order for Payment of Tithes, and relating to Friendly Societies, and all other Orders not provided for in this Table,
£.1. d.

Order of Suspension, and Duplicate, each 0 1 0

Taking off Suspension 010

Making out Kxpenses on Ditto, and Oalh, and Magistrate's allowance of Ditto 0 2 6

Allowance of Parish Certificate, and Oath of execution 0 2 6 *Recognizance.*

Every Recognizance to appear to prosecute, or give Evidence, (except in Felony), and to find Sureties of the Peace,... 0 3 6

Notice to Parties bound under 3 G. IV. , c. 46 0 10 *Summons.*

Every Summons except in cases of Relief, whether containing one or more Names 0 10 *Soldier.*

Information against a Deserter, Warrant, Commitment, Letter to the Secretary at War, Discharge on delivery to the Military, and Order of Payment of Reward-0 3 0

Attesting of a Recruit 0 10

Allowance of Regimental or other Military Accounts 0 10

Warrant to press Waggons, each, if separate Warrants 0 10

Order for Relief of Families of Non-commissioned Officers,

Drummers, &c. of Militia, including Complaint and Oath... 0 2 0

Certificate of Ditto 0 10

Allowance of Account and Order to Reimburse 0 2 6 *Vagrants.*

For every Information in Writing 0 2 0

For every Examination 0 10

For every Commitment 0 10

For Drawing and Ingrossing the Conviction, and Parchment... 0 3 0 *Warrant.*

For every Warrant to apprehend, (except in Felony) 0 10

Indorsing from another Jurisdiction 0 1 0

For every Warrant of Distress 0 2 0

Return indorsed thereon and Oath 0 1 0

Warrant to search for Game or Engines 02 0 *Lent Assizes,* 1826.—*The above written Table of Fees was ratified and cmfirmed by* us,

J. BURROUGH.

S. GASELEE.

SCHEDULE I.

TREASURERS' ACCOUNTS.

The Amount of Money expended by Treasurers, from the Year 1740 to the Year 1823 inclusive, specified under the respective Heads, to which the Public Stock of the County is applicable by Law: and likewise the Money received by Rates, or otherwise making the County Stock, within the same period, to meet such Expenditure.

EXPENDITURE.

I. —County Bridges. *£. t. d.*

By Cash for Building and Repairing Old Bridges 42751 16 8$ for Bridges since the Year 1796 6259 4 0$ to Bridge Surveyors 3706 5 11 for Contracts, defending Indictments, Fees, &c.... 1267) 7 7 for Bound Stones 415 0 II. —Gaol And House Cf Correction.

By Cash for Building, Enlarging, &c. inclusive of Tread Mill 25798 9 6 for Improvement and Kepairs 12184 II 24 for Salaries to Chaplain 3912 6 0 to Surgeon 1982 16 8 to Gaoler and Keeper, and Assistants 10668 10 4 for Food and Maintenance to Prisoners (Bread)... 16395 4£ ... Extra Diet to Working Ditto 7316 g 4

Sick Ditto 2069 17 fig ... Prisoners Clothing 1990 12 9J

Bedding 1342 6 7j

Furniture 1266 7 7J

Washing

Bathing 1922 8 4

Fumigating, *J*

Firing and Candles 2614 7 OJ

Funerals 72 15 7i ... to Gaoler and Keeper for conveying Prisoners to

Assizes and Sessions 1543 4 4j ... to Ditto on Acq. of Prisoners from 1774 to 1790 515 5 5

... to Ditto for Executing Sentences of the Law... 297 9 3

... to Ditto for Calendars, Stationary, Packets, Postages, and Taxes 1281 15 4 *£.,. d.* to Prisoners for Rewards and Extra Earnings... 97 5 10 to Ditto for removing Ground, 744 15 3£ to Gaoler for setting Prisoners on Work,... 2650 0 0 for Interest on,£10,000 borrowed to build Gaol, at 4 *V* Cent 4765 19 0 for Casual Payments 640 12 S III.—Shire Hall.

By Cash on Account of Building... 5796 2 4$ of Repairs 941 3 jj of Furniture 534 14 gj of Airing and Cleaning 10 0 0 of Quit Rent to Corporation of Dorchester, at 1 Guinea, from 1792... 23 8 8 of Hall-Keeper's Salary 105 0 0 of Casual Payments 23 7 2 IV.—Rogues And Vagabonds.

By Cash on Account of Apprehending 546 0 0 of Conveying 10025 15 3j of Relieving and Maintaining 2488 16 3 V.—Felons And Transports.

By Cash for conveying Persons accused of Crimes to Gaol and House of

Correction 6885 17 7i for Prosecuting and Convicting at Assizes... 5417 17 14 at Sessions... 2924 19 1 for Fees to Clerk of Assize on Account of Transports 1039 15 3

Clerk of the Peace do... 149 8 10 to Gaoler for removing Transports to their destination 2043 3 2 to Public Officers from 1815 836 14 2 VI.—Militia And Soldiers.

By Cash for Relief of non-commissioned Officers and

Drummers

to bal lotted Men and Substitutes of other Counties, reimbursed to Treasurers of this County to ditto and ditto of this County, reimbursed by Parish Officers for Relieving Sick Militia Men on their March... 32 12 8 to Clerk of Lieutenancy Expenses and Business... 867 13 8 16384 11 3 £. i. d.

By Cash to Clerk of the Peace for sending Officers' Names to

Gazette 294 5 1 for Kent and Repairs of Militia Depots 688 1 7i for Relieving Soldiers 14 0 0 ..... for Conveying 75 5 3j for removing Baggage 90 16 4 for Treasurers' Salaries 700 10 0 VII. — Coboners.

By Cash for Inquisitions and Travelling Charges 4190 10 6 VIII. —Debtobs, *Insolvent,* and *Prisoners' Relief.*

By Cash to poor Prisoners in King's Bench, Marshalsea, and

Fleet Prisons 355 8 0 for Pees 9 8 7 IX. —Salaries to *certain Officers.*

By Cash to Treasurers 1830 0 0 to Clerk of the Peace 827 10 0 to Corn Inspectors to 1822 2916 12 7 to Crier of the Court of Quarter Sessions 192 13 6 X. —Contingencies.

By Cash to Clerk of the Peace for Printing, Advertising, &c. 4203 18 5$ for Stationery, Books, &c.... 794 19 8 for Orders, extra Business, &c. 7211 7 8j to Treasurers for extra Business & attending Sessions 947 1 2£ ... to Ditto for Interest of Money advanced...103115 10 to Ditto for Stamps, Postage, &c. 147 17 10 *for procuring Returns and settling General Co. Rate, 1740* 65 0 4 on Acc. of Distemper among Horned Cattle, 1746 to 1754 444 0 6 of making Returns relative to the Poor 379 9 4 ... Charitable Donations... 122 3 2

Army and Navy... 270 4 10 County Election Act... 103 17 10 Posse Comitatus... 292 14 10 Population Acts... 94 7 6 for providing Standard Weights, and Examiner's Allowance, from 1802 101 7 7 for fitting up and repairing Sessions Halls 37 10 4 for prosecuting Persons plundering Shipwrecked Goods 0 0 0 for Parish Apprentices bound to Sea Service, conveying, &c 0 0 0 for Loss by defaulting Constables, 1741, 1742, 1784, 1792, and 1800 72 16 4 for Relief to Paupers taken 111, 22 G. III. c. 83... 31 4 2 for conveying and maintaining Lunatics 180 19 10 for Damage done to Land near the County Gaol... 21 0 0 for publishing Treasurers and Gaol Accounts... 280 11 9 for Loss to Eastern Treasurer (Walter ErU) in 1775... 175 8 3i for Casual Payments; 7 10 1

Total Payments....£242342 18 4 RECEIPTS.

The amount of Money, received by Treasurers within the above period, to meet the above Expenditure, and making the County Stock, is specified below, under the respective Heads, viz.

I.—County Rates.

To Arrears in 1740,1741,1742, and 1751 333 4 6£ ... 14 Rates, at £500 each, from 1741 to 1754 7000 0 0 ... 9 at 499 8s. each, from 1754 to 1760... 4494 12 0 ... 15--at 498 Is. 4d. each, from 1760 to 1770... 7471 0 Hi ... 19 at 496 19s. OJd. each,from 1770 to 1779... 9442 2 2J .. .398 at 496 5s. 0d. each, from 1779 to 1823... 197507 18 3.1 11.—Bridges.

To Cash for Old Bridge Materials, in 1787

Yeovil Bridge, half Repairs from County of *Somerset,* 1802 653 II II of Feoffees on account of Hay ward Bridge, 1819... 31 14 9 III— Gaol And House Of Correction.

To Cash for old Gaol Land, and Materials, in 1795 1220 0 0 .... old House of Correction, 1794 470 0 0

Land, Entrance to the Gaol, 1806 155 0 0

Rent of Ground, Castle Field, to Mids. 1805... 45 0 0 IV.— Gaoler.

To Cash of Gaoler, Money borrowed for setting Prisoners on

Work 2650 0 0 .,.... of Ditto, on Ac-

count of Profits of Trades in the Prison 1200 0 0 £. t. i.

To Cash of Gaoler, on Account of Debtors' Fees, from 1791 to 1815 302 5 6 of Ditto on Account of Cravings, from Epiphany

Sessions, 1741 to 1806 534 4 11 V Militia.

To Cash of Treasurers and Parish Officers on Account of the Relief of Families 477 1 1 VI. —Corn Returns.

To Cash of Receiver-General of Customs on this account, from 1793 to 1822 2327 0 0 VII.—Weights And Measures.

To Cash on sale of defective Weights and Balances, 1813 to 1823 63 12 4

Total Receipts £ 240683 14 5J HEADS of EXPENDITURE.

1. —County Bridges 53989 19 3 II. —Gaol and House of Correction 1020/3 8 10$ III. —Shire Hall 7433 16 11$ IV. —Rogues and Vagabonds 13060 11 6J V. —Felons and Transports 19297 15 2% VI. —Militia and Soldiers 19147 15 10J VII Coroners 4190 10 6 VIII Insolvent Debtors, &c 364 16 7 IX. —Salaries to certain Officers 5766 16 1 X. —Contingencies 17017 7 5j

Total Payments £.242342 18 4 HEADS of RECEIPTS.

I. —County Rates and Arrears, &c 226248 17 11j II. —Bridges sold, &c 691 12 8 111 Gaol and House of Correction 1890 0 0 IV. —Gaoler 4686 10 5 V. —Militia 4776 1 1 VI. —Corn Returns 2327 0 0 VII. —Weights and Measures 63 12 4

Total Receipts,£240683 145£

Balance due *from* the County to Treasurers' .-n-.n am at *MiUummr,* 1823 . 1659 3 11 *Note.*—Since the year 1815, the Treasurers' Accounts have been published in the Newspapers annually. —55 G. 111. c. 51, s. 18.

SCHEDULE K. TABLE of ALLOWANCES to CONSTABLES and TITHINGMEN,

For keeping, maintaining, and conveying Felons and other Malefactors and Offenders, committed to the Gaol and House of Correction, and the Charges of those that guard them thither, adjudged to be reasonable, and settled at Michaelmas Sessions, 1826.

Note.—These Charges are to be borne by each Prisoner (if able); but in case he shall not have sufficient Money or Goods within the County to bear the said Charges of himself and those who convey him, any Justice of the Peace may, on Oath, examine into the truth thereof, and by his Warrant, specifying the Offence for which he is committed, order the Expenses to be paid by the Treasurer of the County Stock; and should any extraordinary circumstance happen to make it necessary to increase the above Allowances, the Magistrate will insert the cause of such increase *specially* at the foot of the said Order.

PARISH ALLOWANCES.

18 G. ill. c. 19, s. 4.

For the necessary Expenses the Constables and TithingMen shall incur in doing the business of their Parish, Township, or Place.

Constables and Tithingmen are, within every three Months, and in fourteen Days after they shall go out of Office, to deliver to the Overseers of the Poor of the Parish, Township, or Place, for the time being, *a just Account in Writing, fairly entered in a Book, to be kept for that purpose, and signed by them, of alt sums, to by them expended, on Account of the said Parish, fyc.* in all Cases not hitherto provided for by the Laws heretofore made, or by the said Act. *And also of all Sums received by them on account of the said Poru/i, SfC.*; such Accounts to be laid before a Vestry within the next fourteen Days, and if approved of to be paid out of the Poor's Rate; but if such Accounts shall be disallowed, then any J ustice of the Peace may settle and determine the game upon reasonable Notice to be given to the Overseers.

SCHEDULE L.

7 *G.* IV. c. 64, s. 26.

TABLE for the REGULATION of EXPENSES in all Prosecutions at the Assizes and Quarter Sessions for the County of Dorset.—*Epiph. Sessions,* 1830.

The Fees of Court to be allowed the Prosecutor.

The Prosecutor to be allowed the sum of Four Pence per Mile for travelling Expenses to and from *Dorchester.*

The Prosecutor to be allowed Five Shillings per Day for Expenses at the Quarter Sessions, and Seven Shillings per Day at the Assizes, during his or her necessary abode at *Dorchester;* such sum to include his or her loss of time and trouble.

Each Witness to be allowed the sum of Four Pence per M ile for travelling Expenses to and from *Dorchester.*

Each Witness to be allowed Five Shillings per Day for Expenses at the Quarter Sessions, and Seven Shillings at the Assizes, during his or her necessary abode at *Dorchester;* such sum to include his or her loss of time and trouble.

If, from infirmity or other circumstances, any Expenses beyond the travelling allowance be incurred, either by Prosecutor or Witness, an account of such Expenses actually incurred, and verified upon oath, shall be delivered to the Court for its approbation or rejection, at the time when the Prosecutor applies for the Expenses of the Prosecution.

If any extra demand be made for loss of time by any professional Man, it shall be delivered to the Court at the time when the Prosecutor applies for the Expenses of the Prosecution, and the sum of one Guinea per *diem,* and no more, shall be allowed him for the same.

Every Order on the Treasurer of the County for the payment of the Expenses of any Prosecution, shall specify the particular Expense incurred, *and the Allowance made to each Individual,* whether Prosecutor or Witness, and the *Treasurer* shall pay to each *Person individually,* the sum so specified, on his producing a check from the Clerk of Assize, or Clerk of the Peace, for the same, corresponding with the sum set forth in the general order.

No Constable to be allowed his Expenses in more than one Prosecution at the same Quarter Sessions or Assizes, unless he proves satisfactorily to the Court that he has been detained by other Prosecutions at *Dorchester.*

No Witness to be allowed for any Expenses whatever, unless he or she appear on Recognizance or *Subpana,* except a special request be made in open Court for that purpose, and a special order be given in consequence by the Court.

That every Prosecutor, Witness, and Constable, do receive his order or check on the Treasurer, as soon as possible after the Trial in which they were concerned be ended.

(Signed)

D. O. P. OKEDEN, *Chairman.*

WILLIAM BOLLAND,

One of the Justices of Gaol Delivery.

The NAM ES of the principal RIVERS and BROOKS, which Water this County, are hereunder mentioned, from whence, it will be perceived, many of the Places derive their Names from them. The course of these Rivers is delilineated in a Map prefixed hereto.

ALLEN—rises above Wimborne All Saints.

Axe, or Exe.

ttirt.

Bride.

Bredy.

Cole.

Car, or Chare.

Cerne.

Corfe.

Combsbrook (a Rivulet) falls into the Stour.

Devilsbrooke (ditto) falls into the Frome.

Dewilish, or Dewlish.

Ewerne, cr Iwerne.

Frome.

Hooke, or Owke.

Holbrook (a Rivulet) falls into the Stour.

Ivel, or Yeo.

Liddon.

Laddon (a Rivulet) falls into the Stour.

Luckford Lake.

Lyme.

Alilborne.

Newelle.

Osmersayte (a Rivulet) falls into the Stour.

Piddle, or TitEifT.

Ferret, or Parrot.

Shreenwater (a Rivulet) falls into the Stour.

Sherford.

Simtne.

Seate (a Rivulet) falls into the Liddon.

Sydling.

Stower, OrSTOTJR.

Sturkell (a Rivulet) falls into the Stour.

Tarent, or Tarrant.

Trill (a Rivulet) falls into the Stour.

Terrig (a Rivulet) falls into the Allen.

Way, or Wey.

Winterborne North. South.

In 1328, 3 Bdw. 111. John de Whitfield granted the Bailiwick or Custody of the Rivers Frome and Stour, or Stower. to the Brian's, of Woodsford.

In 1446, 25 Hen. VI. James, Earl of Wills, held the Custody of the above Rivers.

In 1456, 35 H. VI Alice, Countess of Wilts, held the same.

In 1540, 32 H. V1IL the Free Fishery of the River Stower was granted to Daccombe, and his Heirs.

In 1595, 38 Eliz. *Sir* Giles Sirangways, *lint,* held the Custody of the said two Rivers.

THE NAMES OF ALL THE *mvotbua maee,* WITHIN THE COUNTY OF DORSET, IN ALPHABETICAL ORDER, ALSO THE *TOWNS, TITHING S, VILLAGES, HAMLETS, FARMS, ahd LANDS* WITHIN THE SAME WITH EXPLANATORY NOTES AND OBSERVATIONS.

7.—Tithing in conjunction with Thompson Parish 9— Eggerton, firom whence the Hundred takes its name, 10.— United with Burleston Parish. 10—Bardolfeston, part in Fiddletown Parish. : i-This Parish i s united to Frome Vauchurch.and is a Tithing in conjunction with Melbury Bubb. 12—This Parish is united with Fifehead Neville Vari. h. 13—Bugbarrow; A Charity School built here.

Beet Regis Parish removed to this Place) Order quashed, for that it appeared there were no Parish Officers—Easter Sessions, 1766-This Place is rated to Beer Regis, but maintains its own Poor separate. *r*-1 Tithing in conjunction with Lillington Parish.

ranee/ put in Btoverpaine Parish,—Nut lord, part in Fimpenit Parish. 31— Monkwood Hill, part in Mappowder Parish. 32— A Tithing, sometimes in-

cluded with Broadway.—Tatton, E. & W., part in Fortisham Parish. 33— Inzacrts, part in Loders Parish. 47—Brownshall, from whence the Hundred takes its name. 56—This Village is now dipopulatcd, and consists only of one House. 68—Coombs Ditch, merely a Ditch, from whence the Hundred takes its name. 71—Bindon, Great, gives name to the Liberty. It formerly belonged to, and made part of the Hundred of Rush more. 77—Aylewood, in Langton Wallis Tithing. 77— Blatchenwell: this Tithing includes Slape and Norden, and pays 29.8d. to Arne Chapelry County Rate. 78— Pipsford, part in Mapperton Parish. TL.-AIderholt.Boveridge.and Monkton-up-Wimborne Chapelries included in this Parish, and Ihe Chapels of Aldeiholt and Monlcton-up-Wirnborne are ruinated. 89—This Parish claims to be extra-parochial; the Village U entirely depopulated, and the Church ruinated b eyond the memory of man, and pays the Poor Rates to Came Winterborne. 97—East Mill, in Bindon Liberty. 99—This Parish united to Batcombe Parish. Tollerford, a Ground, near a Ford, at the entrance of four Cross wajs ftcm Maiden Newton to Toller Fratrum, from whence the Hundred takes its name. 114— This Place was Abbey Land, and extra-Parochial, haTing no connexion with any Parish, and been exempt from any Payments in support of the Poor. It was granted this Privilege by Hen. VI-II. only one House—Return to House of Commons, 1775.

Wyke, formerly a Tithing in Knowlton Hundred.

and has always 110—This Place claims to be extra-Parochial. The Vill isdepopulated; but few Houses now standing. The Chapel is entirely destroyed, and Duty performed at Came Winterborne. 121—Gaunts, part in Wimborne Minster Parish. 124-This Vill depopulated and the Church destroyed. 126-Baggridge, now extinct. Knowlton: This Place gives Nameto the Hundred; « was autientlj a *Vill,* but now depopulated, and the Chapel destroyed. 127—Chapel ruinated. 141—A Tithinff In conjunction with H erst on. In Swanwich Parish. Kingswood, in Studland Tithing. Knit-

son, in Afflington Tithing, Cor ft Castle Parish. Lens ton, included in the Tithing of Herston. !44—This Place claims to be extra-Parochial; hut one House only, included in, and pays Land-Tax to Holnest Tithing. 14i—Stockbrldge, in LiUington Parish, and Holnest Tithing. Kingsmill *Margaret Marsh, see. Iwerne M. Marshwood, see Whitechureh Can IGl-MARTiN'sTowN,or wiS'"....*

Carrants

AshdonWint.'

Clandon

Park

Rew 162-Melbury Abbas

Melbury, East

West 163-Melbury Bdbb 164-Woolcomb Matravers, 1g5-melbury Osmond, Lower...

166-Melbury Sampford, Higher 167-Melcombe Horsey

Nettlecomb Tout

Melcombe, Bingham

Harper's, or Harefoot Lane...

Melcombe Regis, see Weymouth.

Milbome Stileham, see Beer R'

108-milborne St. Andrew

Milborne Churchstone

Deverell, or Cary

Mamford

Michaels tone

Symondstone

Dewlish

Gundrey's, *m*

Michel's, *m* 170-milton Abbas

Bagber

Churchcomb, or Chescomb

Delcomb

Huish

Lescomb

Ifl2—Melbury West Tithing partly in this Parish, partly in Holy Trinity Parish, Shaflon, and the remainder in ann, alias Shafton &t. Rumbold's, and is a Tithing in conjunction with Cann. 163—A Tithing in conjunction with Batcombc. 101— Woolcomb Matravers Chapel destroyed. S06—No Parish Officer! appointed.

17—LoTetown, loraetirnei separate Tithing, but generally included lathii Parish. 190—Nutford, part in Blandford Forum. 191—Redhone, from whence the Hundred takes its additional Name. 192— Loscombe, part in Netherbury.

Woolcombe Bingham, part in Toller Porcorum. 193— This Parish is depopulated, and the Church destroyed, it is Joined with Hook Tithing, but pays Church and Poor to Poorstock. j95 Tatton, part in Buckhvnd Rlpers. Uggscombe lies in a Valley now called Mysteeomhe, from whence the

Hundred takes its Name.„, 198—Bardolfeston, part in Athelhampstone. Troytown— Cars Troi (Welch)—Troi signifies to turn, and taer denotes Banks or Walls, as well as a City; it is therefore supposed that this Place derires its Name from the winding Banks or Maze, rather than any allusion Co Troy.

202—Bexington i this Vill is long since depopulated, and the Parish united to Puncknowle, trhtrv It pays to Church audPoor. 207—Dean, part in Keinston Tarrant. 210— Alceater, this Liberty and Tithing are included in the out-Parish of St. James's, I 211— This Parish is included in the Tithing of West Melburv, in Sixpenny Hundred. 216— Frome Belet, a Tithing in conjunction with Stinsford and Bockhampton: formerly a Pari&b, and Vill now depopulated; only one House, and the Church destroyed; united to this Parish, about 1470. 218-United to Tynehara Parish, 6 G. 1, c. 8.

Stoborough, part of this Tithing lies in Stoborough Liberty and in the

Newton, in the Manor of Corft Castle,but belongs to this Parish' 234— Cogdean, from whence the Hundred takes its Name.

236—Organford, patt in the Parish of St. Martin's, Wareham.

239—Herston is included in Langton M &tiavers Tithing.

241—Sydling Fifehead, formerly a separate Tithing, now included in Sydling St. Nicholas.

Sydling-Up, in Cerne, &c. Hundred. Mageston, Little, in Fraropton Parish.

244— A Tithing in conjunction with Anderson Parish.

247— Redlane, from whence the Hundred takes its Name. 248— Southover, alias Troop, a Tithing in conjunction with Tincleton and Cliff. 1—Woolcomb Bingham, part in Poorstock Parish. 274— Bradford Bryan, part in Kingston

Lacy. Petersham, in Cranbome Hundred.

Gaunts, part in Hinton Martell Parish. Holt, this Chapelry lies partly in the Tithing of Stone and

Thornhill. Badbury, from-whence the Hundred takes its name.

275— Burton, East, formerly a separate Tithing, now included in Winfrith. SYNOPSIS OF THE SEVERAL AND RESPECTIVE DIVISIONS, HUNDREDS, LIBERTIES, AND BOROUGHS,

WITHIN THE COUNTY;

SHOWING THE

OLD AND NEW DIVISIONS, NUMBER OF TITHINGS IN EACH, ACCORDING TO THE NEW ARRANGEMENT THEREOF, MADE IN PURSUANCE OF THE ACTS

The DIVISIONS were originally Jive, namely—

I-DORCHESTER.

II.-BRIDPORT, OR BEAMINSTER. III.-BLANDFORD, NORTH AND SOUTH. IV.-SHAFTON, EAST AND WEST.

V.-SHERBORNE, (INCLUDING STURMINSTER AND CERNE.)

Ill the Year 1740, at the settling of the County Rate, they were altered and made agreeably to the Land Tax Divisions, consisting of the Nine following:—

I.-DORCHESTER.

II.-BRIDPORT, OR BEAMINSTER. III.-BLANDFORD NORTH, OR BLANDFORD. IV.-SOUTH, OR WAREHAM.

V.-SHAFTON EAST, OR WIMBORNE.

VI.-WEST, OR SHAFTESBURY. VII.-SHERBORNE. VIII.-STURMINSTER. IX.-CERNE.

In the Year 1830, the new Arrangement was made, viz.— I.-DORCHESTER.

II.-BRIDPORT.

III.-CERNE.

IV.-WAREHAM.

V.-BLANDFORD.

VI.-WIMBORNE. VII.-SHAFTESBURY.

VIII.-STURMINSTER.

IX.-SHERBORNE. THE NAMES OP THE KEW DIVISIONS, AND THE HUNDREDS, LIBERTIES, And BOROUGHS COMPRISING THE SAME, ALSO, THE TITHINGS WITHIN EACH HUNDRED, LIBERTY, AND BOROUGH, IN ALPHABETICAL ORDER, ACCORDING TO THE NEW ARRANGEMENT, MADE AT THE

MIDSUMMER SESSIONS, 1830, IN PUR-

SUANCE OF

THE STATUTES

9 Geo. IV, c. 43—10 Geo. IV, c. 46. PART II.

I.-DORCHESTER DIVISION.

Cerne, Totcombe, and Modbury Hundred.

Compton Abbas, or West.

Culliford Tree Hundred.

Ashdon and Clendon.

Broadway cum

Buckland Ripers. (1)

Cripton and Farringdon.

Chickerell, West.

Herringston and Clapcotts.

Knighton, West.

Littlemayne.

Monkton, Winterborne.

Osmington.

Radipole.

Stafford, East, and Lewell.

Stafford, West.

Stotingway.

Vhitcombe.

Eggerton Hundred

Abbas, Winterborne.

Longbredy.

George Hundred.

Bockhampton, Stinsford, and

Frome Belet. Bradford Peverell and Muckle ford. Broadmayne. Charminster. Colliton Row. Frome Whitfield, Forston. Grimston. Stratton.

St. Martin, Winterborne.

Piddletotcn Hundred.

Athelhampston.

Burleston.

Chesilborne, Little.

Ilsington.

Lovard.

Piddletown.

Piddle, Little.

Tincleton Cliff and Throop.

Tolpiddle.

Walterson.

Tollerford Hundred.

Chilfrome.

Cruxton.

Evershot.

Frome Vauchurch.

Maiden Newton.

Melbury Sampford.

Rampisham.

Toller Fratrum.

Toller Porcorum.

Winford Eagle.

Uggscombe Hundred.

  Abbotsbury.

  Corton.

  Fleet.

  Friar Waddon.

  Littlebredy & Kingston Russell.

  Langton Herring.

  Litton Cheney.

  Portisham.

  Puncknowle.

  Rodden and Elworth

  Shilvinghampton.

  Steepleton, Winterborne.

  Swyre.

Winfrith Hundred.

Galton.

Poxwell.

Ringstead.

Warmwell.

Woodsford.

f 1)—A separate Tithing, but frequently included in Broadway Tithing.

Bindon Liberty,

Bexinoton. .

  Fordiugton Mill-Street.

Lewlish Liberty. Dewlish. *Frampton Liberty.* Bincomhe.

Compton Vallence, or East. Came, Winterborne. Frampton.

Forthington Liberty. Fordington.. *Oivermoigne Liberty.* Owermoigne. *Piddlehinton Liberty.* Piddlehinton. *Portland Liberty.* Portland. *Sutton Pointz Liberty.* Preston. Putton and East Chickerill. Sutton Pointz.

Waby house Liberty.

Wabyhouse. (2) *Wyke Regis and El-wellLiberty.*

  Elwell.

Wyke Regis.

Dorchester Borough.

  All Saints.

Holy Trinity.

St. Peter.

Weymouth and Melcombe Regis Borough.

  Melcombe Regis.

Weymouth.

II.-BRIDPORT DIVISION.

Beaminster Hundred.

Ash.

  Beaminster.

  Bowood.

Cheddington.

Chardstock, North.

Chardstock, South.

Corscombe.

Langdon.

Melplaish.

Netherbury.

Stoke Abbas.

Wambrooke.

Beaminster Forum andRedhone Hun-dred.

Brad pole.

  Kingcombe, Over.

  Mapperton.

  Mosterton.

  Poorton,North.

  Poorton, South, *cnm* Loscomb.

(21-This Tithing, Stotingiray In Cul-lifeld Tree Hundred, and EhKll in Wjks Regis, Sr. Litertj, cenrpo,? the Parish of Upway,

  Perrott, South.

Windsor, Little.

Cerne, Totcombe, and Modbury Hundred.

  Wylde Court. (3) *Eggertm Hundred.*

  Askerswell.

  Hooke, and Witherston.

Kingcombe, and Vraxall.

Matravers, North and South.

Milton, West.

Nettlecombe.

Godderthorne Hundred.

  Allington.

Loders, Up.

Shipton Gorge.

Sturthill.

Walditch.

Uggscombe Hundred.

  Chilcombe.

Phillyholme. (3)

Whitechurch Canonicorum Hundred.

  Burstock.

Chideock.

Charmouth.

Catherston Lewston.

Colway.

Marshwood.

Pilsdon.

  Stockland, North.

Stockiand, South.

Stanton St. Gabriel.

Symondsbury, North.

Symondsbury, South.

Wootton Fitzpaine.

  C3—Tbcsf two Tiihlsgi ecu poae ths Parish of H»nkcbwcb

  Gridleshay,

  Sarum,

  Stoke Atram

  Wells ild

  Wootton Abbas...

Broadwinsor Liberty.

Broadwinsor.

Childhay.

Dreinpton.

Dibberford.

Forthington Liberty.

  Dalwood.

Frampton Liberty.

Benville.

Bettiscombe.

Burton Bradstock.

Halstock Liberty.

  Halstock.

Lothers and Bothenhampton Liberty.

Bothenhampton.

Loders.

Poorstock Liberty.

  Poorstock.

Bridport Borough.

Bridport.

Lyme Regis Borough.

Lyme Regis.

III.-CERNE DIVISION. *Buckland Newton. Hundred.*

Brockhampton.

  Buckland Newton.

  Duntish.

  Knowle.

  Mappowder.

  M interne Parva.

  Plush.

  Pulham, East.

Pulham, West.

Wootton Glanville, and

Newland.

Cerne, Totcombe, and Modbury Hundred.

  Cattistock.

Cerne Abbas.

Cerne, Nether.

Godmanston.

Hilfield.

Middlemarsh.

Sydling-Up.

Sydling Fifehead. (4)

Sherborne Hundred.

Cerne Up.

Tollerford Hundred. Frome St. Quintin.

Whiteway Hundred.

Chesilborne.

Melcombe Horsey.

Yetminster Hundred.

    Batcombe, *cum* Melbury Bubb.

    Newland.

    Woolcombe.

Alton Pancras Liberty.

Alton Pancras.

Bindon Liberty.

Pulham, East.

Forthington Libertg.

Hermitage.

Piddletrenthide Liberty.

Piddletrenthide.

Minterne Magna.

Sydling St. Nicholas Liberty.

    Sydling St. Nicholas.

IV.-WAREHAM DIVISION. *Beer Regis Hundred.*

Beer Regis.

Kingshold.

    Kingston, Winterborne.

Coombs Ditch Hundred. Bloxworth.

Hasilor Hundred. Ame.

Blatchenwell.

    Bradle.

    Creech, East

    Church Knowle.

    Eggleston. (5)

    Earls Mead and Haymoor.

    Encombe.

(4) _ A separate Tithing, but gener«llj included in Sydling St. Nicholas Tithing. (5) —Ditto, lometimes included in Tyneham Tithing.

    Holme, East.

    Holme, West.

    Kimmeridge.

    Povington. (6)

    Steeple.

    Stoborough.

    Tyneham.

Hundredsbarrow Hundred.

Affpiddle.

    Briantspiddle.

    Hyde.

    Shitterton.

    Tonerspiddle.

    Worgreit.

Rowbarrow Hundred.

Afflington.

    Herston & Langtou Matravers.

Kingston.

Lan&ton Yvallis.

Ower.

Rempston.

Kollington.

Swanwich.

Studland.

Whitecliff.

Worth Matravers.

Winfrith Hundred.

Burton, East. (7)

Combe Keynes.

Chaldon, East.

Hohvorth.

Lulworth, East.

Moreton.

Stoke, East.

Winfrith Newburgh.

Bindon Liberty.

Chaldon Herring.

    Creech Grange. (8)

Lulworth, Y est.

Longcotts.

Wool.

Stoborough Liberty.

    Stoborough.

Corfe Castle Borough.

Corfe Castle.

Wareham Borough.

Holy Trinity. (9)

Lady St. Mary.

St. Martin.

    V.-BLANDFORD DIVISION.

Beer Regis Hundred. Milborne Stileham. *Cogdean Hundred.* Charlton Marshall. *Coombsditch Hundred.*

Anderson and Thompson.

Blandford St. Mary.

Clenston, Winterborne.

Law Lee.

Muston.

    Whatcombe, Winterborne.

Whitechurch, Winterborne.

Cranborne Hundred.

    Gunville Tarrant.

    Turnw ood, *alias* Turnworth.

(6) —A separate Tithing, sometimes included in Tyneham Tithing. (7) —Ditto, sometimes included in Winfrith Tithing (B)-A separate Tithing, generally included in Steeple Tithing, Hasilor Hhndred. (9)—These three Parishes make but one Tithing. *Loosebarrow Hundred.* Spettisbury *cum* Crawford Mag. *Monkton-Up-Wimborne Hnn.'* Chettle.

Monkton Tarrant.

Piddletoum Hundred. Milborne St. Andrew. *Pimperne Hundred.*

Ashe.

Bryanston.

    Durweston and Knighton.

Eastbury.

Hinton, Tarrant.

Houghton, Wintei borne.

Keinston, Tarrant.

Launceston, Tarrant.

Langton long Blandford.

Pimperne.

    Pimperne Warnership.

Rawson, Tarrant.

Steeple ton Preston.

Stickland and Quarleston.

Stowerpaine.

Rushmore Hundred.

Zelston, Winterborne.

Whiteway Hundred. Hilton.

    Milton Abbas.

Dewlish Liberty. Milborne, Churchstone. *Blandford Borough.* Blandford Forum. VI.-WIMBORNE DIVISION. *Badbury Hundred.*

Abbottstreet.

    Barnesley.

    Cowgrove.

    Chalbury *cum* Didlington.

Critchell Moore.

Gussage St. Michael.

Hinton Martell.

Hinton Parva.

Horton.

Leigh.

    Preston, *cum* Crawford.

    Shapwick.

    Stone.

    Thornhill.

    Wimborne Borough.

Wimborne Minster.

Cogdean Hundred.

    Canford Magna,

Coombe Aimer.

Corfe Mullen.

Ham worthy.

Kingston and Parkston.

Lytchett Matravers.

Lytchett Minster.

Longfleet.

    Sturminster Marshall.

Cranborne Hundred.

Alderholt.

Cranborne Borough.

Cranborne Priory.
Cranborne Tithing.
Edmondsham.
Farnham.
Hampreston
Holwell.
Lovetown. (10)
(10)—A separate Tithing, no» included in Monkton Tarrant.
    Parley, West.
Pentridge.
Petersham.
Rushton, Tarrant.
Wimborne All Saints.
Witchampton.
Knowlton Hundred.
    Bowerswayne. (10)
Critchell, proves,?
Critchell, Lucy, J g
Gussage All Saints.
Phillipson. (11)
Knowlhill. (12)
Woodlands.
Wyke. (12)
Looscbarrow Hundred.
    Aimer and Mapperton.
Charborough.
Morden East.
Monkton-Up-Wimborne Hund'.
    Blagdon.
    Boveridge.
    Boveridge Heath.
    M o n kton-U p-W imborne.
Rushmore Hundred.
Morden, West.
Sixpenny, and Handley
Hundreds. (18.)
Gussage and Minchington.
Handley.
Wimborne St. Giles's Hundred.
    Saint Giles.
Woodyates, West.
Bindon Liberty. Worth, West.
VII.-SHASTON   DIVISION.   *Cranborne*
Hundred.
Ashmore.
Redlane Hundred.
Kington Magna.
Silton.
    Sutton Waldron.
Stower, East.
Stower, West.
Tod here.
    Weston, Buckhorn.
Sixpenny, and Handley

Hundreds. (13)
Cann, *cum* Melbury West.
Compton Abbas, E. & W. (14)
Fontmell Magna.
Hargrove, *cum* Bedcister.
Iwerne Minster.
Melbury, East.
Orchard, East.
Orchard, West.
Sturminster, Newton Castle
Hundred.
    Margaret Marsh.
Alcester Liberty.
Alcester.
Gillingham Liberty.
Bourton.
(U)—The-e were separate Tithings, now included in Gussage All Saints. (19)—Ditto. now included in Woodlands. (18)—These Hundreds were united before 1254.
(14)—These are separate Tithings, but generally lncluded in one.
Gillingham.
Gillingham, Free. (15)
Milton and Pierson.
Motcombe.
Slower Provost Liberty. Stower Provost.
Shafton Borough.
Holy Trinity. (10)
Saint Peter.
Saint James.
VIII.-STURMINSTER DIVISION.
Brownshall Hundred.
Caundle Stourton & Woodrow.
    Caundle Wake.
    Gomershay.
    Stalbridge.
    Stalbridge Weston.
    Stock Gaylard.
    Thornhill.
Cranborne Hundred.
Bagber.
Belchahvell.
    Okeford Shilling or Shillingston.
Pimperne Hundred.
Fifehead Neville.
Haramoon.
Hazelbury Bryan.
Iiedlane Hundred.
    Fifehead Magdalen.
Hanford.
    Iwerne Courtney, *alias* Shroton.
    Manston.
    Okeford, Child.

Sherborne Hundred. Lydlinch. *Sturminster Newton Castle Hd.* flinton St. Mary.
Marnhull.
Okeford Fitzpaine.
Sturminster Newton.
Whiteway Hundred.
    Ibberton.
Stoke Wake
Woolland.
IX.-SHERBORNE DIVISION.
Sherborne Hundred.
Abbotsfee.
Fastbury. J
I loundstreet. I
Nethercombe. VsheriK.TM Town.
Newland Boro.' I
Overcombe. 1
Westbury. *J*
Beer Hackwood (17)
Bradford Abbas.
Caundle, Bishop.
Caundle, Purse.
Castleton.
Compton, Over.
(15)—Formerly a distinct Tithing, now included in Gillingham.
(16)—Distinct Parishes, but only one Tithing, and the Parish of St. James is included in the Tithing of Alcestcr. (17) —A Tithing in conjunction with Lillington.
    Compton, Nether.
    Down and Marsh.
    Folke, *cum* Alweston.
    Hay don.
    Holnest.
    Lillington.
    Lewston. (18.)
    Longburton.
    Oborne.
    Pinford.
    Thomford.
    Wootton, North.
Tollerford Hundred.
Chelborough, E.,orLuccombe. Chelborough, West. (19.) *Yetminster Hundred.*
    Chetnole.
    Clifton.
    Leigh.
    Melbury Osmond.
Yetminster.
Byrne Intrinseca Liberty.
    Ryme Intrinseca.
Sutton Pointz Liberty.

Stockwood.

(lB)—Included in the Tithing of Holnest. (id)—Separate Tithings, though generally included in one. THE NAMES OF THE TITHINGS & PLACES, WITHIN ETERY PARISH, PAROCHIAL CHAPELRY, TOWN, VILL, &c. &c. IN ALPHABETICAL ORDER; SHOWING AT ONE COMPARATIVE VIEW, THE PROPORTIONS OF THE LAND TAX, AND COUNTY RATE. PART III. (a) See Thompson Parish.—(b) See Corfe Castle Parish,—(c) See Holy Trinity Parish, Wareham.—(d) See Doand Stole East Parish—(e) See Langton Matravers and Corfe Castle Parishes.—(f) See Melbnry Bubb Parish.

—Batcombe v. Melbury Bubb—Appeal to the County Rate, see Orders of Session.—(gl See Mapperton and Corse cm be Parishes.

-Cann, see Shafton St. Rumbold. 37-Canford Magna 38-Catherston Lewston 39-Cattistock 40-Came Winterborne Cripton (h) 41-Castleton 42-Caundle Bishop

Caundle Wake

Down and Marsh 43-Caundle Marsh or Down & Marsh 44-Caundle Purse 45-Caundle Stourton and Woodrow.. 46-Cerne Abbas 47-Cerne, Nether 48-Cerne, Up 49-Chalbury and Didlington 50-Chaldon Herring

Chaldon, E 51-Charborough, see Morden East ..

52-Chardstock, N

Chardstock, S 53-Charmouth 54-harminster

Burton, Higher

Burton, Lower

Forston 55-Charlton Marshall... S6-Cheddington 57-Uhelborough West (i) 58-Chettle 59-Chetnole 6O-Chesilbome 01-Chickerill West

Chickerill East, and Putton.

02-Chideock -Child Okeford, see Oheford ChiM. 63-Chilcombe 64-ChiH"rome 65-Clifton Maubank 66-Clenstone Winterborne...

Parish, Sec. 1740—COUNTY RATE.

Tithing.

(h) See Farringdon Winterborne Parish Came v. Winterborne Farringdon-Appeal to the County Rale—?ee

Orders of Sessions.—(i) Sec Luc-

combe, alias Chelborough East.

TITHINGS AND PLACES. 67-Compton, Over 68-l'ompton, Nether 69-l'ompton, Abbas 70-Compton, West, or Abbas 71-Compton, East, or Vallence 72-Coombe Keynes 73-Corfe Mullen 74-Corfe Castle...

Afflington (i)...

B lute him well

Encombe

Kingston

Ower

Roil in.,'ton

Lang (on Wallit (k)

Reinpston

75-Corscombe

Benrille Mapperton(l) 76-Cranborne.

Cranborne Borough

Cranborne Priory

Cranborne Tithing

Alderholt

Blagdon

Boveridge

Boveridge Heath

Hoi well

Monckton-up-Wimborne 77-Critchell, Long

Critchell, Goves

Critchell, Lucy...

78-Critchell, Moore...

(i) See Langton Matravers and Swamrich Parishes.—(k) See Arne and Langton Matravers. (1) See Mapperton and Beaminster Parishes. TITHINGS AND PLACES. 87-Farringdon Wint' and Cripton. 88-Farnham 89-Fifehead Neville (m) 90-Fifehead Magdalen 91-Fleet 92-Folke and Alweston 93-Fontmell Magna, and...

Hartgrove and Bedcister 94-Fordington

Fordington Mill Street...

95-Frampton 96-Frome St. Quintin 97-Frome Vauchurch

G.

98-Gillingham

Magiston, alias Free...

Milton and Preston

99-Godmanston 100-Gussage All Saints

Bowerswayne...

Wyke 101-Gussage St. Michael 102-Gunville Tarrant

Kastbury

H.

108-Hal stock 104-Uampreston 105-

Hamworthy 106-Hammoon 197-Hanford (extra parochial) 108-Handley Gussage and Mincliington 109-Haselbury Bryan 110-Hawkchurch

Phillyholme

Wylde Court 111-Haydon 112-Hermitage 113-Herringston & Clapcotts (ex. pa.) 114-Hilfield 115-Hilton 116-Hinton Martell 117-HintonParva 118-Hintou St. Mary 119-Hinton Tarrant 120-Holme, East 121-Holnest and Leweston (n) 122-Hooke and Witherstone (o) 123-Horton j24-Houghton Winterbome (m) Fifehead Neville v. County Rate—Appeal by this Parish, (n) See Leweston Parish,—(o) See Poorstock Parish.

see Orders of Sessions, TITHINGS AND PLACES.

I.

125-Ibberton 126-1 werne Courtenay, alias Shroton 127-1 werne AHnster

K.

128-Keinton Magna 129-Keinston Tarrant 13ii-Kinson, and Parkston (p) 131-Kingston Russell, see Littlebredy 132-Kingston Winterborne...

M uston 133-Kimnieridge 134-Kninhton, West... 1...

Littlemayne

Friarmayne

Stafford, East, and Lewell 135-Knowle(q)

Bradle

Creech, East 138-Langton Matravers and Herston

Langton Wallis

Afflington (r)...

137-Langton Herring 138-Langton Long Blandford...

139-Launceston Tarrant 140-Leweston, see Hoinest 141-Leigh 142-Lillington and Beer Hackwood 143-Litton Cheney 144-Littlebredy, see Kingston Russell 145-Longbredy 146-Longburton 147-Longfleet... -Long Critchell, see Critchell, Lg. 148-Lothers Matravers, N. and S....

Uploders...

149-Luccombe, alius Chelbro'. E. (s) 150-Lullworth, East 151-Lullworth, West 152-Lytetiett JMatraverse 153-Lytchett Minster 154-Lyme Regis

Colway 155-Lydlinch

M.

156-Maiden Newton

Ouxton 157-Manston 158-Mappowder 159-Mapperton (t) (p) See Parkston—(q) Knowle T. County Rate—Appeal by this Parish—see Orders of Sessions.

(r) See Corfe Castle and Swanwich Parishes— (s) Pays County Rate separately. See Chelborough West. (t) See Beaminster and Coyscombe Parishes. TITHINGS AND PLACES. 160-Marnhull Thorton 161-Margaret Marsh 162-Marshwood 163-Martinstown

Ashdon and Clentlon...

164-Melbury Abbas, or West *Cann St. Rumbold*

Melbury, E

165-Melbury Bubb *Batcoinbe* Woolcombe 166-Melbury Osmond 167-Melbury Sampford 168-Melcombe Horsey 169-Milborne Stileham 170-Milborne St. Andrew

Milborne Churchstone...

171-Milton Abbas

Hoi worth 172-Minterne Magna Middlemarsh -Moore Critchell, *see C. Moore* 173-Moreton 174-Morden East

Morden, *W Charborough* 175-Mosterton 176-Motcombe 177-Monkton Tarrant 178-Monkton Winterborne (v)

N.

179-Netherbury

Ash

Bowood

Melplaish -Nether Cerne, *see Cetne Nether. O.* 180-Oborne 181-Okeford, Child...

182-Okeford, Fitzpaine 183-Okeford, Shilling... 184-Orchard. E. 185-Orchard, W. 186-Osmington

Ringstead 187-Owermoigne

Galton (?) Winterborne Monkton and Winterborne Farringdon Appeal to County Rate—see Orders of 188-Parley, W 189-Parkston, *(Hamlet)* (w)...

190-Pentridge (x) 191-Perrot, S 192-Piddlehinton 193-Piddletown

Bardolfeston llsington

Little Chesselborne

Little Piddle

L-ovard

Walterston 194-Piddletrenthide 195-Pilsdon *Marshwood* (y) 196-Pimperne

197-Poorton, North 198-Poorstock

Poorton, S. and l/oscombe

Nettlecombe *Witherstone* (a)

Milton, W 199-Portland 2U0-Portisham

Gorton

Friar Waddon

Shilvinghampton 201-Poxwell 202-Preston *cum* Crawford 203-Preston

Sutton Pointz 204-Funcknowle

Bexington 205-Pulham, E

Pulham, K. in *Bindon...*

Putnam, W

R.

206-Radipole... 207-Rampisham 208-Rawson Tarrant 209-Rushton Tarrant 210-Ryme lntrinseca

O) Kinsonv. Parkston.—Appeal to County Rate—see Orders of Sessions, (x) Pentridge v. Woodyates—Appeal to County Rate—see Orders of Sessions. (' Sec.Manhwood and Whitechurth Cannonicorum. (?) SeeHooke.

(f) This yum is assessed on the three Parishes, iz. Holy Trinity, Lady St. Mary, and St. Martin.

(g) Ladj St. Mary v. County Rate.—Appeal by this Parish—see Orders of Sessions, (h) See Maishwood and Pilsdon Parishes, There is a difference of 6»d. more than the Sum given in the Act of Parliament, (4 W. & M. c 1), which must be owing to the subdividing the fractional parts in each Tithing, &c. t This Sum is now reduced by Appeals to,£496 5s.-j, viz.—on Fifehead Neville Parish, 12s.—Steepleton Preston 14s.-Jd.—Lady St. Mary Parish, in Wareham, £ 1 (is, 7d.—and Knowle Parish, £ 2s. 4d. OF THE NEW DIVISIONS, AND THE PARISHES, PAROCHIAL CHAPELRIES, AND PLACES,

MAINTAINING THEIR OWN POOR, WITHIN EACH,

IN ALPHABETICAL ORDER;

SHOWING AT ONE VIEW, THE ANNUAL VALUE OF REAL PROPERTY; AND THE AMOUNT OF THE POOR'S RATE, RAISED IN THE YEAR 1815 j THE COUNTY RATE ASSESSED IN 1740, AND CONTINUED TO THE PRESENT TIME;

WITH THE

POPULATION OF 1831, IN EVERY PARISH, CHAPELRY, PLACE. AND DIVISION. PART IV. NOTE—For the purpose of com-

pressing this List in the present size, the fractional parts of a pound have been omitted in Cols. 2 and 3—Col. 2 contains the total amount of the estimated annual Value of Real Property, upon which the Assessments were made at 2s. In the Pound, in the Year 1815; and Col. 4 contains the Total Amountof the Poor's Rates raised in the same Year, which averaged about 3s. 3d. in the Pound, on tbe Amount of the preceding Column. 21 Col. 2 included in Came.—20 Col. 2 included in Ditto—27 Col. 2 included In Littlebredy. PARISHES AND PLACES. 3-Beaminster 4-Bettiscombe 5-Bothenhampton 6-Bradpole 7-Bridport 8-Broadwindsor........ 9-Burstock 10-Burton Bradstock... 11-Cathersron Leweston 12-Chardstock 13-Charmouth 14-Cheddington 15-Chideock 16-Chilcombe 17-Corscombe 18-Dalwood 19-Halstock 20-Hawkchurch 21-Hooke 22-Loders 23-Lyme Regis 24-Mapperton ».... 25-Marshwood 26-Mosterton 27-Netherbury 28-Perrott, South 29-Pilsdon 30-Pborton, North 31-Poorstock 32-Shipton Gorge 33-Stanton St. Gabriel... 34-Stockland 35-Stoke Abbot :M5-Symondsburv 37-Walditch :0-Wambrooke 39-VVhitechurch Cann'. .. 40-Witherston 41-Wootton Fitzpaiue .. 42-Wraxall 40— Columns *2, 3,* and *b,* included in Poorstock. PARISHES AND PLACES. iU-Kimmeridge 11-Kingston, Wint' 12-Langton Matravers 13-Lulworth, East 14-Lnlworth, West 15-Moretou 16-Steeple

Stoborough, (a) 17-Stoke, East IH-Studland 19-Swanwicta 20-Tonerspiddle 21-Tyneham 22-Wareham, Holy Trinity...

Stoborough ... 2:!-Lady St. Mary 24-St. Martin 25-Winfrith 26-Wool 27-Worth Matravers

V—BLAND FORD

DIVISION.

1-Anderson 2-Blandford Forum 3-Blandford St. Mary 4-Bryanston 5-Charlton Marshall 6-Chettle 7-C1enstone, Winterborne...

8-Durweston 9-Gunville, Tarrant 10-Hilton 26-Included in Anderson. 4—Columns 2,3, and 5, included In Monko. 11—Supposed to be partly in the Count; of Wilts PARISHES AND PLACES. 12-

Gussage All Saints... 13-Gussage St. Michael 14-Hampreston 15-Hamworthy 16-Handley 17-Hinton Martell 18-Hinton Parva 19-Horton 20-Kinson 21-Longfleet 22-Lytchett Matravers... 23-Lytchett Minster 24-Morden 25-Parkston 26-Parley, West 27-Pentridge 28-Rushton, Tarrant 29-Shapwick 30-Sturminster Marshall 31-Wimborne Minster... 32-Wimborne St. Giles... 33-Witchampton 34-Woodlands 35-Woodyates, West... VII—SHAFTON DIVISION.

Alcester, (b).

1-Ashmore 2-Bourton 3-Compton Abbas, 4-Fontmell Magna. 5-Gillingham G-Hartgrove 7-Iwerne Minster 8-Keinton Magna £. 1903 2065 2520 793 5640 1299 430 1369 2226 1604 2224 1769 1190 729 1114 821 940 4100 3406 12358 2166 1993 1453 1740.

Amount of the
County Rate.
Population. 11 G. IV., 1 12 6
1 12 11
-16 5i 35—Columns 2 and 3 included in Pentridge. 6—Columns 2 and 4 included in Fontmell Magna. (b) This Liberty and Tithing included in St. James's, Shafton, out-Parish 1-Beer Hackett 2-Bradford Abbas 3-Castleton 4-Caundle, Bishop 5-, Marsh 6-Purse 7-Chelbro', E. or Luccomb!
8-Chelborough, West 9-Chetnole 10-Clifton 11-Compton, Nether 12-.., Over 13-Folke 14-Haydon 15-Holnest 16-Leigh 17-Leweston 18-Lillington 19-Longburton 20-Melbury Osmond 21-Oborne 22-Ryme lntrinseca. 110 595 186 376 70 180 83 62 236 60 415 139 281 123 159 400 18 205 361 380 83 171 1—Column 2, included in Lillingtotv 17—Column 2, included in Lillington. Divisions. i.-dorchester
Ii.-bridport...
Iii.-cerne i iv.-waeeham...
v.-blandford...
Vi.-wimborne...
Vii.-shafton
Viii-sturminster... ix.-sherborne...
Poole, Town and
County
Total See Remarks in next Page.
Note—The County Expenditure has of late years been about 18 Rates of

£496: 5s.-id. per Rate, or £8932: 10s. 4jd. per annum, (about 3d. in the pound): and it is a singular fact, that by the annual amount of the four preceding Taxations, it appears that the said sum of £8932 is about i of the land-tax, (being Hid. in the pound throughout the County), about I of the Property Tax, Sch. A., (which, at 2s. in the pound, amounted in this County to £69839), and about of the Money raised by Poor Rates (being 2s. 8,d. in the pound); though it should be observed that the County Rates are paid out of the Poor Rates, which probably should have been borne by a distinct Rate made for this purpose.

OF THE NEW DIVISIONS, AND THE PARISHES AND PLACES WITHIN EACH, IN ALPHABETICAL ORDER, SHOWING ALL THE STONE BRIDGES WITHIN SUCH PARISHES AND PLACES, AND BY WHOM TO BE REPAIRED, EXTRACTED FROM THE RETURNS OF THE CONSTABLES AND TITHINGMEN, IN PURSUANCE OF AN ORDER MADE AT THE EASTER SESSIONS, 1791, DISTINGUISHING THOSE WHICH ARE COUNTY BRIDGES, AND WHEN ORDERED TO BE REPAIRED BY THE COUNTY. 40-Portisham 41-Portland 42_Poxwell 43-Preston 44-Puncknowle.. 45-Radipole 46-Rampisham.. 47-St. Martin, Wint.'.. 48-Stafford, West 49-SteeDleton, Wint.'.. 50-Stinsford 51-Stratton 52-Swyre 53-Tincleton 54-Toller Fratrum 35-Toller Poreorum 56-Tollpiddle... 57-Upway 58-Warmwell 59-Weymouth, and... 60-Melcombe Regis... 61-Whitcombe fi2-Winford Kagle 63-Woodsford 64-Wyke Regis

Il_BRIDPORT DIVISION.

1-Allington 2-Askerswell
Deverell Coombe
Town
Backwater
Caye Pond
Chinehill
Dog Kennell...
Druce...
Horsepool
Ditto

New Mill
Paine's
Stone
Higher Bridge... Horsman's Lodmoor Preston Bridges Sutton Ditto...
Symes
Chick's
Codsbridge
Great Ditto
Stapestones
Stafford.... BOCKHAMPTON GRIMSTON...
Boyce's
Baker's
Crooked Bridge
Mill Ditto
Hull's
Portsmouth
Meader's
Mill
Stroud's Bridges I Weymouth...
Late George Gould, Esq.
Turnpike.
The Parish.
Turnpike.
The Parish.
Ditto.
Turnpike.
Ditto.
The Parish.
Ditto.
Ditto.
Ditto.
Late Thomas Willis.
The Parish.
Turnpike.
The Parish.
Ditto.
Ditto.
The Parish.
Ditto.
Ditto.
The Parish.
The County—1823.
Ditto —1813.
W.T.L.P.Wellesley. Esq.
The Parish.
Ditto.
Late John Mitchell.
The Parish.
Ditto.
Ditto.
Ditto.
Built by Subscription. The Inhabitants of the Boiough.

PARISHES AND PLACES. 23-Lyme Regis. .. 24-Mapperton... 25-Marshwood... 26-Mosterton... 27-Netherbury... 28-Perrott, South 29-Pilsdon 30-Poorton, North 31-Poorstock... 32-Shipton Gorge 33-Stanton St. Gabriel.. NAMES OF BRIDGES.

Colway...

Names of Bridges	By whom repaired
Weight and Measure..	Hund' of Whitec' Cann'.
Boarding	The Parish.
Stockham	Ditto.
Bettiscombe, al' Beac'	Ditto.
Bingham's	Messrs. Symes & Cox.
Broom Close	Late — Hawker, Esq.
Bittlelake	Late W. T. Cooke, Esq.
Cursey...	Late Dr. Tucker.
Clenham's	Late Daniel Case.
Mill	Sir W. Oglander, Bart.
Eales	Ii.ite J. Kussell, Jun.
Furley	Late John Clare.
Horsepool	The Parish.
Lanebrook	Ditto.
Longmead	Ditto.
Loscombe	Late W. T. Cooke, Esq.
Mason's	K. Knight & J. Hallett.
Mermaid	Messrs. Pitfield & Sabine.
Melplaish	Late Wm. Clarke, Esq.
Millham's	The Parish.
Ox or Ax	Kobert Old.
Purcombe	Messrs. Cook & Gollop,
Sheepslight	Late John Adams.
Slape ... Mill	Late W. T. Cooke, Esq.
Stone	Ditto.
Ware	John Steddam.
Watford	The Parish.
Whittystone	Robert Old.
Winsom Water	The Parish & Bradpole.
Binhim	Daniel Case.
Castle Mill	Ashley&Lethbridge, Esq.
Ditto	The Parish.
Common Close...	Ditto.
Crate	Nettlecombe Tithing.
Dun's Mead...	Mrs. Joan Reader.
Ellery's	Ditto.
East Water	Henry Conway.
Gore	Robert Eorsey.
Lampground...	The Parish.
Merret	Richard Hansford.
Mill Water...	Thomas Brine.
Milton	The Parish.
Oakhay's...comb	Ex'orsof P. Bid well, Esq.
Smokeham, or Smoke-	The Parish.
Studlands, or Shutlands	Late Lady C. Darner.
Tomshay	Nettlecombe Tithing.
Whitley Parks-	The Parish.

Wise Park

BY WHOM REPAIRED.

Late Henry Wallbridge.
Late Joan Reader.
Late Mary Stevens.

PARISHES AND PLACES.

NAMES OF BRIDGES. 5-Gitlingham O-Hartgrove... 7-lwerne Minster 8-K. einton Magna 9-Margaret Marsh 10-Melbury Abbas 11-Motcombe... 12-Orchard, East 13-Orchard, West 14-Shaston, Holy Trinity 15-... St. Peter's 16-... St. James's 17-... St. Rumbold, aV Cann 18-Silton 19-Stower, East 20-... Provost 21-... West 22-Sutton Waldron. 23-Todbere 24-Weston, Buckhorn.

VIII.-STURMINSTER DIVISION.
1-Belchalwell 2-Caundle, Stourton... 3-Fifehead Neville... 4-Fifehead, Magdalen

Porridge Bay...
Spekett's
Townbridqe
Wyke Street
　Cattley
　Frogmoor
Humber
Hidshay, or Hutshay...
Marsh Lane...
Turnbridge
Bow, East end...
Five Bridges, *E.end*
Gope's
　Lane Bridge...
Luxer's Lane...
Motcombe-Street
New-Lan»
　Puxey
　White's Corner
Gulliver's
　House
　Heybridge
Keibrook...
　French Mill
　Spragg's
　Burlton's
　Mill
　Stour
　Stocken
Five Bridges, *West end*
Woodlake
Harput's
Highbridge
Hilless
Small Ford
Kitford, see *Ibberton*
Garved
Rawden Mill...
Fifehead
　Holbrooke Green
Cale, or Caule, see *Statb'l*
　Trill
　Mill BY WHOM REPAIRED.

Feoffees of land in the Par'
Ditto.
  County—1809.
Ditto —1808.
  The Parish.
  Ditto.
  Ditto.
  Ditto.
  Ditto.
  Ditto.
  The Parish.
  The County—1633.
  The Parish.
  Marquis of Westminster.
  The Parish.
  Ditto.
  Marquis of Westminster.
  The Parish.
  Ditto.
  Ditto.
  Ditto.
  Ditto.
  The County—1829.
  The Parish.
  Ditto.
  Ditto.
  Ditto.
  Ditto.
  Ditto.
see Keinton Magna.
Parish.
Martin Toogood.
Turnpike.
  Late Walter Whitaker.
  The Parish.
  Parish and Caundle Bish'. Do. and
Holwell, Somerset. Do.
  Do. and Lydlinch.
  The Parish.
Owner of the Mill.
EXTRACTS OF PARTICULAR RULES AND ORDERS OF THE APPEALS.
The Inhabitants of St. Peter, in Shas ton, v. The late Constables and Overseers of the same Parish.—On an appeal to the accounts of the said constables and overseers— it appearing, that the lands, charged in the rate for the relief of the poor of the said parish, lie part within the said borough and part without; and that the same ought to have been allowed by the Justices of the *county* and borough; but was allowed only by one Justice of the borough.— Ordered, That the said appeal be dismissed. *Mids. Ses.*

1761. BAILIFFS.
Ordered, That the Sheriff or Under Sheriff do, from time to time attend this Court, at every General Quarter Sessions; and they are to have, at such times, six Bailiffs at the least, with their staffs of office, attending; and that the Clerk of the Peace is to serve every Sheriff with a Copy of this order. *Mids. Adj. S.* 1736.

Ordered, That Robert Hallett and Stephen Lush, bailiffs, be fined 20s. each, for not attending this Court. *East. S.* 1742.

BRIDPORT HARBOUR. *Corporation of Bridport* v. *the Owners and Occupiers of Lands at Bridport Mouth.*—On the oath of Andrew Way, gent, it appears, that by order of the Corporation of Bridport, he had allotted and piled out 8 acres, 3 roods, 13 perches of laud, at the place mentioned in the act for the intended building of an harbour; and it was moved by Counsel that the precept, under the hands and seals of two Justices, be read and filed; and notice was given of such allotment to the occupiers of such lands, and proved on oath; and it was also proved on oath by the testimony of witnesses that 6 acres 3 roods 25 perches, part of the premises, were in possession of John Best, who claimed the same by lease from George Pitt the elder, Esq. for a term of twentyone years, of which CJ years were then in being; and the reversion and inheritance thereof belonged to Sir Anthony Sturt, Knt. George Chafin, George Pitt the elder, and George Pitt the younger, Esquires, upon and subject to several trusts and uses tneulioned in the settlements of the lands and estates of the said George Pitt the elder, and that the annual value thereof was 45s. and no more; and that upon the said land there is built a small hut, rented at 27s. a year:—that 2 acres 25 perches, other part of the said lands so allotted, was the inheritance of Thomas Strangwayes Horner, Esq. and Susanna his wife, Stephen Fox, Esq. and Susanna his wife, and Sir Robert Long, Bt. being part of the lands of Thomas Strangwayes, Esq. dec.; that on part thereof there was also a hut built, and that

against the said hut there were two sheds erected; and that 25 perches, part thereof, was occupied with the hut, and were claimed by Robert Chilcott, who held the same from the Strangwayes family by lease on lives, of which two were then in being; that the said Robert Chilcott was in possession of 2 acres, part of the same; and that William Lawes was in possession, as tenant to the said Chilcott, of the said hut and the 25 perches; and the sheds were erected and possessed by John Lea, John Bishop, William Bishop, and John White; and that the said 2 acres, 25 perches were situate on the east side of the river there, and weie part of the lands so allotted:—that the two acres of ground (all sandy lands) in the possession of Robert Chilcott, was worth 3s. a-year, and not more; that the hut, now in possession of the said William Lawes, was then let for and worth 35s. a-year; and the 25 perches belonging to it was worth 5s. a year; but the sheds were not worth 12d. a-year.

That the remainder of the lands thus allotted contains about one acre more, and was part of the common meadow on the west side of the river there; and that the feeding of the aftershare of the said acre of meadow, from Monday next after the first day of August until Monday next after the first day of February, yearly, was claimed by the said Thomas Strangwayes Horner, and others, being part of the lands of the said Thomas Strangwayes, deceased; and the same was also held by the said Robert Chilcott by virtue of the said lease, and was in his occupation. And that one quarterpart of the fore-share of half an acre and five perches of the said premises thus allotted, was the inheritance of William Waldron, Esq. and then occupied by Henry Davie, as tenant at will to the said William Waldron; and the other three-fourth parts of the said half acre and five perches was the inheritance of John Bragg, Esq. and Elizabeth his daughter, then the wife of George Bethell, Esq. or of the said George Bethell in her right, and now occupied also by said Henry Davie; and that the fore-share of 20 perches of the said acre was the inheritance of Simon Taylor, Gent, and was occupied also by the said Henry Davie, as tenant to the said Simon Taylor; and the residue, being the fore-share of about 30 perches, was the inheritance of Matthew Hounsell, Gent, and was occupied also by the said Henry Davie, as tenant to the said M. Hounsell; and that the value of the whole acre thus allotted is worth 20s. a-year and not more: And it was also proved that the said Henry Davie was willing and desirous to release all profits and advantages accruing to him as tenant thereof, so as the whole would be equally divided between his landlords, the owners and proprietors of the same. Jurors—Walter Mullens, Robert Symes, Christopher Marsh, Richard Henville, Robert Hansford, Robert Greening, Edward Lawrence, John Beer, Samuel Hoskins, John Marsh, William Greening, Henry Gould. The said Jurors on their oath say, That 45s. is the yearly value of the 6 acres 3 roods 25 perches, part of the said premises thus allotted as aforesaid, and then in possession of the said John Best; and they assess the same to the sum of £45, and say, that they award and give unto the said John Best, in lieu of his damage and recompense for his interest therein, to be paid by the said bailiffs and burgesses, the sum of £13: 10s. and the remainder thereof, being £31:10s. unto the said Sir Anthony Sturt, George Chafin, George Pitt the elder, and George Pitt the younger, to be paid by the bailiffs, &c. subject to the trusts, and to the same uses, intents, and purposes, as the lands belonging to the said George Pitt the elder and George Pitt the younger are limited, *prout* the settlements: And they assess the hut built on some part of the said 6 acres 3 roods 25 perches, to the sum of £28: 4s. and award that 40s. part thereof, be paid unto the said Jonathan Hayden; and that £6 other part thereof, be paid unto the said John Best; and the residue thereof, being £20: 4s. be paid unto the said Sir Anthony Sturt, and others; subject as aforesaid, in full for their several and respective estates and interests in the same. And the jurors further say, that they assess the said two acres on the

east side of the said river thus allotted, to the sum of £3, and they award and give 36s. part thereof, unto the said Thomas Strangwayes Horner and Susanna his wife, and Stephen Fox, Esq. and Susanna his wife; and one shilling, the residue thereof, unto the said Sir Robfrt Long; to be paid by the bailiffs and burgesses, in full of their respective estates and interests in the same. And that they assess the hut, and also the 25 perches adjoining, other part of the said premises, and then in the possession of William Lawes, to the sum of £24: 10s. and award and give the sum of £5 part of the said £24: 10s. unto the said William Lawes; and the sum of £9: 15s. other part thereof, unto the said Robert Chilcott; and the sum of £9:15s. the remainder thereof, unto the said Thomas Strangwayes Horner and Susanna his wife, Stephen Fox and Susanna his wife, in full recompense for their respective interests therein. And that they assess the two sheds built against the hut, to the sum of 20s., and award that 5s. be paid to each of them the said John Lea, John Bishop, William Bishop, and John White, in full recompense for their respective interests in the same; to be paid by the said bailiffs and burgesses. And the jurors further say, that they assess the acre of meadow on the west side of the said river, to the sum of £20, other part of the lands thus allotted, and award the sum of £7 to be the value of the after-share thereof, and give the sum of £3: 15s. part of the said sum of £7, to the said Robert Chilcott; and £3: 5s. the other part of the said sum of £7, unto the said Thomas Strangwayes Horner and Susanna his wife, Stephen Fox and Susanna his wife; to be paid by the said bailiff and burgesses, in full recompense for their several estates and interests of the said acre: and also assess the foreshare of the said acre, to the sum of £13, and award the sum of £5: 5s. part thereof, to be given to the said John Bragg, George Bethell, and Elizabeth his wife; and assess the sum of £1:15s. other part of the said £13, to be given to the said William Waldron; and assess the sum of £2:10s. other part of the said £13, to be given to

the said Simon Taylor; and the sum of £3:10s. the residue of the aid £13, to be given to the said Stephen Hounsell; to be paid by the said bailiffs and burgesses, in full of their several estates and interests in the said acre of ground: And they find all other facts to support their award and order, and thereon judgment is given according to the said verdict. — *Mich. Sess.* 1740.

BRIDGES—see *County Bridget.* CLERK OF THE PEACE.

The Justices of the Peace assembled at this sessions, being informed of the death of Thomas Coward, h'sq. late Clerk of the Peace for this County, and the most Noble Charles, Duke of Bolton, having omitted to appoint a Clerk of the Peace, (no person appearing to execute the said office,) to the end that there might be no delay in the execution of justice, have unanimously elected and appointed Bryan Combe, of South Mapperton, in the county of Dorset, Clerk of the Peice for this County, pursuant to the *statute,* To hold, &c. until another Clerk of the Peace shall be duly appointed. 37 H. VIII. c. 1.—*Epip. Sess.* 1726.

COUNTY CLERK.

Wm. Harris, Esq. the senior Justice of the Peace of the *Quorum* now present in Court, in the absence of the *Custos Rotulorum* of this County, in pursuance of the *statute,* doth appoint and name Robert Browne, George Richards, Sydenham Williams, and Thomas Haskett, Esqrs. four of his Majesty's Justices of the Peace of this County, or any or either of them, to inspect the County Clerk's books, and to put the *statute,* 11 Henry VII. c. 15, in execution.— *Mich. Sess.* 1743.

An Act of Parliament passed fn 17M, 8 G. I. to restore and rebuild this harbour; hot It doesnot appeal that the Act Was put in execution till this present quarter sessions. The pier was begun by Mr. Reynolds, engineer, and finished in 1743: towards the expanse of which, lotd Deertaurst and Geo. Richards, Fm. the two Representatives, gave £3,600; Richard Brodrepp, Esq. gave 41000, and the Town £300, making in the whole the sum of £6000.—Hutchins's

Hist, of Dorset.—It appears by the ace unu of tha bailiffs and burgesses of Bridport, passed at Mich. Sess. 1744, that the sums of £3500, £500, and 10 guineas, for plans, 4c. was paid to Mr. Reynolds; and the sums to diee.s other persons in that *yen* amounted to £4231: 8s. 8d.; that the receipts for harbour duties for the year preceding did not amount to more than £18: la lid. The average expenditures for keeping in repair the harbour and pier for ten rears from 1786 to 1795, amounted to £230:17a. 7d. and the avextff of the Moeinta of the tattUft and buigeacw *in the* umi period, to £830117t. Odd. In each year. CORONERS.

That to prevent any dispute which for the future mayarise on account of taking any inquisition on any person dying in the county gaol—Ordered, That the sum of 5s. hall be allowed the Coroner for every inquisition, and no more.—*Mich. Sess.* 1761.

COUNTY BRIDGES.

Whereas, for want of cleansing and widening the river, which runs through Little Mohun's bridge, and below the same, the waters are obstructed, and overflow the King's common highway adjoining to the said bridge—Ordered, That the Clerk of the Peace do forthwith give notice to the occupiers of lands adjoining to the said river, that in case the same is not sufficiently cleansed and widened, so as to prevent any future obstruction, within *ten* days from henceforth, they are to be prosecuted for such nuisance.—*Adj. Mic. Sess.* 1760.

HAYWARD BRIDGE.

Ordered, That John Saintlo, Esq. one of the feoffees, produce his account at next sessions, relating to *Lady Hayward's charity*, for repairing the bridge.—That Richard Raines, Allen Ford, Mark Grey, William Fry, John Andrews, Martha Vincent, widow, and the other tenants, are to attend at next sessions. That Richard Bingham, Esq. be desired to permit the agents of Shillingston, (in case he has any deeds relating to the donation) to inspect the same. —*Blandford Sess.* 1734.

On reading the above order, and a copy of a decree of the Commissioners of charitable uses, dated 6 Sept. 1600, 42 Eliz., and also examining witnesses on oath—OrDered, That the feoffees of the bridge, called Hayward bridge, are *to* and do amend the highway adjoining to the said bridge leading to Shillingston and Sturminster Newton, as far as the western end of the present hole or puxy there. That Mr. Saintlo's account be referred to Mr. *Martin,* Mr. *Freke,* sen. and Mr. *Bower,* for the time he has acted as one of the feoffees, who are desired to settle the same, and the arrears now due, and to make their report next sessions.— That the Churchwardens of Shillingston and Child Okeford are to have copies of such accounts, and to be heard against the same.—That the referees are to measure the ground that is now to be repaired, and to fix a post at the end thereof for future memory.— That the money in Mr. Saintlo's hands, and the arrears now due from the several tenants of the lands, be applied by Mr. Saintlo, and the other feoffees, immediately, in repairing the said bridge and highway adjoining: and that the referees are to make their report of the whole at the next sessions.—*Sherborne Sess.* 1735.

The report of the three Justices being received and read —Ordered, That the same be confirmed; and the balance in the tenants' hands to be paid forthwith to the feoffees of Hayward Bridge, and by them to be applied pursuant to the direction of the last order. That an arch be forthwith built for the better conveying the water in the place where the horse bridge stood. That the highway next adjoining to. the said bridge, and mentioned in the last order, be better repaired, and that such highway, from the west end of such bridge to the present puxy, contains 22 lugs of 16 feet and half to the lug; and that a stone at the end thereof be fixed, with an inscription thereon, directing that the feoffees of the said bridge are to amend the highway so far. That the said bridge be forthwith put in good repair by the feoffees.— *Shaston Sess.* 1735.

That the feoffees of the bridge, called Hayward bridge, do produce their accounts at the next session of the peace, to be held at Blandford Forum in this county, relating to *Lady Hayward's charity,* and that a copy of this order be served on Mr. Ridout, the steward to the feoffees.—*Bridport Sess.* 1813.

That the Clerk of the Peace do prepare a case, and lay the same before Mr. Serjeant Lens, for his opinion respecting Hayward bridge.—*Easter Sess.* 1815.

That the case concerning Hayward bridge, and Mr. Serjeant Lens's opinion thereon, be entered in the records of the county.—*Mich. Sess.* 1815.

The Eastern Treasurer having reported unto this Court, that an indictment was preferred at the last assizes, against the county, on account of Hayward bridge being out of repair,—Ordered, that the said treasurer do prepare a special plea, stating that the trustees of *Lady Hayward's charity* are bound to repair, and that he take the necessary professional steps thereon.—*Mich. Sess* 1815.

At the Lent Assizes, 1815, an indictment was preferred against the county for not repairing this bridge. The trial came on at the Summer Assizes, 1817, when a verdict was. given for the crown. It appeared on this trial that the said bridge was an ancient bridge, and that John and Robert Eschelling, or St. Vivonia Eschelling, *lady of the manor,* gave certain lands, *(not named,)* situate, lying, and being within the parish of Okeford Shilling, alias Shillingston, and Child Okeford, to certain feoffees or trustees therein named, their heirs and successors, upon trust, and for the purpose of laying out and expending the *annual rents* in the repairs of this bridge, and a certain part of the road and highway at each end thereof. That feoffees had been appointed, and continued to that time, who had received the rents and profits, and expended the same in and about the repairs of the said bridge and road, until about the year 1815, when, after some high floods, the bridge was damaged, and the roads at each end thereof washed away; and the amount of the money in the hands of the feoffees being about £100, was inadequate to the repair thereof, and they offered to pay over this sum to the magistrates of the county in aid of the repairs, but the magistrates refused, not thinking themselves justified in accepting it, until it should be determined in a court of law.

The then feoffees were the Right Hon. George Lord Rivers, Edward Berkeley Portman, Thomas Bowyer Bower, Henry Seymer, Edmund Morton Pleydell, Richard Bingham, William Trenchard, and Lawrence Edward St. Lo, Esquires.

The steward of the feoffees (Mr. Septimus Smith, of Blandferd) has in his possession the several deeds, books, and other documents belonging to this charity: but the original grant from John and Robert Eschelling cannot be found. He has also the inquisition of the commissioners appointed under the Act 39 Eliz. c. 6, taken 6th Sept. 1500 (42d Eliz.) and a copy of the decree thereon. Also, the book of account, in which the expenditure of the rents appear, and the repairs done by the respective tenants and others, who were always paid by the steward. In addition to the lands which at the time of the trial were occupied by William Melmoth, there are four or five cottages with gardens, close to a place called *Bere Marsh,* and near to the said bridge, which are held under the trustees at about £3 or £4 per annum each, making a rental altogether of about £35.

COUNTY RATE.

Resolved, That the sum of £500 be assessed on this County, pursuant to the late Act of Parliament, 12 Geo. II. c. 29. —*East. Sess.* 1741.

Stitisford parish and *West Stafford* parish.—On an appeal to the General County Rate—for that the tiihing of Frome Billett, wilhin the hundred of George, lies within the parish of West Stafford, and not in the parish of Stiitsford; and that 14s. 2d. being the proportion of the said rate for that tithing, ought to be taken off from Stinsford, and added to the assessment on the parish of West Stafford; and the same appearing to be true—Ordered, That We?t Stafford do stand rated in the sum of £L: 3s. 2d. and Stinsford be rated on-

ly £2:14s.—*Epip-Sess.* 1741. *Came* and *WinVerborne Farringdon.*—On an appeal to the General County Hate—for that the whole tithing of Cripton and Farringdon is assessed at £1:5s. and charged to tiie parish of Came; and, that part of the said tithing lies in the parish of Came, and the other part lies in the parish of Farringdon: and the same appearing to be true—OrDered, That 12s. 6d. part thereof be charged to Came, and the other 12s. 6d. to the parish of Farringdon.—*Epip. Sess.* 1741. *Winterborne Monkton* and *Winterborne Farringdon.*— On an appeal to the General County Rate—for that the tithing of Clapcotts and Herringsion lies within the parish of Winterborne Farringdon, and not Moncklon; and that the proportion of that tithing is rated at 13s. 8d.—Ordered, That Monckton be abated the sum of 13s. 8d. and to pay no more than 9s. and that the tiihing of Clapcotts and Herringsion do pay into the said parish of Farringdon the sum of 13s. 8d. so abated on the said parish of Monckton. —*Epiph. Sess.* 1741. *Pentridge* and *West Woodyates.*—On an appeal to the General County Rate—for that West Woodyates is rated at 16s. 5jd. and assessed on the parish of Pentridge; and that West Woodyates is a parish of itself, and maintains its own poor, and lies within the hundred of Wimborne St. Giles, in this county; and the same appearing to be tiue— Ordered, That Pentridge be abated the said sum of 16s. 5id. and to pay only 10s. and that West Woodyates be rated in future the sum of 16s. 5«d.—*Adj. Epiph. Sess.* 1741. *Melbvry Bnbb* parish ami *Batcombe* parish —On an appeal to the General County Rale—for that that part of the parish of Batcombe which *lies* within the tithing of Melbury Bnbb, haih always paid 9s. 0.1. in aid of the said parish of Melbury Bubb, when £1: 9s. 2d. was assessed upon that parish; and that the parish of Batcombe was only rated the sum of 3s. 8d. in respect of Newland tithing', within the said parish of Batcombe: and the same apppring to be true—OrDered, That the said parish ot Batcombe be rated in future the sum of 13s. 5d. viz. for and in respect of that part of the

parish lying in the tithing of Melbury Bubb, the sum of 9s. 9d. and for and in respect of Newland tithing, within the said parish, the sum of 3s. lid. And also that the said parish of Mflburv Bubb be rated in future the sum of £1:17s. 3d. viz. for the parish of Melbury Bubb, the sum of 19s. 5d. and for Woolcombe tithing, within the said parish, the sum of 17s. lOd.—*Mich. Sess.* 1741. *Parhston hamlet,* within the tithing or village of Kingston, in the parish of Great Canford, and hundred of Cogdean, and *the tithing or village of Kingston,* within the same parish and hundred.—On an appeal to the General County Bate—for that the hamlet of Parkston and village of Kingston are rated each to the said rate, the sum of 19s. lOd. amounting in the whole to the sum of £1:19s. 8d. and that the annual value of the whole hamlet of Parkston is no more than the yearly sum of £320, and that the tithing or village of Kingston is of the yearly value of £1000: and the same appearing to be true—Ordered, That the hamlet of Parkston be assessed and pay the sum of 9s. lid. and the sum of £1: 9s. 9d. being the residue of the said sum of £1: 19s. 8d. be for the future assessed and rated on the said village of Kingston.—*Epiph. Sess.* 1750.

Ordered—That on Appeals to the County Rate, *eight days' notice* of such appeals be given to the Treasurer of that part of the county wherein the said parish so appealing lies.—*Easter Sess.* —1754.

Fifehead Neville parish.—On an appeal to the General County Rate, by ihe parish of Fifehead Neville, in the hundred of Pimperne, in this county—for that the said parish was rated in and by the said rate the sum of £1:5s. 6Jd., and that no more than 13s. Old. ought to be assessed on the said parish. And on hearing counsel on the part of the said parish—Ordered, That the sum of 12s. be abated, and that the sum ot 13s. 6Jd. be in future rated and assessed on the said parish.—*Easter Sess.* 1754. *Lady St. Mary* parish, in Wareham.—On an appeal, respited from the last sessions, to the General duunty Rate, by the parish of Lady St. Mary, in the borough of Waieham, in this county, setting forth that the said parish was rated in and by the said rate the sum of £2: 9s. 7id., and that no more than £l:3s. ought to be assessed on the said paiish, and on hearing counsel on the part of the suid parish—Ordered, That the sum of £1: 6s. *VA.* be abated, and that the sura of £1: 3s. be in future rated ami assessed on the aid parish.—*Mich Sess.* 1700. *Church Knowle* parish.—On an appeal to the General County Kate, by the parish of Church Knowle, in the hundred of Hasilor, in this county, setting forth that the said parish was rated in and by the said rate the sum of £1:19s. ad. and that no more than 17s. 4d. ought to be assessed on the said parish: and on hearing counsel on the part of the said parish—Ordered, That the sura of £l: 2s. 4d. be abated, and that the sum of 17s. 4d. be in future rated and assessed on the said parish.—*Epiph. Sess.* 1771. *Stecpleton Preston* parish or place.—On an appeal to the General County Rate, by Nimrod Bailey, the only churchwarden and overseer of the parish or place of Steepleton, in the hundred of Pimperne, in this county, setting forth that the said parish or place was rated in and by the said rate the sum of £1: 5s. Od., and that no more than lis. u'd. ought to be assessed on the said parish or place: and on hearing counsel on the part of the said appellant—Okdered, That the sum of 14s. Ojd. be abated, and that the sum of lis. *(id.* be in future rated and assessed on the said parish or place. —*Epiph. Sess.* 17B0. Kxx v. Ikeiabitamti or St. Paut, Cotbut Gardkn.—This was an appeal against the Genera County Kate, at the M iddleex quarter sessions, which rate was confirmed at the next general quarter session, and a special case was stated for the opinion of the Court of King's Bench: after hearing counsel on both tides, and it appearing that the allegations in the petition and appeal were true, I/O RD MANSFIELD said, there is great hardship in this case, but the point is tea led in Parker's Reports, 74, and we can gire no relief—we have no authority to alter the proportion, notwithstanding hange of cir-

cumstances, and though conTinced that the equity ot the case it with the appellant.— Cald.Cases, 106— 83 Geo. III. Hil. Term, 1782. But now, by the 55 Geo. Ill: c. 51, a. 14, Justice *im* Sessions are empowered to correct sueh inequalities, disproportions, or omission as shall, on appeal, be proved, to oxtet. EXTRA-PAROCHIAL PLACES. *Sixpenny Handley* v. *West Woodyates.*—Upon examining witnesses on both sides, it appeared that the churchwardens and overseers of Handley had obtained an order of removal, and had executed the same by delivering the orders and the paupers to Nathaniel Bestland, at West Woodyates—that West Woodyates is situate within this county, and has a church where the service of the Church of Kngland is performed, but there are no churchwardens or overseers, and only one inhabitant, viz. the said Nathaniel Bestland and his family; and therefore for the reason aforesaid—OrDered, That the said order be filed.—*Epiph. Sess.* 1741. *Rex* v. *John Shank.*—Appeal respited to t!ie next sessions. — *Epiph. Sess.* 1744. n *John Shank* v. *Okedon* and *Hooper,* Justices.—An appeal to a warrant for nominating Shank overseer of West Woodyates, respited until the next sessions, and no order of removal to be served on the said parish by the parish of Handley until after the next sessions.—*Mids. Sess.* 1744. *Rex v. John Shank.*—On reading the order of last sessions, and hearing counsel on behalf of the king; and the same not being opposed by the appellant—Ordered, that the same be respited until the next sessions, and either party may in the mean time apply to his Majesty's Court of King's Bench, to make the said order an order of that Court, if they shall think fit.—*Easter Sess.* 1745. *John Shank* v. *Appointment of Justices.*—Upon reading the said orders, and on hearing counsel—Ordered, That the appointment of the two Justices be confirmed. —*Midi. Sess.* 1745. *Note*—An appeal was made by N. Bestland to an ap point-ment of overseer, by the same Justices, for the year ensuing: and upon proof of the service of the said warrant of appointment, and upon reading a copy of

a record from the augmentation office, and examining witnesses on oath on both sides, it appearing that he was the only inhabitant and householder in West Woodyates—Ordered, That the said warrant of appointment be confirmed.-/! *dj.Mich. Sess.* 1745. *N. Bestland* v. *two Justices.*—Confirmed the order.— *Mids. Sess.* 1746. FAIRS. An order in council having been received and read unto this Court, and in obedience thereto—Ordered, That the fair usually held at Stalbridge the 14th instant, and the fair at Shroton the 14th September next, be *stopped—Adj. Mids. Sess.* 1751.

The petition of Sir William Hanham, Bart, and others, relating to the fair kept at Wimborne Minster, in this county, on a *Good Friday,* being read—Ordered, That proclamation be made for keeping such fair for the future on *Easter Monday* yearly.—*East. Sess.* 1727. HIGHWAYS.

Ordered, That the heir-at-law of William Gould, Esq. deceased, do attend this Court, to shew how the monies for repairing the highways of the parish of *Broadway,* given by the will of the said William Gould, have been appropriated; and that the title to the lands in question be referred to three Justices, who are desired to inspect the same, and make a report thereof at the next sessions.— *Mich. Sess.* 1728.

Ordered, That the Justices' report be received and filed, and that the heir at-lavv of the said William Gould do pay to the present surveyors the sum of £2: 8s. being the balance of his account; and to be applied towards the repairs of the highways, &c.—.*Epiph. Sess.* 1728.

N. B.—Report not delivered by the Justices into Court. INROLMENT.

The inrolment of a deed, dated 27 March, 1731, made between Samuel Smethem, *alias* Martin, Robert Loder, Robert Willis, Gents. William Gould, vintner, Priscilla Taylor, widow, and James Chaffey, Gent, all of Dorchester of the one part, and James Syndercombe, of Stratton, in the said county, Gent, of the other part, was acknowledged by all parties, and prayed to be in rolled, pursuant to the *statute* in that case made.—*Mids. Adj. Sess.* 1731.

The inrolment of a deed of bargain and sale between Thomas Bishop and Dorothy his wife, Edward Patten and Ann his wife of the one part, and Matthew Knight of the other part, ».—*Mich. Adj. Sess.* 1762.

The inrolment of indentures of lease and release, made between William King and Jane his wife of the one part, and Mary Barnes, Betty Barnes, and Pennel Kitig of the other part, and witnessed by George Hayward, Gent, and George Green.—*Epiph. Adj. Sess.* 1766.

The inrolment of an agreement between the several owners and occupiers of lands, tenements and hereditaments, being the major part thereof in number and value, lying within the manor and parish of Bloxworth, in this county, dated 31 May, 1766, for a piece of heath ground, called Woolbarrow Hill, part of Bloxworth Heath or Common, to be inclosed, and kept iu severalty by Jocelyn Pickard, Esq. his heirs and assigns, for the growth and preservation of timber or underwood, *stat.* 29, *G.* 2.—12 June, 1766.

RATES OF WAGES.

The Rates of Wages were made and settled in pursuance of the stat. 5, Eliz. c. 4, and entered among the Records of the Sessions.—*East. Sess.* 1757.—This act was repealed by stat. 53, G. 3, c. 40.

RATE OF CARRIAGE OF GOODS.

The Rates of the Carriage of Goods were made and settled in pursuance of the stilt. 3, W. & M. c. 12. and enterf d among the Records of the Sessions. —*East. Sess.* 1757.— This act was repealed by stat. 7 and 8, G. 4, c. 39.

SESSIONS.

Ordered, On due consideration of former orders, that the several *Jurors.* Bailiffs, Constables, and other officers, which are to be summoned by the Sheriff to serve at the respective General Quarter Sessions of the Peace, according to the new Regulations and Appointments of his Majesty's Justices of the Peace of this County, be returned out of the several Hundreds, Liberties, and Boroughs following, that is to say—

At the Sessions which is now ordered to be held at Blandford, *on Tuesday in the first week after the Epiphany in each year,*

From the Hund. of *Badbury*
Beer Regis *Cogdean*
Hasilor
Hundredsbarrow *KnowUon*
Loosebarrow *Monkton-up-Wim'*
Liberty of Owermoigne
Stoborough
From the Borough of Blandford.
From the Hund. of Piddletown
Fimperne
Rowbarrow
W!iiteway *Wimb' St. Giles*
Winfritii
Coombsditch
Liberty of Bindon
Piddletown

Uewlish, and By the Act 6 G. 4, c. 60, s. 13, It is directed that every Precept to be issued for the Returnof Jurori before Courts of Quarter Sessions, shall direct the Sheriff to return a competent Number from th e Body of his County, and not from any Hundred or Hundreds, or from any particular Venue within the County.

At the Sessions which is now ordered to be held at Sherborne, *on Tuesday in the first week after the Clause of Easter, in each year,*

From the Hund. of Ceroe Tote' and Modbury
Yetminster
Liberty of Piddletrenthide
Svdling St. Nie'
Halstock, and ıWinterne Magna.

At the Sessions which is now ordered to be held at Shaston, *on Tuesday in the first week after the Translation of Si. Thomas the Martyr, in each year,*

From the Hund. of Sixpenny Hand Sturm'-N'-Castle
From the Hund. of Sherborne
Brownsliall
Buckland Newton
Liberty of Alton Pancra3
Ryme Intrinseca
Forthington
From the H und. of Cranbome
Redlane
Liberty of Alcester
Stower Provost

Liberty of (xillingham, and Boro'. of Shaftesbury.

At the Sessions which is now ordered to be held *at* Bridport, *on Tuesday in the first week after the Feast of St. Michael, in each year,*

From the Hund. of Beaminster
Eggerton (Jodderthome
Tollerford
George
Liberty of Broadwindsor
Portland
Poorstock
Wabyhouse
From the Hund. of Beaminster For'm and Redhone
WliitechurchCan'
Uggscombe
Culliford Tree
Liberty of Framp ton
Wyke Regis and
Elwell
Lothers & Both'n
Sutton Pointz.

Micft. *Adj. SesS.* 1729—2 H. 5, St. 1, c. 4, s. 2 *Note.*—At the Epiphany Sessions, 1825, the Justices then and there assembled, ordered that the General Quarter Sessions of the Peace should in future be held at the County Town of *Dorchester,* instead of being held at the four towns above-mentioned: and afterwards, in 1831, in pnrsuance of the Act 1 W. 4, c. 70, s. 35, the General Quarter Sessiotis of the Peace were directed to be held at the *times* hereinafter mentioned, viz.:— TROPHY OR WHITE COAT MONEY.

It appears unto this Court, that there is of the arrears of the money commonly called *White Coat Money,* in the hands of the Honourable Colonel Strangwayes, the sum of £470: 6s. 2d. proved on oath by Mr. Thomas Mansell; and in the hands of Mr. Arthur Cosens, £100, as by his receipt dated 26 August, 1693, which receipt was produced by the said Mr. Mansell, and is left in his hands; and in the hands of Mr. George Parker, the sum of £71: 6s. 10d., amounting in the whole to the sum of £041:13s.—It also appears that John Fisher had received in the year 1688, of the said White Coat Money, £1489: 8s. of which he had paid £997: 7s. lOd. and a balance remained in his hands of £570: 6s. 2d. —Mid. *Adj. Sets.* 1712.

Ordered, That the money commonly called *Trophy* or *White Coat Money,* according to a power given by *statute,* (Militia Act, 1712,) be applied to the building or purchasing one or more charity schools at *Dorchester,* or some other convenient place or places in this county, for the use and benefit of the same, in educating poor children in the doctrine of the Church of England: and that the further consideration thereof be deferred until the Right Rev. and Right Hon. the present Bishop of this Diocese be made acquainted therewith, humbly to know his Lordship's directions; he having formerly signified a desire to have the said money so disposed of.— *Mich. Sess.* 1712.

Ordered, That payment of the *Trophy* or *White Coat Money,* be made to Denis Bond, Esq. amounting to £641:13s. for buying of arms for the militia of this county; and he is impowered to receive it for that purpose.—*Mich. Sess.* 1715. The sum of £70,000 per Month was directed to be raised according to the proportioni and in such manner as by an ordinance of both Houses made in his Majesty's absence.—The sum for this county was £1311:10s. 6d. nearly equal to a land-tax of 28. in the pound—The last of these subsidies *mm* raised in 1670. FOR THE

REGULATION OF THE PRACTICE

of THE

COURT Of GENERAL QUARTER SESSIONS or The PEACE,

FOR THE COUNTY OF DORSET,

Made at the Sessions held at Dorchester,

July 12, 1825,

AND

Altered and amended at the Michaelmas Sessions,

1830.

ffiontents:

Motions... No. 14—Pa.174

Appeals 2 to 13— *lb.*

Jurors..... 27— 180

Indictments to be preferred 15— 176

Traversed, for Criminal Offences?,-in Custody or ou Baili l0-17 177

on Highways and Bridges 18— 178

on Presentments of ditto 19— 7J.

County Bridges Repairs to be ordered by?

Magistrates, when not exceeding £20 TM

Improvement or Erection to be re-?-P ferred to the Bridge Building Committee 180

Prosecutors and Witnesses 26— *lb.*

i

©r&er of roteeotng: 1.-The Court will proceed with the business of the Sessions in the following order:— 1st.-Motions. 2nd.-Appeals. 3rd.-Misdemeanors which have been Traversed. 4th.-Other Misdemeanors, where the party is not in Custody. 5th.-To deliver the Prison.

But when two Courts are opened for the dispatch of the business, the Chairman of the Quarter Sessions shall make such an arrangement, and appoint such portion thereof, to be disposed of in the second Court, as may best suit the general convenience.

APPEALS. 2.-It Is Ordered, That the appealing Party, by himself, or his attorney, shall '*personally* serve or deliver, at the usual place of residence of one, at least, of the Parish Officers, or to the party against whom any appeal is intended to be made, a written notice of the intention of trying such Appeal, at the next General Quarter Sessions of the Peace, on or before the *Monday* in the week next before the week in which such Sessions shall take place (save and except where a certain time is limited by Act of Parliament,) and shall, if required so to do, prove the service or delivery of the notice, on the hearing of tire Appeal. 3.-That all Appeals (except those for respite and adjournment) shall be entered with the Clerk of the Peace, on the first day of the Sessions, *by eight o'clock at night;* and that all applications for the entry and respite of Appeals, be made by motion of Counsel. 4.-That in all Cases where an Appeal against an Order of Removal shall have been entered and respited, a copy of the Order of Court, directing such entry and respite, or a notice containing the substance thereof, shall be personally served or delivered at the usual place

of residence of one, at least, of the Parish Officers, or of the party or persons against whom such Appeal has been entered and respited, on or before the *Monday* previous to the week in which the ensuing Sessions shall take place: and that the *personal* service or delivery of such copy, or of such notice as aforesaid, shall be proved, (if required,) on the hearing of such respited Appeal, and no further notice of trying the said Appeal, shall be required on the part of the Appellants. 5.-That when a reasonable time for giving notice of Appeal has intervened between the confirmation of any *Poor Hate* and the Sessions next ensuing, no Appeal shall be entered for the purpose of being respited, except such special reasons be stated as shall prove satisfactory to the Court, or unless the consent of the party respondent to the proposed respite, be expressly stated in Court. 6. —That, where an Appeal has been entered, and the Parties Appellant and Respondent shall consent to adjourn the hearing of the merits till the next Sessions, no notice of trial shall be given or required; and the production of the record of such adjournment shall be sufficient evidence of the consent of both parties, who then may proceed to the trial of the Appeal; and that no further adjournment shall be allowed without special leave of the Court, on motion, and consent by Counsel. 7. —That; all respited and adjourned Appeals be continued in the Minute Book of the proceedings, in the order of their original entry, and be called on for hearing accordingly. And when any Appeal shall be called on in the order in which it stands in the paper, if no person shall appear for either of the parties, and no cause shall be assigned for continuing the said Appeal, then the order for adjourning the hearing of the same shall be struck out of the paper. 8.-That when any Appeal shall have been entered and respited by the consent of the Court, and the Appellants shall, before the trial thereof, think (it to withdraw such Appeal, or the Respondents shall determine to quash their order, cither party shall be empowered to do so, on giving to the other party *six clear days' legal notice in writing,* of such intention respectively; and no Costs of Suit shall, in such case, be paid on either side, excepting such costs as may have been necessarily incurred *by the Respondents,* subsequently to the service upon them of the order of entry and respite, and previously to the notice of withdrawing the Appeal; or by *the Appellants,* previously to the notice from the Respondents of quashing their order; the allowance of such cost being limited to 40s. unless upon special cause shewn to the satisfaction of the Court. 9.-That when a notice of Countermand of the Trial of an Appeal shall have been duly served, it shall not be necessary for the Respondent Party to attend at the next Sessions, but Ihe Court will order the Appeal to be struck out of the paper, with an entry that it was abandoned. 10. —That when the Respondents shall have given due notice of their intention to quash their order, the A ppellant may move to have the order quashed as a matter of course. 11.-That in all Appeals against Orders of Removal, the Appellant shall produce the Pauper, or in default of so doing, the Order appealed against shall be confirmed, unless some reasonable cause be shewn why the Appellants have not been able to produce the Pauper, in which case, the Court may, on motion of Counsel, adjourn the hearing of the Appeal; and the Court may, in any case, make such order with respect to the payment of the costs of the day, or such apportionment of the costs attendant upon the production of the Pauper at the trial, as they may deem reasonable under the circumstances of each particular case. 12. —That all *Foreign* Appeals shall be heard first, except under special circumstances, at the discretion of the Court. 13.-That in all Appeals against Orders of Removal, the Respondents shall begin with their proofs in support of their Order. MOTIONS. 14.-1t Is Ordered, That no application be heard by the Court, whether the same be for the entering, respiting, adjourning, or discharging, of any Appeal, or Order of Court, or respiting the proceedings on any ndictment or Presentment, or to continue or discharge any Recognizance, or for furiher punishment of persons convicted under the Vagrant Art, or upon any other subject in which the Court is called upon to make any *Order,* or pronounce any *Judgment,* unless the same be made by Counsel in open Court. INDICTMENTS. 15.-it Is Particularly Recommended, That all persons having Bills of Indictment to prefer, would attend with their witnesses, at the office of the Clerk of the Peace, with instructions for the same, or deliver the same already prepared, (if upon any special matter,) at his office, either on the *first* day of the Sessions, or early on the following morning, so that the Grand Jury may proceed to enquire thereon, immediately after the charge has been given by the Chairman. And to induce an early attention to their recommendation, all Indictments for Felony or Misdemeanors, where the Defendants are in custody, will be tried in the order in which they are found, and for that purpose the Foreman is requested to number each Bill as presented. The Court reserves to itself the power of refusing the Costs of Prosecutors when they have not attended on the first day, or on the opening of the Court on the second day of the Sessions, and do not shew satisfactory reasons for having omitted to do so. Provided always that the Court are not understood to preclude themselves from altering the order in which the cases shall be tried as they may think fit, on the ground of general convenience. TRAVERSES. 16.-Where a party has been held to Bail to appear and answer to any Indictment to be preferred against him, *twenty days* at the least, before the Sessions, at which such Indictment shall be found, or where an Indictment having been preferred and found at a previous Sessions, process therefore shall have been served upon the Defendant, *twenty days* at the least before the next Sessions, in both such cases the Defendant shall plead to such Indictment, and the trial thereupon shall proceed at the same Sessions.

But where a party shall *not* be held to Bail to appear twenty days at the least before the Sessions at which an Indictment is preferred and found against him, or, an Indictment having been found at a previous Sessions, process thereupon shall *not* have been served upon him twenty days, at the least, before the ensuing Sessions, such party shall be called upon to plead, and shall be intitled to Traverse, or put off the trial till the ensuing Sessions.

17.-Where any Defendant being intitled to his Traverse, shall appear and plead to an Indictment preferred against him, at the same Sessions at which such Indictment shall be found by the Grand Jury, he shall be at liberty to try such Indictment at the same Sessions, without giving any notice to the party prosecuting of his intention so to do. But where the Indictment shall have been found at a previous Sessions, and the party be intitled to his Traverse; See 60 Geo. III. c. 4. . 3. 5. or in case of a voluntary appearance without process; such party shall not be allowed to try, unless he shall have given notice of his intention so to do, to the Prosecutor or his Attorney, on or before the *Monday'va* the week preceding the week in which the Sessions shall be held, and shall have left a duplicate of such notice at the office of the Clerk of the Peace *four whole days,* at the least, before the first day of such Sessions. HIGHWAYS AND BRIDGES—TRAVERSED. 18.-Parties presented or Indicted for the Non-Repair of any Bridge, or Highway, shall be at liberty to Traverse to the next Sessions, whether or not the process was served upon them twenty days or more, before their appearance. HIGHWAYS AND BRIDGES—INDICTED. 19.-1T Is Ordered, That whenever the Inhabitants of any Parish, Tithing, or Place, or any Party supposed to be chargeable, shall be presented or Indicted for not Repairing any Highway or Bridge, the Clerk of the Peace shall, within twenty days next after the first day of the Sessions at which such Presentment shall be made, or such Indictment be found, make out process to the proper Officers, to the intent that the parties Presented or Indicted, may enter into Recognizances for their appearance to plead to the same at the next following Sessions, at which

Sessions they shall so appear and plead, or move the Court to respite their plea; but that only one respite shall be allowed, unless the Court shall, on some special cause, duly shewn to their satisfaction, deem it expedient to giant a further respite. 20.-That if the party or parties Presented'or Indicted shall plead guilty, or shall be convicted, the Court may impose such a Fine as they may deem sufficient, according to the justice of the case, or may require proof on oath of some competent person, of the sum necessary to put into complete Repair the Highway or Bridge so Indicted or Presented, and impose such sum as shall be so proved by way of Fine, and in both cases, cause process to be issued for levying the same on the Inhabitants, Party, or Parties liable to such Repair, which Fine or sum so proved to be necessary, when levied, shall be paid into the hands of such person or persons as the Court shall think fit to appoint. 21.-That no Presentment or Indictment for Public Nuisances, respecting Highways or Bridges be discharged, until proof be made that such Highway or Bridge is in Repair, or that the nuisance has been removed, which proof shall be made in some one of the following ways, viz. :— lst.-By Certificate of the Justice who has presented the same, if the proceeding be by Presentment. 2nd.-Where the proceeding is by the way of *Indictment,* in the case of *Highways,* by a Certificate under the hands of *two* Justices of the Division in which such Highway lies; and in the case of *Bridges,* by a Certificate under the hand of *one* of the Justices of the Bridge Committee for that Division in which the Bridge is situated, countersigned by the Chairman of the Geueral Bridge Committee. 3rd.-Tn the case of *Highways,* by the Certificate of *one* Justice, and the *viva voce* evidence of *one* witness. 4th.-In the case of *Presentments* and *Indictments* of *Highways,* and *Bridges* by the *viva voce* of *two* witnesses, provided that due and satisfactory proof be offered, that notice in writing has been given *eight clear days* before the Sessions, to all Justices acting or residing in the Division wherein such Highway or Bridge may be situated, re-

questing them to view the same. 22.-That in *all* the before-mentioned cases, proof shall be made, that *Jour clear days*' Notice in Writing has been given to the Prosecutor of such *Presentment* or *Indictment,* as well of the time appointed for viewing the Highway or Bridge, for the purpose of obtaining such certificate, as of the intention to move the Court to discharge such Presentment or Indictment, upon the production of such certificate, to the intent that the Prosecutor may object to, or shew cause against, the discharge of such Presentment or Indictment. 23.-That in all cases, the Certificate shall state, that the Highway, Bridge, or Nuisance, has been actually viewed by the person or persons certifying, and that the same, at the time it was so viewed, was in Substantial Repair, and likely so to continue, or that the Nuisance complained of was then effectually abated and removed. COUNTY BRIDGES, REPAIRS, &c. 24.-That whenever any alteration, repair, or improvement of any *County* Bridge shall be required, the expence of which will not exceed the sum of £20, any Magistrate acting within the Division where such Bridge is situated, may, at his own discretion, order such repairs to be carried into effect, without any order of Sessions, and the sum so expended shall, upon the certificate of the Magistrate so ordering the repairs, and upon production of the bill at the next Sessions after the repairs are completed, be ordered to be paid, the same being first also referred to the Bridge and Building Committee, for their inspection and approbation. COUNTY BRIDGES—*Improvement tf Erection of* 25.-That all matters relating to the Repair, Improvement, or Erection of any *County* Bridge or County Building, or to the County Road, over and at the ends of County Bridges, be referred to the General Bridge and Building Committee, to be by them reported, with their opinion thereupon, to the Court of Quarter Sessions, PROSECUTORS AND WITNESSES. 26.-That all applications for the payment of the expences of Prosecutors and Witnesses, be made openly in Court; and if the same be granted, that

the allowances be paid according to the Table submitted to, and approved of by one of the Judges of Assize, under stat. 7, Geo. IV. c. 64, s. 26. JURORS. 27.-No person summoned to serve on Juries shall be excused from giving *personal* attendance, without reasonable cause to be allowed by the Court; and all Certificates of Sickness or Inability, must be produced, and verified upon oath or affidavit, if the Court shall so require. BOUNDARY ACT, 2 and 3, W. IV. c. 64. KNIGHTS OF THE SHIRE.

The isolated parts of the counties of *Devon* and *Somerset,* described in Schedule M, to be considered as forming part of the county of Dorset, within which they are included, and which are expressed in the same Schedule, sec. 26 of the said act.

The several Parishes, Tithings, and Places comprised in the several Districts hereinafter mentioned, have been assigned and set out by his Majesty's Justices of the Peace, assembled at the General Quarter Sessions of the Peace, holden at *Dorchester,* in and for the said County, on Tuesday, the 16th day of October, 1832, and annexed to the respective Polling Places, mentioned in Schedule N, sec. 29 & 30, pursuant to the said act, so far as respects the Election of Members to serve in Parliament, as Knights of the Shire.

DORCHESTER DISTRICT. Holy Trinity
Abbotsbury
Abbas, Winterborne
Ashdon and Claudon
Athelhampstone
Bexington
Bincombe
Bockhampton, Sticsford, and
    Dorchester—
All Saints
St. Peter's
Frome Billett
Bradford Peverel & Muckle-
ford Ripers
Broadway and Buckland
Broadmayne
Burlestone
Came, Winterborne
    Cattistock
    Charrainster
    Chickerill, West

Chessilborne
Chessilborne, Little
Colliton Row
Compton Abbas, or West
Compton Vallence, or East
Corton
Cripton and Farringdon
Cruxton
Dewlish
Elwell
Fleet
Frome Vauchurch
Frome Whitfield
Forston
Fordington
Fordington, Mill-Street
Frampton
Friar Waddon
Grimston
Godmanston
Herringston and Clapcotts
Ilsington
Knighton, West
Langton Herring
Littlemayne sell
Littlebredy & Kingston Rus
Litton Cheney
Longbredy
Lovard
Maiden Newton
Melcombe Horsey
Monkton, Winterborne
Osmington
Owermoigne, *with Galton*
Piddletown,
Piddlehinton
Piddletrenthide
Piddle, Little
Portesham
Poxwell
Preston
Puncknowle
Putton and East Chickerell
Radipole
Kings tead
Rodden and Elworth
Saint Martin, Winterborne
Stafford, East and Lewell
Stafford, West
Steepleton, Winterborne
Stotingway
Stratton
Shilvinghamptou
Sutton Pointz
Swyre

Sydling St. Nicholas
Sydling, Up
Tincleton, Cliff, & Throop
Tollpiddle
Up way
Walterson
Weymouth Melcombe Regis
Warmwell
Whitcombe
Woodsford
Wyke Regis
Wynford Eagle.

II.-CIIESILTON DISTRICT. Isle Of Port-
land. I lll.-WIMBORNE DISTRICT.
Wimborne Minster
Abbots treet
Alderholt
Barnesley
Blagdon
Bowerswayne
Boveridge
Boveridge Heath
Canford Magna
Corfe Mullen
Cowgrove
Chalbury *cum* Didlington
Cranborne Borough
Cranborne Priory
Cranborne Tithing
Edmondsham
Gussage All Saints
Gussage St. Michael
Hampreston
Hamworthy
Holwell
Horton
Hinton Martell
Hinton Parva
Kinson and Parkstoii
Knowlhill
Leigh
Lovetown
Longfleet
Long Critchell
Monkton-up-Wimborne
More Critchell
Parley, West
Pentridge
Petersham
Poole
Phillipston
Rushton Tarrant
Saint Giles
Shapwick
Stone

Sturminster Marshall Thornhill
Wimborne Borough Wimborne All
Sainls Witchampton Woodlands
Woodyatcs, West Worth, West.
V.-WAREHAM DISTRICT.
Wareham—
Holy Trinity
Lady St. Mary Saint Martin
Affpiddle
Afflington
Arne
Bere Regis
Blatchenwell
Blox worth
Bradle
Briantspiddle
Burton, East
Chaldon, Herring
Chaldon, East
Charborough
Church Knowle
Coombe Keynes
Corfe Castle
Creech, East
Creech, Grange
Earls Mead and Haymoor
Eggleston
Encombe vers Herston & Langton
Matra
Hol worth
Holme, East and West Hyde
Kimmeridge
Kingshold
Kingston
Kingston, Winterborne
Longcotts
Langtcn Wallis
Lulworth, East
Lulwnrth, West
Lytchet Matravers
Lytchet Minster
Morden, East and West
Moreton
Ower
Povington
Rollington
Rempstone
Shitterton
Steeple
Stoborough Tithing
Stoborough Liberty
Stoke, East
Studland
Swanwich Tonerspiddle Tyneham
White Cliff

Winfrith Newburgh
Wool
Worgret
Worth Matravers.
V.-BEAMINSTER DISTRICT.
Beaminster
Allington
Ashe
Askerswell
Benville
Bettiscombe *Binhall Downs and Earthay in Axminster, co. Devon*
Bothenhanipton
Bowood
Bradpole
Bridport
Broadwinsor
Burstock
  Burton Bradstock
  Catherston, Leweston
  Chardstock, North
  Chardstock, South
  Charmouth
  Cheddington
  Chelborough, East
  Chelborough, West
  Chideock
  Childhay
  Ohilcombe
  Chilfrome
  Culway
  Corscombe
  Drempton i)ibberford
  Evershot
  Frome St. Quiutin
Halstock
  Hooke and Witherstone
Kingcombe and Wraxall
Kingcombe, Over
Langdon
  Little Windsor
Loders
Loders, Up
Lyme Regis
Mapperton
Marshwood
  Matravers, North and South
  Melplaish
  Melbury Bubb
  Melbury Osmond
  Melbury Sampford
  Milton, West
  Mosterton
  Netherbury
  Nettlecombe

Perrot, South
Phillyholme
Pilsdon
Poorton, North
Poorton, S. *cum* Loscombe
Poorstock
Rampisham
Shiplon Gorge
Stanton St. Gabriels
Stoke Abbas, *alias* Abbots
Sturthill
Symondsbury, N. and S.
Thorncombe, co. Devon
Toller Fratrum
Toller Porcorum
Wambrook
Walditch
  Whitchurch Cannonicorum
Wild Court
Wootton Fitzpaine.
  N. B—Stockland Parish and Dalwood Chapelry arejorae.l to Devonshire. Sch. M. I. i.
  VI.-SHERBORNE DISTRICT.
  Sherborne Town.
  Alweston, *cum* Folke
  Alton Pancras
  Batcombe, and Nevvland
  Beer Hackett
  Bradford Abbas
  Brock ham pton
  Buckland Newton *Buckshaw Tithing, co. Som'*.
  Castleton
  Caundle, Bishop
  Caundle, Purse row
  Caundle, Stourton & Wood
  Caundle, Wake
  Cerne, Abbas
  Cerne, Nether
  Cerne, Up
  Chetnole
  Clifton
  Compton, Nether
Compton, Over
Down and Marsh
Duntish
Gomershay
Hay don
Hermitage
Hilfield
  Hoi nest *Holwell Parish, cn. Somerset*
  Knowle
  Leigh

Leweston
Lillington
Longburton
Lydiinch
Mappowder
Middlemarsh
Minterne Magna
Minterne Parva
Oborne
Pinford
Plush
Pulham, East and West
Ryme Intrinseca
Stalbridge
Stalbridge Weston
Stockwood or Stoke
Stock Gaylard
Thornford
Thornhill
  Woolcombe land
Wootton Glanville & New-Wootton, North
Yetminster.
  VII.-SHAFTESBURY DISTRICT.
  Shaftesbury
  Holy Trinity
  St. James, with AlcesterT.
St. Peter
A shmore
Bagber
Bourton
Buckhorn Weston
Cann, *cum* Melbury, West
Compton Abbas, E. & W.
Fifehead Magdalen
Fontmell Magna
  Gillingham
Gillingham Free
Hammoon
  Hargrove *cum* Bedcister
Hinton St. Mary
Iwerne Minster
Keinton Magna
Manston
Margaret Marsh
Marnhull
Melbury, East
Milton and Pierston
  Motcombe
Orchard, East
  Orchard, West Cann
Shastun St. ltumbuld, *alias* Silton
  Stower, lias!
  Slower, West

Stower Provost
Stunninster Newton
Sutton Waidion
Thorton
Todbere
  Vlll.-BLANDFORD DISTRICT.
  Blandford Forum
Aimer and Mapperton
Anderson and Thompson
Ashe
  Blandford St. Mary
Bryanston
Belchalwell
Charlton Marshall
Chettle
  Clenstone, Winterborne
  Coomb Aimer
  Crawford Tar', *cum* Preston
  Durweston and Knighton
  Eastbury
  Farnham
  Fifehead Neville
  Gunville Tarrant
  Gussage and Minchington
  Hanford
  Handley
  Hazelbury Bryan
  Hilton
  Hinton Tarrant
Houghton, Winterborne
Ibberton
Iwerne Courtn',*alias* Shroton
  Keinston Tarrant
Langton Long Blandford
Launceston Tarrant
Law Lee
  Milborne Churchstone
Milborne St. Andrew
Milborne Styleham
Milton Abbas
Monkton Tarrant
Muston
  Okeford, Child
Okeford Fitzpaine
Pimperne
  Pimperne Warnership
Rawson Tarrant
Shillingston
Spettisbury
Steepleton Preston
Stickland and Quarleston
Stoke Wake
Stowerpaine
Turnwood
  Whatcombe, Winterborne

Whitechurch, Winterborne
Wool I and
  Zelston, Winterborne.
23urgesses

The several Boroughs, Towns, and Places following, as to the Election of Members, or a Member to serve in Parliament respectively, shall include the Places specified in Sch. O. s. 35 of the said Act, and be comprized within the Boundaries, which in such Schedule is specified and described, in conjunction with the Names of such Boroughs, Towns, and Places respectively.

BRIDPORT.

From theToll-Bar on the Exeter toad, in a straight line to the uorthern extremity of the Fence which separates the Field called " Marland Five Acres," from the Field called " Higher Girtups and Dogholes;" thence along the western fence of the field Higher Girtups and Dogholes to the point at which the same reaches a Lane leading into Mead Lane; thence along the said Lane leading into Mead Lane to the point at which the same reaches Mead Lane; thence along Mead Lane to the point at which the same joins the Chard road; thence, northward, along the Chard road (o the point at which the same is joined by the first Lane on the right, called "Green Lane;" thence in a straight line to Allington Mill; thence in a straight line to the point at which Conygere Lane joins the Pymore road; thence along Conygere Lane to the point at which the same joins the Beaminster road; thence in a straight line to the Bridge over the river Asher, close by the Flood Houses; thence along the river Asher to the point at which the same would he cut by a straight line to he drawn from the Eastern extremity of Coneygere Lane to the Turnpike Gate on the Dorchester Road; thence along the said straight line to the Turnpike on the Dorchester Road; thence, southward, along the Dorchester road to the point at which the same is joined by Bothenhampton Line; thence along Bothenhampton Lane to the point at which the same is met by the stream which forms the boundary between the respective Parishes of Walditi h and Bothenhampton; thence along the said

stream to the poiut at which the same falls into the river Asher; thence down the river Asher (following the easternmost branch thereof at the points at which the same divides into two branches) to Squib's Bridge; thence in a straight line to the south-eastern corner of Kremy Cottage, on the Bothenhampton road; thence in a straight line to the eastern extremity of Wonderwell Lane; thence, westward, along Wonderwell Lane to the point at which the same joins the Burton Bradstock road; thence, southward, along the Buiton Bradstock road to Wich Gate; thence in a straight line through the Bombardier's house to the Sea Coast; thence along the Sea Coast to the eastern extremity of West Cliff; thence, northward, along West Cliff, and along the western boundary ot the Ship Yard of Messrs. Matthews and Co. to the point at which the same meets the boundary at the Field called "Pitfield Marsh;" thence northward, along the boundary of Pitfield Marsh to the point at which the same meets the river Brit at Ire Pool; thence up the river Brit to the point at which the same is joined by the stream which forms the boundary between the respective Parishes of Symondsbury and Allington; thence along the last-mentioned stream to the point at which the same meets the Fence which runs down thereto from the Toll Bar at the Exeter road; thence along the last-mentioned Fence to the Toll Bar on the Exeter Road.

DORCHESTER.

From the second or middle bridge on the Sherborne road, along the northern branch of the river Frome, passing under Grey's bridge, to the point at which such northern branch is met, near Stanton's Cloth Factory, by the boundary of the pari-h of Fordington; thence, southward, along the boundary of the parish of Fordington, to the point at which the same meets the Wareham road; thence, westward along the Wareham road to the Turnpike Gate; thence in a straight line to the centre of the Barrow, called " Two Barrows;" thence, in a straight line to the centre of the Amphitheatre, called " Maumbury Ring;" thence in a straight line to the centre of the Barrow, called

" Lawrence Barrow," near the Exeter road; thence in a straight line to the south-western corner of the Barrack Wall; thence, northward, along the Barrack Wall and Palisade to the pointat which such Palisade meets the southern branch of the river Frome; thence in a straight line to the second or middle Bridge on the Sherborne road.

LYME REGIS.

The respective Parishes of Lyme Regis and Charmouth. POOLE.

The Connty of the Town of Poole, the Parish of Hamworthy, and the respective Tithings of Parkstone and Longfieet.

SHAFTESBURY.

The old Borough of Shaftesbury; the several Out-Parishes of Holy Trinity, St. James, and Sf. Peter; the several Parishes of Cann St. Rumbold, Motcomb, East Stower, Stower Provost, Todbere, Melbury Abbas, Compton Abbas, Donhead St. Mary, and St. Margaret's Mnrsh; and the Chapelry of Hartgrove.

WARE HAM.

The old Borough of Wareham; the Parishes of Code Castle and Bere Regis; the several Out-Parishes of Lady St. Mary, Holy Trinity, and St. Martin, ami the Chapelry of Arne; that part of the Parish of East Stoke which adjoins the eastern boundary of the old Borough of Ware ham; and also such part of the Parish of East Morden as is comprised within the following Boundary, that is to say:

From the point at which the boundary of the Parish of East Morden meets the southern boundary of Morden Park Wood, southward along the boundary of Morden Park Wood, to the point at which the same meets the Sherford Lake; thence, eastward, along the Sherford Lake to the point at which the same meets the boundary of the Parish of East Morden; thence, southward, along the boundary of the Parish of East Morden, to the point first dt scribed.

WEYMOUTH And MELCOMBE REGIS.

From the old Sluice on the Wareham Road, in a straight line to the point at which the northern Wall of the old Barrack Field meets the Dorchester Road; thence along the said northern Wall, and

in a line in the direction thereof, to the point at which such line meets the boundary of the old Borough; thence, northward, along the boundary of the old Borough, to the point at which the same meets the Upper Wyke Road; thence, westward, along the Upper, Wyke Road to the point at which the same is joined by a

Cross Road leading to the Lower Wyke Road, otherwise called Buxton's Lane; thence along the said Cross Road to the point at which the same joins the said Lower Wyke Road; thence along the said Lower Wyke Road to the point at which the same joins the Sandsfoot Castle Road; thence, northward, along the Sandsfoot Caslle Road to the point at which the same is met by the Footpath leading by Lovel's Farm to Bincleves; thence along the said Footpath to the point at which the same reaches the edge of the Cliff at Bincleves; thence along the Sea Coast to the old Sluice aforesaid.

POOLE.

Town and County. 36 Edw. HI.— *Charter.* 10 Elk. 1568.

At the Election in 1807, John Jeffery, Sir Richard Bickerton, and Joseph Garland were returned, the latter two having an equal numbe of Votes, but on anew Writ being issued, Sir H. Bickerton was returned without opposition. *Note.*—This Town and County, being a County Corporate, having Its own Sheriff and other Magistrates, is distinct from the County of Dorset; and the Civil Officers of the County at lare, have no power to intermeddle therein.

The Amount of real Property and Poor's Rate is given,.

Land TaK

Polling Place for this Town is VV'imborne,

Page 141 142 183

Names of Gentlemen inserted in the Commission *at* the Peace, by a Cold Seal, since the issuing thereof in December, 1830:— ABSTRACT OF RETURNS OF *Charitable Donations,*

&c.

Made in pursuance of the Act 26 *(i.* 3, c. 58, " For procuring, upon Oath, "Returns of all Charitable Donations for the

Benefit of Poor Persons, "in the several Parishes and Places within that part of Great Britain "called England." AND ALSO OF THE SUPPLEMENTARY RETURNS

Which were ieceived in consequence of Circular Letters written by the Chairman of the Committee of the House of Commons, in 1787, the former having been found defective, reported by the Committee in 1788, and ordered to be printed the 26th June, 1816, so far as relates to the County of Dorset, and corrected to the Year 1832.

ABSTRACT OF RETURNS MADE BT THE MINISTERS AND CHURCHWARDENS, OP ©fcarttafrte Donations, IN THE COUNTY OF DORSET, FOB THE BENEFIT OF POOR PERSONS,

In Pursuance of the several Acts of Parliament relating thereto, 26 Geo. III. c. 58—52 Geo. III. cc. 101, 102 59 Geo. III. c. 91.

1 & 2 W. IV. c. 34.--2 43 VV. IV. cc. 57, 115. CORRECTED TO THE YEAR 1832. DESCRIPTION of the CHARITY, *by* whom, when, and for what Purpose 1-ABBOTSBURY. SCHOOL.

Mrs. Susanna Strangways Horner, by will, dated 28th February, 1754, gave an annuity or rent-charge, payable out of the manor of Abbotsbury, with a school-house, wherein the master now dwells, £20 per annum for the salary of a proper schoolmaster to teach thirty boys to read, write, and cast accounts, and navigation—vested in the Earl of llchester...

Ditto, by will of the same date, gave £100 in money, for the relief of the poor of this parish, at the discretion of her executors—vested in ditto

——, (supposed by a Strangways, or by some ancestor of the late Countess Dowager of llchester) by, dated —, gave £— in money, for the relief of the poor—vested in ditto , (supposed by the heirs of William Strangways, *Esq.)* by, dated, gave some Land, situate at *Haselbury Bryan,* for the relief of the poor, &c.—vested in the overseers of this parish

Bernard Mitchell, by will, dated 22d March, 1640 gave a rent charge out of his freehold house, called the King's Head Inn, in Melcombe Regis, for the benefit of the poor, &c.—vested in the overseers of this parish 2-ABBAS WINTERBORNE.

Bernabas Whittle, by will, dated _, gave £80 in" money, for the use of the poor of this parish, and

Hypollvto (called Henry) Mockett, by will, dated (20th September, 1653, (died in 1659), gave „£25 in j money, for the same purpose—vested in the heirs of' Warren Lisle, Esq. deceased 3-AFFPlDDLE.

SCHOOL.

Mrs. Johanna Milbourne, by will, dated, 1808,' gave £150, 3 f Cent. Red. Ann., the interest, dividends, profits, and produce thereof, to be paid towards the maintenance of a School for teaching and instructing the poor The Overseers have always received and applied this Money; but whether the Land is vested U them is uncertain,—It has. siace been let for £G 10s. a-year.

ESCRIPTION of the CHARITY, by whom, when, and for what pnrposej given.

Annual Produce.

children of this parish, in reading, writing, and saying their catechism, &c. vested in James Frampton, Esq. lord of the manor, the vicar, or officiating minister, and churchwardens *(See Moreton Parish.)* ALCESTEH—*see St. James's, Shafton.* 4-ALLlNGTON—*see Bridpoit.* 5-ALMEB—None. 6-ALTON PANCRAS—*None.* 7-ANDERSTONE—None.

ARNE—*None—see Holy Trinity Parish, Wareham.*

8-ASHMORE-AW. 9-ASKERSWELL. by, dated —, gave in land, situate in the Parish

Field, for the repairs of tht church of this parish—vested in

Joseph Stone

, by, dated —, gave £10 in money, since laid out in the purchase of a small tenement, of one Charles Bagg, 26th March, 1743, and which is occupied by the poor of this parish —vested in the heirs of the Rev. Gregory Syndercombe, *L. It.* 1). and John Tucker, Gent, in trust for the parish 10-ATHELHAMPSTONE—None.

B.

11-BATCOMBE—None. BEAMlNSTER—see *Netherbury.* 12-BELCHALWEL.L. , by, dated —, gave £15 in money, for the

use of the poor of this parish who do not receive alms; distributed in *Easter* week—vested in the Rector of this parish 13-BEER REGIS. SCHOOL.

Thomas Williams, Esq. by deed, dated, 1719, gave the inheritance in fee-simple of seven acres of land in Beer fields, a dwelling-house, orchard, and six acres of pasture at Rye Hill, two dwelling-houses, two gardens, one orchard, and two grounds containing four acres, a cottage at *Bug. barrow,* with half an acre of land thereto belonging; toge.

A school-house was afterwards built bj Mr. Williams, at this place, which he the use of a master and the said children.

DESCRIPTION of the CHARITY, by whom, when, and for what purpose, g given.

I;g 1 ther with common of pasture for 50 sheep and XO cows belonging to the same; and also the tithe of hay of a moor on the west side of a little meadow on the south end of Rush Mead; in trust, that the rents and profits of the said premises should always be applied and disposed of for the teaching and clothing of *tix* poor children born in this parish—vested in the vicar and others, trustees of the said school

Henry Fisher, Clerk, by will, dated-, 1773, gave,£1001 in money, to the use of the said school—vested in John Bond, esq....

Mrs. Nevill Pleydell, by will, dated —, 1785, gave £5 in money to the use of the said school—vested in the vicar for the time being

George Daw, gave in money, *£W*
James Penny, ditto 5
William Penny, ditto 10
John ProMe, Gent ditto 10
Thomas Clinch, ditto 5
Matt. Turberville, Gent. ditto 5

How or when these Sums weie given is not mentioned, but the interestthereof is distribU'

ted tothe poor!

of this parish at stated periods.

Richard Mitchell, Gent....ditto..
Wm. Gould, Merchant, ditto..

Bernard Mitchell, by will, dated 22d March, 1646, gave a rent charge, issuing out of his freehold house, called the King's Head inn, in Melcombe Regis, for the benefit of the poor—vested in

the overseers of this parish...

Mrs. Barbara Skinner, by will, dated —, 1769, gave,£200 to the *dissenting* poor, at the discretion of her exe. cutor—vested in Mr. George Brugh, her executor t A table in the church mentions this £120; but £16 appears to have been lost, as no account of it can be given. £110 is now in tlie hands of the heirs of the late Thomas Erie Urax, Esq. t Said to have been distributed; therefore no annual produce.

DESCRIPTION of.the CHARITY, bj whom, when, and for what purpose' given. 14-Kingston Winterborne—*None.* 15-Milborne Stileham.

Lady Morton, by deed, dated —, gave an annuity to the

poor of this place of *V* annum—vested in £. M. Pleydell, Esq....

Bernard Mitchell, by will,dated 22d March, 1646, gave a rent charge, issuing out of his freehold house, called the King's Head Inn, in Melcombe Regis, for the benefit of the poor—vested in the overseers of this tithing...

16-BEER HACKET—*None.* 17-BETTlSCOMBE—*None.* 18-BlNCOMBE—*None.* 19-BLANUEORD l'ORUM. FREE SCHOOL.

Removed to this town from Milton Abbey in 1785.—*see M. Ab.* SCHOOL.

Archbishop Wake, by deed, dated 17th April, 1728, gave,£1616 5s. 5d. in money, for and towards erecting a charity school, and cloathing and instructing 12 boys, and tor, other charitable purposes in this town, and which he con firmed, by his will, dated 12th Feb. 1731—vested in the bailiff and burgesses...

ALMSHOUSE.

George Ryves, Esq. of Ranston, by will, dated 8th May, 1685, gave the residue of his personal estate, since laid out in lands, situate at *Litton Cheney,* in the county of Dorset, towards maintaining ten poor persons in the almshouse, at 2s. 6d. a week, and a garment, viz. eight out of Blandford, and two out of Pimperne—vested in the bailiff and others GENERAL CHARITIES.

Richard Rogers, by, dated—, *he died about* 1643), gave £'290 in money, the produce of which is disposed of in clothing poor people, and in binding boys apprentices— vested in the bailiff and burgesses.

Mary, widow of John Gundry, Esq. by will, dated —J 1692, gave a rent charge, issuing out of vvalford Farm, in Wimborne Minster, to be paid to a poor man of this town,! 10s. every quarter day—vested in the bailiff and burgesses

Robert Ridout, by, dated —, 1698, gave £50

O. S. S. Ann. the interest to be applied in teaching poor children to read—vested in the bailiff and burgesses...

Annual Produce.

£. s. d.

48 9 8 120- 11 1 10

History of Dorset, Toi. 1, pp. 145,146, DESCRIPTION of the CHARITY, by whom, given.

wheti, and for what purpose

Annual Produce.

Priscilla Dennett, spinster, by will, dated —, 1703, gave £50, O. S. S. Ann. to three poor families at Christmas, who attend constantly at church—vested in the bailifl' and burgesses

Borert Pitt, M. D. by will, dated — , 1711, gave £100,1 O. S. S. Ann. for binding out poor boys apprentices— vested in the bailiff and burgesses

Walter, Ridout, by. dated —, (supposed *to have been given about the year* 1690), gave £15 in money, the interest of which is laid out in buying wheat for the poor, when more than 5s. bushel— vested in the bailiff and burgesses

Margaret, wife »f Thomas Pitt, by will, dated 17th July, 1719, gave „£600 to be disposed of to and amongst such and so many poor housekeepers, inhabitants of the said town of Blandford, as are not pensioners, and do not receive alms from the said parish—vested in Thomas Fit herbert, John Dale, and John Harrison, *(since dead,)* as feoffees

William Pitt, their son, by will, dated 20th December, 179, gave in land, at, to be disposed of in like man, ner as the above—vested in the said Thomas Fitzherbert, John Dale, and John Harrison, *sincedead,)* as feoffees

William Pitt, by, dated —, (came info *the hands oj the corporation about the*

year 1690), gave £50 in money, for binding out poor boys apprentices— vested in the bailiff', and burgesses....... .....

Christopher and Rorert Pitt, by, dated, *(came into the hands of the corporation about the year* 1690), gave,£150 in money, since laid out in the purchase of lands at Kingston. The sum of I0s. is paid quarterly to a poor person in the church alms-house, the remainder in alms at Christmas—vested in the bailiff and burgesses

Sir Warwick Hele, by, dated —, *(came into the hands of the corporation about the year* 1690), gave in money, £ 150, which nets £5 I0s. per annum; of which 50s. is expended yearly in bread for the poor, and 60s. in cloathing and alms at Christmas—vested in the bailiff and burgesses...

Francis Kingston, by will," dated 1st February, 1777, gave „£300 in money, to five poor men and five poor women, DESCRIPTION of the CHARITY, by whom, when, and for what purpose given.

who have been respectable housekeepers, and go to church —vested in the bailiff and burgesses WmiAM Williams, Gent. of this town, by will, dated 30th June, 1621, directs his executors to raise out of his estates „£i000, to purchase lands to the value of „£140 per annum, within two years after his decease, to be conveyed to them and their heirs, in trust for the purposes therein mentioned. The Lands hereinafter mentioned were purchased, and in the year 1690 the rents and produce were as follows:—

Clenstone Winterborne, *Little Clenstcne Farm,£110 -*, 100 *Acres of Wood...- .* £240 2 8

With the rents and profits of the above a certain number of poor boys are to be bound apprentice to the sea service, viz,

Two out of this town the first year;

Two out of Shaftesbury the second year; and

Two out of Sturminster Newton the third year, And so on successively; and £14 to be yearly paid with each, and for cloathing them. The residue to artificers of the said towns, *£b* at the least, and not

more than £8 at the most, to be distributed to each yearly; if any of them shall be impoverished by fire, &c. to be relieved out of part of what is given to the tradesmen. Un the death of an executor, a feoffment shall be made by survivors, and always 4 fe. offees to remain, to eachjof them yearly the sum of £1:16s.8d. and to the chief officers of this place, Shafton, and Stur. minster Newton, 6s. 8d. each. The executors were, Sir Thos. Freke, of lwerne Courtnay, Knt. Richd. Swayne, of Blandford Forum, Esq., Arthur Squibb, of Westminster,

Borough of Blandford Forum for the time being, and their successors, upon trust, to apply and dispose of the said principal sum of *£3000*, and the interest, profits, and produce thereof, as the same shall from time to time become due and payable, for and towards erecting, establishing, and supporting of an Hospital or Infirmary, for the use and reception of sick and infirm persons in the said county; the same tobe built at or as contiguous to the said town of Blandford Forum as may be. And in the mean time, until a sufficient sum or money can be raised for supporting the said hospital, the interest, dividends, and produce of the said £2000 shall front time to time be vested in the names of the said trustees, their heirs and successors, in the further purchase of Government Securities, towards establishing a fund for the purposes aforesaid; which legacy has not been demanded of the executors.

Gent., and Brune Williams, of Tyneham, Esq. By codicil he gives *£h* yearly, out of the £140 to be paid the Schoolmaster of Blandford. The remainder of his goods and chatties to be employed by the executors in maintaining the almsmen and women in the aforesaid towns, to be appointed by them, and who are to receive £5 a-piece yearly for ever, —vested in F. J. Browne, James Frampton, John Herbert Browne, Esqrs. and others *M* rs. Ann, Anne, or Man, of Blandford, by will, dated1737, gave the interest of,£100, to be paid in a certain time to the schoolmaster of this town, for assisting the vicai of the said town ten Sundays in the year, in the administration of the Sacrament, and appointed the rectors of Pim perne and Bryanston her trustees. The principal was for some years lost, but part being afterwards recovered by John Gannett, Esq. late of this town, he, by will, dated 1773, ordered it to be made up,£50; this has since accumulated and £200, 3 cent, consols have been purchased, and are now standing in the names of the rectors of *Pimperne* and *Bryanston*—vested in the said rectors

John Bastard, by deed, dated, 1768, gave,£600 3 cent, consols, for lighting the town lamp, teaching children to read, and to purchase bread for the poor—vested in the bailiff and burgesses by ——, dated—, gave, *Gratis Money,* supposed to have been given by Dr. Haymore and others, about 1618, was originally £60, but by losses and otherwise, re duced to *£25,* has generally been lent to poor tradesmen of this town; sometimes, when provisions have been dear, the interest has been given to poor families—vested in the bailiff and burgesses

Ann Pitt, by will, dated 21st June, 1783, gave £3, to be distributed by yearly instalments among poor men and women of the said town, until the whole was expended.

20-BLANDFORD ST. JUARY-tfmc 21-BLOX WORTH., by, dated —, gave £5 in money to the use of the poor of this parish—vested in James Jellett, blacksmith 22-BOTHENHAMPTON—*None.*
Annual Produce £. s. d.
ESCRIPTION of the CHARITY, by whom, when, and for what given.
The Rev. William Preston, rector of Clifton, by will, dated —, 1758, (founded in 1781), gave some land at Nether Compton, for a charity school—vested in the rector of Bradford Abbas...........
.... 14- SI Auk West, Esq. and William Read, Gent., by deed, dated, —, 1781, purchased £350, 4 cent, towards the support of the said school—vested in the late Mr. James West, Thomas Thompson, and Mark Fooks......» 4 _ _

Sir John Hele, serjeant-at-law, of Wembury, co. *Devon,* by, dated —, *(he died 4th June,* 1608), gave a rent

charge, to be paid out of his estate at Clifton, for the benefit of the second poor of this parish—vested in the Marquess of Anglesea, and the minister, churchwardens, and overseers...............
... 2 12 24-BRADFORD PKVKRELL.

William Churchill, by will, dated 17th April, 1039, gave £10 in money, for the benefit of the poor.

Thomas Meggs, Esq. by deed or will, dated 26th June, 1696, gave £20 in money for the same purpose—vested in —

John Thistlewayte, M. A. rector, by will, dated, 1724, gave a rent charge upon the tithes of Pilton and Farley, co. *Wilts,* to be distributed annually amongst the poor of this parish—vested in Winchester College... (2 10 25-BRADPOLE-Arone.

The Bailiffs and Burgesses, by deed, dated, 1620, gave, (with trust monies vested in their hands) acres of land, called Broad Oak, in Symondsbury; three-fourths of There is a Tablet in the Church that mentions these two Donations, and for what purpose given. The late Thomas Meggs, Esq. is supposed to have had this 30 in his hands.

B DESCRIPTION of the CHARITY, by whom, when, sod for what Fuip-se the profits to be employed by the direction of the bailiffs and burgesses for the maintenance of a *schoolmaster,* within the borough, and the other fourth for the benefit and main tenance of the poor people of the said borough, for ever—vested in the said bailiffs and burgesses

Daniel Taylor, (a Quaker,) by deed, dated, 1708, gave in land, a house called *The Bull,* for the purpose of supporting a Free-School at Bridport; the number of scho- lers to be twelve of the poor inhabitants there, or so many as the clear annual produce of the premises should exceed or fall short of *£U;* vested in late Thomas Nicholson, Samuel White, and Thomas Westcombe HOSPITAL.

James Napper, by will, dated, gave, in money to the use of the poor people of the house or hospital of St

Mary Magdalen, in AUington; vested in, (uncertain, the same not having been paid for several years)

Robert Salter, by will, dated, 1642,

gave,£300 in money, (since laid out in lands called Cattleborough, in the parish of Whitchurch Cannonicorum, in pursuance of the will,) one-third part of the annual produce to the poor of the almshouse at *Allingion.* (belonging to Bridport,) i third part to the poor of *Whitchurch Canntnicorvm,* and one-third part to the poor of *Charmouth*; vested in late Henry Sherive, LL. D. rector, Thomas Bishop, and Wm. Orchard, surviving trustees...

Almshouse.

Thomas Jessop, Esq. by deed, dated 1602, gave a rentcharge, issuing out of a tenement in Bridport, for the better sustentation of the poor of the southernmost almshouse in Bridport; vested in the bailiffs and burgesses...

Daniel Tatlor, (a Quaker) by deed, dated 1696, gave a house, called the *Quaker's Almshouse,* in trust, for the use of such poor persons of the borough of Bridport to dwell in, as should be appointed by the trustees and their successors; vested in the late Moses Neeve, Thomas West- combe, John Hill, Isaac Hann, John Jeffery, and others.

The following Lakds and Premises are supposed to have been heretofore granted to the Bailiffs and Burgesses of the borough of Bridport, in trust for the poorof the almshouse there, called *The Higher Almshouse,* leases either for lives absolute for years, or years determinable on lives, having been granted time out of mind by the said Bailiffs and Burgesses, or by the Bailiffs with the Assent of the Burgesses, of the premises respectively, as trustees of the lands belonging to the same almshouse; and counterparts of leases being in their custody, granted in like manner, some of them dated upwards of 160 years since, but no trust, deed, or grant to them, of any of the said premises can be found:—

One Tenement, &c, situated on the west side of South-street, on lease to John Margrie, determinable on lives, under the yearly rent of

One Tenement, &c. situate on the south side of the Weststreet, on lease to Mr. Daniel Gundry, determinable on three lives, under the yearly rent of...

One Messuage, &c. situate on the west-side of the South, street, on lease to Wm. Beam, determinable on lives, un der the yearly rent of.............

One piece or plot of Ground, situ ate at the south end of the South-street, on the west side of the road leading to the sea, in the occupation of Mr. Samuel Gundry, on lease at rack rent, for the remainder of a term of 14 years, (of which 11 were unexpired, on the 25th of March, 1785) under the yearly rent of

One Tenement, &c. with the garden and spinning ways belonging, and also the south part of the spinning way. bounded out, with the work-house at the end thereof, in length 80 feet, and in breadth 18 feet, situate on the west! side of the South-street, on lease to Andrew Crabb, deter, minable on lives, under the yearly rent of

One Dwelling-house, with the garden plot, situate on the west side of M ichael's-lane, in the possession of Mr. Jo. seph Gundry, who holds the same on lease granted to his late father, in con- sideration of rebuilding, for the residue of a term of!19 years, determinable on three lives, under the yearly rent of

The above rents are reserved to the use of the poor of the above alms-house, which have ever been supposed to have been invested in the said Bailiffs and Burgesses as overseers andtrustess thereof, and they have time out of mind repaired the same; but no.grant can be found of it.

A certain little House on the north- side of the East-street, in

Bridport aforesaid, which was always deemed and taken to be an *almthouse,* and now used as such, and which has been repaired by the said Bailiffs and Burgesses, is like wise presumed to have been invested in them by some grant, which cannot be found.

A certain other *Almsaouse* in Brid- port,called, the *Lowei Almshouse,* of which there is no account extant, but is re paired at the expense of the parish.

GENERALCHABITIES.

Bailiffs And Burgesses, by deed, dated 1632 gave (with trust monies vested in their hands) 14 acres of land called Broad *Oak,* in Symondsbury, one-third

part for raising and maintaining of a stock of money, to set on work the poor artificers of the said borough; the other two thirds for the relief and mainte- nance of other poor people within said borough; vested in live of the capital burgesses

Ditto, by deed, dated, 1650, gave (with trust monies vested in their hands) in land, two messuages in Bridport, called *The Malthoiise* and *Brewhouse,* for apprenticing poor children, comfort- ing poor housekeepers, and buying them materials to labour upon in their profession; vested in the bailiffs and burgesses...

Charles Pitfield, of floxton, in the county of Middlesex, Esquire, by deed, dated 5 July, 1765, gave a rent-charge, on an estate in the parish of Symonds- bury, called *Thorncombe, £15* annum; £7:10s. annum, part thereof, to be be- stowed in bread, to be distributed by DE- SCRIPTION of the CHARITY, by whom,; when, and foi what purpose g 1 given. g . the churchwardens and overseers of Bridport, every *Sunday* morning, imme- diately after Divine service, unto 40 poor and impotent people of Bridport, Symondsbury, andJAllington, a penny loaf to each, under the direction of the bailiff and burgesses of Bridport; and 10s. *?* annum, other part thereof, for- preaching a charity sermon'at.Brid. port on the 2d *March* yearly, 2s. 6d. ts the clerk,",ls. 6d. to the sexton; „£6:16s. an- num, the other part thereof, to provide eight coats,.sixjfor men.and two for women, to be distributed yearly on the 2d March; vested in the church, war- dens and overseers of Bridport, under the directions of the bailiffs and burgesses...

.rorert Bull, by will, dated, (about the year 1726, or 1736) gave £200 in mon- ey, £i annum, for teaching twelve poor children to read, £3 annum to twelve poor men at Christmas, and if any over- plus, to be laid out in books called "The Whole Duty of Man;" which sum was laid out in the 3 *V* cent. Consols, and; yielded £ 250; vested in the rector of Bridport, and his successors for ever Bernard Mitchell, by will dated 22d March, 1646 gave a rent-charge,

payable out of *The King's Head Irnti* Melcombe Regis; the share to this parish is 20s.; vested inj the Overseers of this parish—see *Weymouth* 27- BROADMAYNE.

Matthew Darby, by will, dated 13th Dec., 1655,gavea rent-charge issuing out of land in this parish, the profits thereof to be disposed of in manner fol- lowing, viz. the sum of „£3 once in three years to apprentice out poor chil- dren; and 20s. a-year to labourers of this parish; vested in late Mrs. Shorto, of Piddletown

Elizabeth Costan, by will, dated 6 April, 1763, gavel £ 10 in money to the poor of this parish; vested in Mr. Wil- liam Thresher...

Note.—Lost out of the Parish Chest, £10, the DESCRIPTION of the CHARITY, by whom, when, and for what purpose! giten.

William Gould, Esq. by will, dated, 1624, gave *£5tb* in money, (since laid out in the purchase of lands a), the prof- it thereof to be applied to exempt the poor from statute labour on the high- ways; vested in the officers of this parish

John Gould, Esq. by deed, dated, 1762,gave ahousel and garden to the poor of this parish (o reside in; vested in the parish officers...

29-BROADWINSOR.

Robert Smith, M. D. by will, dated 26th June, 1725, gave a messuage or dwelling-house, called *NewHouse,* in the Tithing of *hildhay,* with several Closes thereunto belonging, unto trustees, to convert the said house into a school-house, fit and convenient for a schoolmaster to live and teach schooltherein; and that the trustees were from time to time to elect such school- master, and to displace him upon rea- sonable cause—which schoolmaster was to teach thirteen poor boys, of the parishes of *Burstoek* and *Broadwinsor,* to be elected and chosen by the said trustees; and in case of deficiency in number in those parishes, such deficien- cy to be supplied out of any of the neighbouring parishes. The master's salary to be £13 annum, and *the over- plus ariiing out of the rents of the es-*

tate,t after maintaining the school-house in proper repair, to be applied as the trustees should think fit for the improvement of the school, and encouragement of learning therein; vested in the vicar of Burstoek, and the vicar of Thorncombe, and their successors - BRYANSTON, *see Blandford.* See Orders of Sessions, Title Highways. t What these Rents are is not mentioned DESCRIPTION of the CHARITY, by whom, when, and for what 30-BUCKLAND NEW-TON.

Rorert Hide, Esq. by gift, dated 24tli March) ,,,

1605, gave, in money.........J lu

William Dunning, of Brockhampton,) a

Gent., by gift, in 1606, ditto *2*

William Jessop, by will, dated—, 1609,ditto 5

Beatrice Donning, by will, 1609, ditto 2

John Stevenson, by will, 1614, ditto 5 24-

The Parishioners added, in money... 2 13 4

Wm.brice, and other Parishioners gave, 1609-13 4

„£27 6 8

Joan Lock gave, in 1619,10s. and the Parishioners, 13s. 4d but this £ 1: 3s. 4d. is since lost, or included in the above sums.

C j' The profits of the above benefactions have been distributed annually, according to the antient custom, and to purchase tools for the poor labourers not receiving parish relief; vested in the Churchwardens.

John Barnes, Gent. of Duntish, by will, dated, 1686, gave „ £ 50 in money; to this sum the Parishioners added £35, and purchased a house and garden, and three acres of land, in the parish of *Huselhury Bryan,* and it was settled that 508. of the rent of the above house and land should be paid yearly to the poor of *Duntish,* and the remainder generally to the poor of this parish. The house has fallen to ruin, but the land at Haselbury lets for £8 *V* annum; vested in the impropriate Rector, and the Parish Officers..

Fits Foy, Esq. by will, dated, 1781,

gave in money ,£100, the profits to be distributed to the poor; vested in his executors

Eli Kabeth Maria Foy, widow of Fitz Foy, Esq. by will dated, 1806, gave,£25 in money, to be distributed as above; vested in her executors

Ditto, by ditto, dited, 1806, gave £200, 3 f Cents to her son-in-law, Samuel Shore, Esq. in trust, to distribute the interest thereof to twelve aged men and women DESCRIPTION of the CHARITY, by whom, when, and for what purpose given.

41-CAUNDLE BISHOP.

Earl of Bristol, by will, dated 6th April, 1687, gave £d0 in mo.-cy, f»r the benefit of the second poor of this parish; vested in the rector and churchwardens. ..

Rey. Mr. Gillingham, by will, dated 30 March, 1719, gave in money, for the like purpose; vested in ditto

Rev. Mr. Gale, by will, dated 9 Dec. 1728, gave £10 Inj money, for the like purpose; vested in ditto...

W. Clavor, Gent. by will, dated 1 August, 1769, gave some land in, for the like purpose; vested in ditto

William Li. Digby, by deed, dated, gave in money, for the like purpose; vested in ditto 42-CAUNDLE MARSH.

Ralph Gollop, by will, dated, 1721, gave a rent charge issuing out of land situate in this parish, for the benefit of the second poor; vested in Geo. Tilley Gollop,

Mr. John Winsor, by will, dated, 1715, gave an an nuity, issuing out of land (land-tax deducted,) in Yeovil, in the county of *Somerset,* for the benefit of the second poor of this parish; vested in Mr. Rough

Sir Rorert Miller, Knt, and Dame Margaret his wife, by deed, dated 20 March, 1620, gave a rent charge issuing out of the tithes in Uploders and Upton; the share to this parish is £10—*see Loders* 46-CKRNE NiSTHER-iVone. DESCRIPTION of the CHARITY,, by wh. given. what purpose c a

Ditto, by ditto, dated 2 Sept. 1752. gave half an acre of land adjoining Holditch Mead, for the like purpose; vested in the same feoffees

Jobn Sampson, Gent. by, (uncertain) dated (uncertain), gave an annuily or rent charge, issuing out of land, supposed to be called Baycroft, in Membury, *Devon.* for the use of J phor of this parish; vested in the parish officers

Rev. Richard White, by will, dated 24 May, 1624, gave some lands, in the parish of St. Mary Magdalen, at Taun ton, *Somerset,* for the relief of the poor of this parish vested in parish officers

Henry Turner, by deed, dated I Feb. 1631, gave a rentcharge out of a field called Jveto *Close,* in Axminster, *Devon,1* for the relief of the poor of this parish; vested in ditto

By Farishioners of this parish, by copy of court roll, dated 1 Feb. 1781, purchased a house and orchard in this parish,, held on four lives, for the benefit of their successors, parishioners, and to be inhabited by persons unable to pay house, rent; vested in ditto...

84-CHEDDINGTON-AW. *Note*—There are certain tenements in this parish, supposed to be given by one Ousley, formerly an owner thereof, to the parish of Shepton Beauchamp, in the county of *Somerset,* which nets £& annually, now used as a poor-house, belonging to Rev. Mr. Coxe, Mrs. Keats, and five others, but in what year uncertain. -CHARLTON MARSHALL—see *Spettisbury.* 55-CHEL-BOROUGH, WEST.

John Drake, Gent, by, dated, 1677, gave £5 in money to the use of the poor in this parish; vested in

Robert Dawe, by, dated, 1677, gave 20s. in money to the same use; vested in —... ... t DESCRIPTION.. of the CHARITY, by whom, when, and for what purpose c ''% given. g 3

Alexander Wellman, by, dated, 1680, gave 20s. in money to the same use; vested in *Note.*—This seven pounds in money was lent to some person who paid interest for the two first sums, till the year 1703, when it was lost.—Wellman's 20s. was paid interest for till 1704, when it was likewise lost on the death of the"person who had it -UHETNOLb. -*See Yetmuisttr.* 56-CHET-TLE:

Edward Smith, by will, dated, 1769, (or thereabouts)!

gave £25 in money, to place out two or more children to a day-school, to be taught to read; vested in 57-CHESSEL-BORNE.

Anne Pitt, by will, dated 1 June, 1783, gave0in money, to be paid thereout 40s. annually, till the whole is expended, for the benefit of the poor of this parish; vested in the poor Of this parish; vested in W.Davis, of Dewlishj

Wili Iam Pope, by will, dated, gave £5 in money, the interest thereof to be laid out in purchasing ten sixpenny loaves, to be distributed to ten poos people of this parish yearly, on *St. Thomas's* Day; vested in John Mitchell

Annual Produce.

George Browne, Esq. by deed, dated 28 Nov. 1774, gave an annuity or rent-charge, issuing out of Little Toller Farm, for endowing a school at Toller Porcorum, for the children of this parish to be sent to school there—*see Toller Porcorum.* DESCRIPTION ol the CHARI-TY, by w given.

n, and for what purpose

Annual Produce.

«0-CHI1XOMBE—AW.

fil-CLENSTONE WINTERBORNE-AW. 62-CLIFTON MAUBANK—AW. fiS.COMBE KEYNES—AW 64-COMPTON, OVER-AW. fio-COMPTON, NETHER.

Several Parishioners, by deed, dated 20 April, 1650, purchased of Giles Fudge, out of monies arising from sale of lands at Sherborne, belonging to this parish, two aues of pasture land, called *Caswell,* now called *Paridi Ground,* and half an acre of arable land in Westfield, both in this parish, in trust for the inhabitants thereof. The yearly rent is distributed at Easter to such of the in habitants as do not receive weekly pay. The land let in 1802 for *J_* :t: 3s. 1 annum. The purchase deeds were in the hands of the late Thomas Thompson; then vested in Thomas Pitman, John Beaton, Thomas Masters, William Taylor, Thomas Hillary, Hugh Green, and Nich. Beaton, t By deed, dated 20 Sept. 1623, the sum of was secured to sundry trustees; afterwards, by deed, dated 12 May, 1637, this sum was vested in other trustees, and, with c£13 added by the Parishioners, the above lands! were purchased,

though not mentioned in the con veyance.

By Subscription, by deed, dated, 1795, a house was purchased and fitted up for a charity school for the poor inhabitants; vested in the late Thomas Thompson fili-CO.UPTON ABBAS, E. or HARGROVE—A'one.

DESCRIPTION of the CHARITY, by whom, when, and for what given. 66-COMPTON VALENCE.

Hyppolet Mockett, by will, dated 20 April, 1653, gavel „£25 in money, to the most industrious and necessitous1 poor of this parish; vested in H. Davis - CORFE MULLEN—see *Sturminster Marshall.* 67-CORFE CASTLE.

ALMSHOUSE.

Sir Edmund Uvedale, Knt. by will, dated, 1612, gave lands called *New Mills,* for the support of the poor in the almshouse; vested in the churchwardens and their successors; but it is said to have been granted in 1786, by the mayor and barons of Corfe, to Henry Bank. es, Esq. for 99 years, at the old rent of *£18* annum, but by what au thority is not known...

Rorert Abbott, by deed, dated, 1610, gave a tenement at Poole, with a garden, &c. the profits thereof to buy 12 pennyworth of bread, for the poor in the almshouse, every Sunday; vested in the churchwardens

Ditto, by ditto, dated,--, 1611, gave another tenement at Poole, the profits thereof to be given to the poor in the almshouse, usually given in money and dowlas, or bread; vested in ditto Green, by, dated gave an acre of land, at Uffington, (not said for what purpose, or how to be applied,) laid out in bread and linen for the poor; vested in the churchwardens, &c.

Bonfield, by, dated, gave a certain sum of money, supposed to have been all expended before 17

—— Stockman, by, dated, gave a sum of money; ditto

John Hardin, by will, dated, 1766, (or thereabouts), gave in money, to be paid out of his estate at Woolston, to 12 poor men, 12 penny loaves; vested in the rector of Corfe Castle, &c....

DESCRIPTION of ihe CHARITY, by whom,

when, and for what purpose' *a -_-Is"* Benjamin Heather, by, dated, gave lands at

Woolston, or Woolgarston, called the *Poor Land,* which was sold by deed, dated, 1700, to the mayor and bai rons of Corfe, in trust for the churchwardens of the poor; the profits thereof is given in bread and linen to the poor, viz. the churchwardens purchase sixty ells of dowlas yearly for the poor in the almshouse, and give them bread on *Good Fridays;* vested in the churchwarden, &c.

70-CORSCOMBE.

Mr. Russeli., by will, dated (unknown,) gave a rent-charge on land, at, of 20s. yearly, for the benefit of the poor of this parish; vested in the late John Floyer, Esq. of West Stafford

Kote—From 1766 to 1775, only 6s. 8d. has been paid,

and since that time the charity is in arrear.

71-CRANBORNE.

Hr. Richard Carter, by will, dated, 1694, gave the rents and profits of a house, garden, and three acres of land in this parsh, to be distributed every *St. Thomas's* Day to 56 poor persons of this parish; vested in Richard Carter..

Rev. Richard Wynn, late vicar, by will, dated 1729, gave „£20 in money, the interest thereof to be dis tributed to the poor of this parish in bread, on *St. The* Kim's Day yearly; vested in the parish officers.....

Thomas Hooper, Esq. of Boveridge, by will, dated, 1661, gave,£30 to be lent, *gratis,* to ten poor tradesmen of this parish, in sums of £3 each, for one year only; vested in the parish officers..

.

Kote—£'12 of this money has been lost out of the principal sum; only £18 remains.

John Hutchins, by will, dated, *(unknown),* gave the rents and profits of a house, garden, and three acres of land, in, to six poor men of the said parish annuallyj and a great coat each at *Christmas;* vested in the parish officers These lands were probably purchased by Uie Mayor and Barons of Corfe, with money formerly given to the use of the poor, and possibly of a Mr. Bonfield, Stock-man, and others, whose names are at present unknown—it was always vested in the churchwardens, who received the rents, and accounted tor the same year-ly.

DESCRIPTION of the CHARITY, by whom, when, and for what purpofe§ given."
ALMSHOUSE.

Thomas Hooper, Esq. of Boveridge, by will and grant,

dated, gave some land at Manston, called *Over Thatch-er's Lease,* for the establishment and support of an alms house at Boveridge, by which three single persons, parti-J cularly old servants and tenants of the family have been paid each „£6: Is. 4d. yearly, including a late addition of 8s. to each; the minister's salary is *£6 V* an-num...

Note—Cash accumulated in the hands of the late steward, Mr. Tarver, £100; and there is an annual income from the almshouse steward, issuing from lands ad joining the almshouse garden, amounting to

72-CRAWFORD TARRANT, or PARVA—
None. 73-CRITCHELL LONG.

The Interest of *£i,* called *Poor Stock Money,* is paid to the! poor of this parish yearly, by the parish officers. —*Query,.* if a charity?

74-CRITCHELL MOORE.

Sir William Napier, by will, dated 27th August, 1745,

gave a rent charge issuing out of his es-tate at Witchampi ton, vested in parish officers...

Sir Edmund Uvedale, Knt. of this place, by will, dated

I Oct. 1621, (proved in Prerogative Court of Canterbury),

gave all his lands, called Rushton 11 ill, Chalcott's, and

Iiittle Hill, in the parish of *Rushton,* pur-chased of Charles

Vaughan, deceased, unto Sir John Ryves, Sir Nathaniel

Napier, Knts. and Richard Swayne, Esq. and their heirs,

towards the maintenance of the poor of the almshouse at

Blandford Forum for ever; vested in the corporation of

Blandford...

This should have been inserted at Blandford Forum

Anno 1781. Extracted from the papers in a cause—

Humphrey Sturt, Esq. informant, t;. Bailiff and Bur.

gesses of the said borough of Blandford Forum, defendants, at the suit of Attor-ney-General.

This charity aioie from the sale of tim-ber many years ago, which was received by one Tarrer, a-steward of the late Ed-ward Hooper, Esq. from the amount of £100, and compound interest. In addi-tion to the other income of the almshouse, Mr. Tarver's representative paid in 1710, to Mr. Webb, Mr. Hoop-er's present steward, £117:10s M. being the amount of the present Charity, with the accumulation, and Mr. Hooper has directed Mr. Webb t» place out an even sum at interest, as won as he can kind a proper security, which he has not been able to do.

Accordmg to Mr. Whlteway and Bond's Chronology, this School was endowed in 1569. They say the great school and library over it, was built in 1618, (after the great fire in 1613), by R. C. (Robert Chick), who was minister and school-master from 1595 until the time of his death in 1627, Sir Robert Napper, or Napier, gave the ground for the build-ings which were added.—Hutchinfs Hut017 of Dorset, To1i *2,* p. 22, DE-SCRIPTION of the CHARITY, by whom, when, and for what given.

Annual Produce THE UNDER SCHOOL.

The Townsmen, by subscription, erected, at about „£100 expense, on the lands of the corporation, in 1623, a School House, (there is no endowment), in the parish of *The Holy Trinity,* where six boys of the town of Dorchester are to be taught reading, writing, and arith-metic. The Master is permitted to live rent free in the house for his trouble in teaching the said boys, and is put in or removed upon just occasion by the cor-poration. The rent of the house is worth about „£8 *W* annum; vested in the cor-poration

Ann Napier, by deed, dated 2 March, 1715, gave some land, at *Melbury,* the

profits thereof to be applied in teach, ing six poor children, viz. a boy and girl belonging to each of the three parishes, to read the Holy Scriptures, &c. and the overplus of the estates, if any, to go to-wards clcathing them; vested in the cor-poration , by, dated, gave in land, be-ing a shop, which was taken down about the year 1823, at the west end of the church, in Holy Trinity parish, the prof-its thereof for teaching and instructing six poor boys, or more, of the parish of Holy Trinity; vested in the Rector of the Holy Trinity for the time being

Mrs. Mary Strangwayes, (wife of Thomas Strangwayes, Esq. and daugh-ter and co-heiress of Edward Vaughan), and Mrs. Lora Pitt, by deeds, dated 7 July, 1737, and 14 Feb., 1740, gave in land, at, for the cloathing and teaching fifteen poor boys of the town of Dorch-ester, to read, write, and cast accounts, (together with five poor boys of the vill of Bockhampton, within the parish of Stinsford, in this county), and finding them books, pens, ink, and paper; and to each of them at their going off from school, a Bible, and "The Whole Duty of Man"; vested in the late Edmund Morton Pleydell, Thomas Gundrey, Esqrs. and William Chafin, Clerk, trustees *Note*—To the Schoolmaster, out of the above charity *,£li*

Mrs. Hussey Fioyer, by will, dated 10 Oct., 1740,gave £150 money, (this money is now, 1828, in the funds, £300,' 3 cent, consols,) for the cloathing and instructing two or) This school Is to be considered as subordinate to the free school, to train up boys, and to prepare them for the head school.

DESCRIPTION of Hie CHARITY, bj whom, when, and for what purpose! more poor boys of the town of Dorchester, three years at school, and binding them out apprentice; vested in the above-named trustees

Whetstone's Almshouse.

John Whetstone, of Rodden, in the parish of Portis ham, merchant, by, dat-ed, (supposed about thej year 1614), gave,£500 in money, with part of which an almshouse was built, called *Whet-stone's Almshouse,* in Church-Lane, in the parish of All Saints, for the maintenance of four couples therein, at the choice of the corporation, to be taken in succession alike out of the three parishes. Part of the money was laid out in the purchase of lands at *Symondsbury* and AJinterne *Magna,* in this county, which let for £29 *V* annum, (in 1786), subject to disbursements, and the remainder to the hospital of this town; vested in the corporation

Chubb's Almshouse.

Biatthew Chubb, of Dorchester, gent, by deed of gift,

about the year 1615, gave £1000, part of which was laid out in re-edifying the old almshouse, near the Priory, in St.

Peter's parish, for nine poor women, and the remainder was laid out in the purchase of an estate at Nottington, in the parish of Broadway, with which the same is endowed;

vested in the corporation

Over the door is this inscription:—' The Gift of Mat

"thew Chubb and Margaret his wife. 1620."

Mr. Chubb founded an almshouse at Crewkeme, co. Somerset, in 1604, and another at Shaftesbury in this county, in 1611—(gee Shaftesbury Donations.) He wasM. P. for Dorchester in 1801, 43 Elir. and 1603, 1 Jac. 1, and was one of the first bailiffs appointed by king Jai 1610, for the borough of Dorchester. See bis pedigree below:— s I, charter

Nora—*The* representati of Mr. Chubb was Mr. Andrew Loder, who w_.....

Wr, Hubert Lodei, an attorney, and afterwards by Messrs. Nathaniel and Robert Stickland, also

MteHiCjv DESCRIPTION, of the CHARITY, by whom, when, and for what purpose g given. 'g J

It is singular that Mr. Chubb's charity is not taken notice of in the Returns to Parliament-

Sir Francis Ashley, Knt. serjeant-at-law, by will, dated!

12 August, 1635, gave an annuity, issuing out of his manor and farm of Frome Whitfield, now in the hands of Williamj Henning, gent. to the poor of the almshouse near his gate, called *Chubb's,* consisting of nine women, 40s. yearly, viz. to each of them 12d. every quarter,

(which amounts to

36s. a year), and 4s. to be disposed among them at *Christ*

mas, for their better benefit at that time; vested in..

Joan Gould, widow of James Gould, by will, dated 4 Feb. 1630, gave some land and houses, on the west side of the town, in Holy Trinity parish, towards the support and maintenance of poor persons, in a certain almshouse called *Chubb's,* situate in the parish of St. Peter, and in keeping the house in repair; vested in the corporation...

John Symonds, by will, (the will not to be found), dated, gave an annuity of 20s. a year, payable out of a dwelling-house in the parish of Holy Trinity, the lands of John Wood, for charitable purposes, for the equal benefit of the three parishes, and is applied by the owner of the house to the poor persons in Chubb's almshouse; vested

The Comoration, by deed, dated 15 May, 1685, (out ofj charity money lodged from time to time in their hands; but what particular sums, or for what purpose given, cannot be ascertained), purchased an estate at *Nottington,* in the parish of Broadway, in this county; the profits whereof have been from time to time applied towards the maintenance of the poor persons in Chubb's almshouse; vested in the corporation

Edmund Dashwood, by will, (which will cannot be found),1 dated, gave an annuity, payable out of a dwelling.

house in the parish of *St. Peter,* now the lands of James Parsons, towards the support and maintenance of the poor persons in Chubb's almshouse; vested in the corporation..

Napper's Almshouse.

Sib Robert Nappeb, Knt., by will,dated 20 August, 1616, 13 Jac' 1, gave, in land, one-fourth part of the manor of *Litilepiddle,* in the parish of Piddletown, then leased for,£50 a year, for the perpetual provision, sustentation, and maintenance of the almshouse then lately erected by the said Sir Robert Napper, in the parish of St. Peter, and near the ftee school, called *Napper's Mite,* in which ten poor men were to dwell. In the said will it is di-

rected, that the heirs of his name and blood shall for ever stand seised of the premises. In 1636, Gerard Napier, Esq. with the advice and consent of the Master of the Rolls and Judges of Assize, directed that each man should have £5 & annum, by weekly payments, and the overplus to him who should read prayers in the chapel, and for reparations; and in 1670, he being then a knt. and bart. gave the manor of Stert, in the parish of *Babcary,* co. Somerset, as a further endowment, and that his heirs should nominate the schoolmaster of the free school, or other proper person, to oversee the almsmen, to read Divine service once a day, and to catechise them once a week, to be paid £5 V year; vested in Henry Charles Sturt, esq....

THE HOSPITAL OR WORKHOUSE.

The Corporation, by benefactions and charities from the inhabitants of the town, in 1616 or 1617, purchased two houses, in the parish of St. Peter, part of the Old Hospital Lands, and the rents and profits thereof is paid or payable to the present hospital, in support of the poor of the three parishes. There are now four houses built, (1833), leased out on lives by the corporation, and the reserved ground rent of these houses net „£25 annum; vested in the corporation

William Whiteway, sen. by deed inrolled, dated 15 October, 1617, gave an annuity or yearly rent charge of £5, payable on the feast of St. John the Baptist for ever, issuing out of an house in the parish of St. Peter, the land on DESCRIPTION of the CHARITY, by whom, when, and for what purpose given.

the Earl of Shaftesbury, now in the occupation of John Gregory, for the equal benefit of the three parishes, for the better endowment of the hospital, &c.; vested in the corporation

John Perkins, by deed inrolled, dated 15 October, 1617 gave an annuity, or yearly rent-charge of £5, payable on the feast of St. John the Baptist for ever, and issuing out of a house situate in the parish of the Holy Trinity, formerly the lands of Peter Templeman, and now of James Hen ning, Gent. for the benefit of the three parishes, for the above purpose of endowing the said hospital; vested in the corporation...

George Trenchard, Esq. by gift, in 1745, gave a small piece of land, in the parish of the Holy Trinity, for a gar den for the New Hospital

On inquiry it was found that the profits of this garden were misapplied and greatly abused, contrary to the in tention of the donor, and he, about the year 1756, re. took the premises into his own possession.

John Gould, sen. by deed inrolled, dated, (he died after 1617), gave an annuity, or yearly rent-charge of £ft payable for ever, out of a house in the parish of St. Peter, now the land of Mr. Thomas Fisher, towards the support of the poor of the three parishes; vested in (he corporation

Richard Bushrod, by will, dated 28 November, 1628, gave „£4 annum, out of lands in the parish of Ifoorton *Glanville,* in this county, towards the support of the poor, to be divided between the three parishes; vested in. (received by the corporation)...

Edward Dashwood, by will, (the will not found,) dated, (he died 5 February, 1666), gave,£50 in money, the interest of which to be equally divided among the poor of the three parishes; vested in the corporation

Juliana Perkins, by will, dated 19th January, 1656, or 1658, (see tablet), jgave the sum of £00, and by inden ture, dated 19 April, 1660, did grant an annuity or rent charge of £6 annum, payable out of then 3 messuages, &c. called the *George, Inn,* to be paid for the benefit of the; it'j DESCRIPTION of the CHARITY, hy whom, when, and for what purpose g = «i'en. *&lH* three parishes, on the 25th March yearly; vested in the heirs at law of Arthur Gould and Susan Grose, the executors GENERAL CHARITIES.

John Samways, by will, dated... April, 1738, gave an an. nuity of £5 annum, for ever, clear of all deductions chargeable on his the testator's dwelling house, in Holy Trinity parish, now occupied by William Watson, schoolmaster, for laying out the same every *two* years, in the cloathing and binding out apprentice a child of some poor inhabitant of the parish of Holy Trinity, or

St. Pe. ter's, such as the person for the time being, who should be seised of the freehold of the said testator's dwelling-house, charged with' the said annuity, and William Belitha and Joseph Damer, Esqis. and their respective heirs, toge. ther with the minister of the parish of the Holy Trinity, should approve; vested in

Thomas Gape, by will, dated 2 Jan. 1677, gave £ 100, the profits of which were for the benefit of the poor of the three parishes, as follows, viz. one moiety to the poor of All Saints parish, *(£1*:16s.) and the other moiety between the other two parishes, St. Peter's and Holy Trinity, (18s, each); vested in the corporation

William Gape, of St. Paul's, Covent-Garden, West minster, by will, dated, gave an annuity, issuing out of land, to the poor of the parish of All Saints, viz. his five messuages or tenements in St. Sythe's Lane, (St. S within's Lane,) London, £5 annum for ever. The first payment to be made after the death of Mary his wife, who died 16

Nov. 1681; vested in, *(unknown)* but received by the churchwardens...

William Churchill, by will, dated 17 April,1639, gave £10 in money, to re-main in stock for the use of the poor, to be laid out in some profitable employment, for their yearly benefit; vested in the churchwardens of Ho!y Trinity parish DESCRIPTION of the CHARITY, by whom, when, and for what purpose)

Thomas Freke, by gift, dated , gave,£69 in money for the use of the poor of this town; vested in ..

Oeorge Lock, by will, *(not to be found),* dated, gave

£20 in money, the interest of which to be paid to the poor of the parish of All Saints, by the overseers of that parish; vested in Robert Stickland, gent. the representative of Robert Loder, deceased

Robert Thorner, by will, dated 31 May, 1690, devised all his real estate in messuages and lands, situate in the city of London, then of the yearly value of,£80, (and after the lease of the same to Sir Peter Vandeput was expired which happened on the 26th March,

1769, might he of the yearly value of £'400.) unto trustees therein named, and to their successors, to be appointed as therein declared.— The share to this town is stated to be,£16:17s. 6d.; vested (1803,) in Thomas Brand Hollis, of In-gatestone, co. Essex, P. Bernard, of Southampton, and James Solley, of St. Mary Axe, London , dated, gave several houses and lands in the town of Dorch-ester, hereinafter mentioned, viz.: one messuage, garden, and premises, in South-street, now in the occupation of Mr. Stephen Gale; one other in High East, street, now in the occupation of Jesse Bushrod. mason;1 one other, in the same street, next adjoining. now in the occu pation of William Masters, baker; one other in Bell-street, leading-towards Gallows Hill, now in the occu-pation of John Hann, cordwainer; one other, and four acres of land in the East Walls, in the occupation of W. Henning, Gent. one other, called the Bell, in Church-lane, now in the occu pation of Mr. Thomas Bower; one other in Church-lane (the Black Horse,) now in the occupation of Robert Troake one other, in Durn-lane, late in the occupa-tion of R. Warren and others, (now in ruins); and one other in the High East-street aforesaid, called the Parsonage, in the occupation of the Rev. Evan Davies, rector, in all nine houses. These lands were vested in certain truscees or feof-fees, and it is said in the deed hereinaf-ter mentioned. to permit and suffer thel parsonage-house to be occupied by the rector for the time being, or to receive the rents and profits thereof; and the' s appears to have been paid to the parish-es 0 All Saints since 1699. The donor died in 20s. was paid to each of the three parishes; but n of Holy Trinity and St. Peter's since the year 1685. nor to *1* 1698, and Cicily, (formerly Hussey), his wife, died in 1703. without issue, the Estates c.

Thomas Pile and Elizabeth the wire of Thomas Freke, of Hannineton, co. Wilts, for their lires. Isle reversion to Lord Rirers, who, in 1714 took posses-sion.'

E and for what purpose j ij DESCRIP-TION of the CHARITY, by whom, when, glvtn.

churchwardens were to receive out of the said lands one annuity or rent-charge of „£6 yearly, for repairing the church, and for other necessary uses, as they, with the con.

sent of the parishioners, shall see convenient and necessary to bestow the same; and all the rest residue and profits of the said premises, both rents and fines, shall be and remain for the sole benefit and behoof of the rector of the said pa.

rish for the time being. No lease to be granted by the trustees but by consent of the rector, nor for more than 99

years, determinable on three lives in possession, &c. The last surviving Trustee was Nathaniel Stickland, Gent. who, by deed dated 31 May, 1824, enfeoffed John Burnet and

Joseph Clapcott, Gents, as trustees of this charity.

Note—It appears that several houses and lands in this town belonged to Monasteries and Religious Houses,

and probably these were purchased at the dissolution,

and by some well-disposed persons granted to trustees for the uses above-mentioned. In the 36 II. 8, six messuages, &c. in this parish were granted to John

Pope.

Mrs..elizabeth Cozens, by will, dated 19th November,

1818, gave,£500 steck, in the navy 5 cent. annuities,

the interest to be applied in January yearly, as follows:—

amongst the poor women aged 58 or above, of good character, and not having received parochial relief within six months' preceding, resident £. s. d.

In St. Peter's............ 6-
In Holy Trinity......... 5-
In All Saints............ g-

And equally amongst the Inhabitants of

Chubb's Almshouse......... 3-
Napper's Almshouse......... 2 10
Whetstone's Do.......... 2 10

Vested in the Rectors of the three Parishes, and James)

Parsons, her surviving executor

76-DUR WESTON -*None.* DESCRIPTION of the CHARITY, by whom, when, and for what given.

77-EDMONDSHAM.

Rev. Witiiington, by will, dased, 1732, gave some land situate in this parish, the profits thereof for the benefit of the poor; vested in Mr. Gilbert

Thomas Huisey, by will, dated, 1664, gave some land and money to two poor women of this parish, the profits thereof for their use; vested in Air. Ph. F. Bower *Note.*—There are four acres of land in this parish, called *Church Lands,* appropriated for the repairs of the church, formerly let for £1: 6s. *V* annum, but the present rector is the occupier, and pays *£A V* annum, BVERSHOT—*see Frame St. Quintin.* this parish, known by the name of *Church Close* or *CrossJ way Field,* held by lease under the Duke of Bolton. The! profit of this acre has always been applied towards the ex expenses of the church; rented by William Adams; vested in the Parish Officers 79-FARRINGDON, WINTERBOURNE.

Snt Rorert Miller, Knt. and Dame Margaret his wife, by deed dated 20 March, 1620, gave a rent-charge issuing out of the tithes in Up-Loders and Upton. The share to this parish is,£5—*see Loders...* 80-F1FEHEAD NEVILLE.

Roger Goodfellow, by will, dated — , 1730, gave some land at, the profits whereof are to be distributed yearly to the second poor of this parish who do not receive *1* pay; vested in late *W.* Salkeld, Esq. and his heirs 81-FL.KJir.

Bernard Mitchell, by will, dated 22. March, 1616 gave a rent-charge issuing out of his freehold-house in Melcombe Regis, for the use of the poor for ever; vested in the 82-FOLKE-AW.

83-FONTMEEL fllAGNA. Still, *(as supposed,)* by, *(supposed by deed,)* dated, gave £6 in money, the interest thereof to be distributed yearly to the second poor of Hargrove and Bed cister tithing, within this parish; vested in the parish! officers 84-FORD1NGTON. . dated, gave some money, the interest thereof to be distributed to the poor of this parish, in bread, yearly; vested in the heirs of John Floyer, Esq late of West Stafford... 85-FRAMPTON. FREE SCHOOL.

Robert Browne, Esq. by will, dated 21st

August, 1734,) founded a Free School, and gave an annuity, or rentcharge of £15 F annum, payable out of lands at Crockway, in the parish of Maiden Newton. Also, a schoolhouse and gaiden belonging thereto; vested in Francis John Browne, Esq.

——, by. dated, (no written account by whom or when given, but supposed by a Mrs. C. Clapcott, of Winterborne Abbas,) gave £20 in money. The interest thereof is applied, every three or four years, to the benefit of the labouring poor of this parish; vested in Francis; John Browne, Esq....

Annual Produem.

-13 4 -10 15- 1- DESCRIPTION of the CHARITY, by whom, when, and for what purpose 86-FROME VAUCHURCH.

George Browne, Esq. by deed, dated 24 Jan. 1774, inrolled in Chancery, gave a rent-charge of ,£5 annum, upon Cruxton Farm; the profits thereof to be equally divided between 20 poor industrious parishioners of this parish and *Maiden Newton,* who do not receive alms; vested in John Whittle and his heirs...

Ditto, by deed, dated 28 Not. 1772, inrolled in Chancery, gave an annuity, issuing out of land called *Little Toller Farm,* for the endowing a school at Toller Forcorum, for the children of this parish, to be sent to school there— *(vide Toller Porcorum.)* 87-FROME ST. QUINT1N—*None.* EVERSHOT (FREE SCHOOL.)

Christopher Stickland, by deed, dated20 Nov., 1628: 4 Car. I, gave in land, at Over Kingcombe, for teaching male children of the name of *Stickland,* and all relations of Stickland bor n within thirty miles of this place; vested in

Principal Inhantants of Evershot, by deed, dated 20 Nov. 1628, 4 Car. 1. gave the church-house, and one acre of land, for a charity school, by Christopher Stickland; vested in

John Wilkins, of this parish, and Grace his wife, by deed, dated 21 Dec. 1732, conveyed to John F'oy, Robert Browne, William Catford, Esq. and others, certain closes and common of pasture in this parish, for the uses follow ing: to lease the premises for any term not exceeding ten years, and out of the clear rents to pay the curate orincum bent of Evershot, annum, for reading prayers, cate chising the children, and preaching two sermons; £1:10s to the clerk; ,£6 to the master and mistress of the school chosen by the trustees for teaching 12 poor children to read, to knit, and to sew; the residue to be laid out in bibles, and buying blue gowns and bonnets for the poor children, vested in Peroeval lngs and his wife, thesurviving trustees In the yenr 1740 the then Attorney-General, at the relation of Thos. Strangwayes Horner, Esq. and other owners of land in Evershot, exhibit-d his information in the Court of Chancery against the heir-at-law of Wilkins, and the then surviving trustees, for the purpose of having the seveial Charities established. The cause was heard the 7th July, 1750, before the Master of the Rolls, and it was declared that the estates comprised in the above conveyance were well granted, and the purposes thereof ought to be can ied into execution, and declared the same accordingly. Notwithstanding this decree, the taunt has been imperfectly complied with, the rents have been withheld by the tenants, or received by persons who, in strictness of law, could have little or ttoci the business, and the occupier refuses to give in the account of the annual produce DESCRIPTION of the CHARITY, by whom, «hn, and for what purpose j giten. g J

Christopher Stickland, by deed, dated 20 Nov. 1628, 4 Car. 1. gave J 411 in money, to be distributed, viz 20s a-yeat for two sermons, and the remainder for the use of the poor of this place; vested in the parishioners...

Thomas Strangwayes, sen. Esq. by will, dated 1714, gave 40 in money, the interest to be distributed to the poor of this place, on St. Thomas's-Day yearly; vested in the Earl of llchester

Thomas Strang W Ayes, jun, Usq. by will, dated—,1720, gave,£40 in money for the like purpose; vested in ditto...

Mrs. Strangwayes Horner, by will, dated 28 Feb. 1754, gave „£50 in money, for the like purpose; vested in ditto..

—— ——, by, dated, gave some

lands, called!

Poor Lands, for the use of the poor of this place; vested in the paris.li officers William Channino, by will, dated 28 Oct. 1731, gave £0 in money, the interest to be distributed yearly to the poor of this place; vested in late Reuben Toogood's heirs j 88-UODMANSTONE— *None.* 89-G1LLINGHAM FREE SCHOOL.!

John Grace, and several other Copyholders in this parish, by respective surrenders in 1516,1526,1527, & 1530, gave di vers customary lands within the said manor, called " Feoffee lands," or " Parish or Free Lands," therein described and particularized, to the use of several persons and their heirs in trust, that out of the issues and profits thereof there might be perpetually maintained within the said town, a schoolmaster; also for the repair of the church, relief of poor people, refreshing of prisoners, *and repair of highways, causeways, and bridges* within the said parish; vested in *i* This is; large old building near the church, with a mean house for the matter, formerly a church house. The founder unknown. This school was formerly in good repute. In the great rebellion if was full of the sons of loyal gentlemen. Lord Chancellor Clarendon had part of his education here, and it was the first preferment of Dr. Fxampton, afterwards Bishop of Gloucester. —Huuhins's History of Dorset, 3, p. 188.

DESCRIPTION" of the CHARITY, by whom, when, and for what purpesej given the vicar for the time being, the late Rev. John Freke, Rev. William Whitaker, and nine other Feoffees

Note.—The schoolmaster, out of the annual produce, receives £18: 6s. 8d. yearly; also, all the bridges on the public roads, and over the rivers, &c. in the said parish, are kept in repair; and the residue is distributed among the *second* poor on the first Tuesday after Candlemas Day yearly. In 1680 Dr. Davenant augmented the school with „£5 annum. In 1698, Mr. Christopher Estmond, with,£8 annum. Commissioners of His Royal Highness the Prince of

Wales, by deed of agreement, dated in 1624, ga»e allot, ments in land for the poor, as a compensation for the privileges they lost upon the Disaforestation; vested in the Lord of the Manor of (iillinghain

Sir Hugh Wyndham, by will, dated27th July, 1684,gave a rent-charge on land, called *Silton Farm,* for the poor, at the discretion of the distributor; vested in the present owner

Mrs. Frances Dirdoe, by will, dated s 1783, gave

£100 in money, charged on *Milton on Stour* Farm, for the poor, at the discretion of the distributor; vested in the owner of Milton Farm

Workhouse.

Mr. — Alsop, by —, dated, *(before* 1739,)gave

„£100 towards providing and furnishing the workhouse at Gillingham, which was paid by his executors.

By a decree in Chancery, Mich. Term, 40 Eliz. 1598, in a cause wherein Richard Estmonde, John Butler, aud other tenants and inhabitants of Gillmgham, and tenants of the manor, as well for themseives, as on behalf of sundry the inhabitants of the said town, plaintiffs, and Thomas Dirdoe, Edward Lawrence, James Frampton, Robert Alien, John Hayward, and William Bartar, defendants:—and also by another decree, dated 28 Sept. 41 Eliz. lt was ordered, adjudged, and decreed, that the interest of the said copyholders should be conveyed from time to time unto twelve of the customary tenants of the said manor, to hold by copy of Court Roll, to them and their heirs, according to the custom of the said manor, *Sic,* which twelve persons, and the survivors of them, should be called by the name of " The Feoffees of the Lands of Gilllnnham, appointed to charitable uses:"—that as often as by death, or otherwise, the number should be decreased, and brought to the number of eight only, the surviving Feoffees, at the next Court, should surrender the tenements to so many other customary tenants, as to make up the deficiency, and complete the number twelve:—that two of the customary tenants of the said manor should be yearly chosen, and appointed receivers of the rests and profits of the said tenements, at the General Law Day, to be holder! within tin-same manor, about the Feast of the Annunciation of our Lady, and to continue until two others should be chosen; and the said receivers were to deliver up a true account yearly in Whitsun week, to the said Feoffees, or to such auditor as they should appoint:—That the sum of twenty marks yearly, of the rents and profits of the said lands, should he paid to the Schoolmaster of Gillingham, who is to teach the children ot the parishioners gratis; his election, placing, and displacing, t0 be in the Feoffees for the time beingand the rest of the rents and profits of the said lands, to be employed yearly to the reparation of causeways, highways, and bridges; and to the relteving and bringing up of poor orphans—and other charitable and necessary uses mentioned in the said decree.

Nots—The former decree seta forth the uses of these rents, anciently, to be for the maintaining a schoolmaster, for the instruction of youth; the repairing the church, the poor relieved, prisoners refreshed, and highways, causeways, and bridges thereabout kept and maintained-but the latter decree, made on hearing the cause, says, that the uses thereof shall be for the maintenance of a schoolmaster, and repairing of bridges, for the relief of the poor, and towards setting out of soldiers.

DESCRIPTION of the CHARITY, by whom, when, and for what purpose given. 94-HAMPRESTON.

Edward Loveix, by gift, dated, *(unknown),* gave £5 in money, to two poor widows not having had relief; vested in the Rector

Note—£5 more has since been saved by the predecessor of the present minister, John Harbin, to whom it was paid.

95-HAMMOON—J/one.

96-HANFORD—*None.*   97-HASELBURY BRYAN.

By Deed of Feoffment dated 22d day of April, 1701, between Nicholas Hill, Thomas Young, Wm. Kaines, Richard Swayne, jun. and John Crosse, surviving trustees mentioned, together with several other persons since dec., in one indenture of feoffment, bearing date 19 March, 1655 of the one part, and John Cunditt, of Haselbury Bryan, yeoman, Thomas Stayner, of the same, victualler, Thomas Young, jun. yeoman, John Hill, yeoman, Richard Hill, clothier, Giles Stoodley, maltfter, Thomas Boyte, yeoman, Ralph Kaines, yeoman, James Loder, woolstapler, William Mitchell, son of Thos. Mitchell, yeoman, Thomas Cross, yeoman, Joseph Edwards, clothier, Richard Dibbin, of West Orchard, gent. John Turner, of Stoke Wake, tanner, James Ham, of Stourton Caundle, yeoman, Richard Lisle, jun. of Blandford Forum, goldsmith, and John Lane, of the same, gent. Did grant all those ten closes or parcels of land, arable, meadow, and pasture ground, called *Cross Chse, Worthingham's, Quar Close, Clark's Mead, Long Mead, Wake Mead, Pidnell, Thick, tlwrne,* and *Calf hayes,* containing in the whole, by estimation, 15 acres and half, (but by admeasurement in 1813, it contained 20a. 1r. 9p.) situate, lying, and being in this parish, which was left about the year 1655, *(the donor un. known),* the profits thereof to be distributed yearly to the most necessitous and best deserving poor of this parish.

DESCRIPTION of the CHARITY, bj i ad for what puipoae

When the trustees are reduced by death, or otherwise, to ten, they may nominate and appoint other trustees, tenants or inhabitants of Haselbury Bryan aforesaid, and their heirs, in trust for this charity...

98-HAWKCHURCH.

Admiral Sir William Domett, O. C. 13. , in 1828, left by will to the school, „£"10, chargeable for ever on his two Estates at Weslhay and Berry, in this parish; vested in JVoie—This benefaction is not to be paid till after the deaths of his brother and sister, viz. Mr. James Domett and Mrs. Templeman, who are tenants for life.

Earl Of Bristol, by will, dated, 1698, gave „fl5 in money, the interest thereof to be distributed for the benefit of the second poor of this parish; vested in the Earl of *O* igby ivO-HERMITAGE-Jvcme.

Mrs. Susan Bingham, by will, dated, 1786, gave *J_2b* for apprenticing poor boys belonging to this parish and Melcombe; vested in the heirs of George Bingham, elk

Ditto, by will, dated, gave *£50* for apprenticing poor children of this parish and Melcombe, at the discretion of the trustees; vested in trustees...

Note.—No yearly benefaction. the city of London, to Bennett Swaine, citizen, fishmonger, Thomas Hollis, jun. both of London, Isaac Watts, and John Brackstone, both of Southampton, clothiers, to hold the said houses and lands to them and their successors in trust for ever, the rents and clear profits of the lands, to be distributed by turn and rotation when it amounts to „£500, deducting „£20 to this parish, and £10 to the trustees and the land-tax, then the remainder to be applied towards aprenticing out and setting up in trade, a certain number of boys in this place, *Dorchester, Southampton,* and *Salisbury,* inclusive of the contingent expenses. The first rotation to Dorchester and this place began in 1693, and ended in 1758. The second, to Southampton, began in 170S, and is proceeding; and the third, to Salisbury, began in 1720, and is proceeding. The money is paid by the occupiers of the premises to the trustees, who have the disposal of the whole, and the choice of the widows of the almshouse at Southampton, whoare paid2s. week by them The boys to be apprenticed are required to be children of pious and sober parents; vested (1lS03) in Brand Hollis, esq. of Ingatestone, co. Essex, Mr. P. Bernard, of South, ampton, James Solley, of St. Mary Axe, London, and a fourth, lately deceased—see *Dorchester General Charities.* Gave „£200, part of the

1 interest thereof to be distributed among the poor inhabitants not receiving

1 weekly pay; vested in

Lt—Gen. John Michel

1J8-LONGBREDY.

Hippolet Mockett, by will. dated 28 Sept. 1653

Dr. K. IroN SI De, by ditto, dated (, died 1683 1

John Michel, esq. by ditto,' dated,

died 1717

Sir Rorert Miller, Knt. and Dame Margaret his' wife, by deed, dated 20 March, 1620, gave a rent-charge, issuing out of the tithes of Uploder and Upton, for the re lief of the poor of this parish; the share to this parish i: *(see Loders)*...... ....

129-lit Tlebredy.

Sir Rorert Miller, Knt., and Dame Margaret his wife, by deed, dated 20 March, 1620, gave a rent-charge, DESCRIPTION of the CHARITY, by whom, whan, and for what purpose given.

issuing out of the tithes of Uploder and Upton, for the relief of the poor of this parish; the share to this parish is, 130-kingston Russell.

Hippolet Mockett, by wilK Gave „£200, part of the

Dr.R. Ironside, by ditto, dated f tributed among the pood

John Michel, 'esq. by ditto, weekly pay: vested in

Sis Rorert Miller, Knt. and Dame Margaret his wife, gave a rent-charge issuing out of the tithes of Uploders and Upton; theshare to this place is *(see Loitrs)*... -LONGBURTON—*see Buiim Long.* -LONGFLEET—*see Canford Magna—None.* 131-LODERS.

Sir Rorert Miller, Knt. and Dame Margaret his wife, (she was the daughter of Robert Freke, esq. and sister of Sir Thos. Freke, knt.), by deed enrolled, dated 20 March, 1020, gave „£40 yearly, issuing out of the tithes of Up Loder and Upton, to the following parishes, viz.—to this parish £i; to Kingston Russell *J*2; to L-ongbredy £*1*; to Littlebredy £2; to Came Winterborne,5; to Farringdon Winterborne £5; to Cerne Abbas „£10; and to UpCerne,£10, for the relief of the poor, and for apprenticing poor children of the said parishes respectively, vested in the owner of the said tithes, &c.

Hugh Hansford, by deed, dated, (about 1679, as supposed,) gave four acres of land in Askerswell, and half a barn and half the mill holms there, to the poor of this parish; vested in Mr. Little, of Bideford, in the county of *Devon.* *Note*— The payment of this charity has been long discontinued.

132-LUCCOMBE, *alias* CHELBOROUGH E.—*None.* DESCRIPTION of ike CHARITY, by i given.

when, and for what purpou 133-LULWORTH, EAST.

Dorothy Pickering, *widow,* by will, dated, 1707 gave some money, since laid out in the purchase of a farm, called Line/i, in Corfe Castle, to be disposed of in manner following, viz.: 20s. for a sermon on the 9th May yearly, and the remainder to 12 poor protestant widows, or maiden? together, of this parish, not exceeding the age of 40, and to be present during the whole time of the service in the church, unless prevented by sickness, &c.; vested in Rev. Denn Bond, N. Bond, esq. Rev. John Clavill, and three others.

-LOLWORTH, WEST-see *Winfiith—None.* 134-LYDLINCH.

Phillis Romaine, *spinster,* by will, dated, 1711, gave in land, situate at Lydlinch, the profits thereof to be applied towards binding out poor children of this parish apprentices; vested in the heirs of Sir William St. Quintin, bart. Rev. W. Chafin, and Philip Henville deceased

Divers Persons, by gift at different times, gave,£150 in money, laid out in the purchase of lands, at the rents and profits of which is distributed to the second poor of this parish; vested in ditto 135-LYMU REGIS.

Matthew Holworthy, by will,dated 9 May, 1677, gave,£100 in money, the interest to be paid to the poor; vested in the churchwardens and overseers

John Tucker, by will, dated, gave in money,£10

Henry Henley, by do., dated 13 Aug. 1695, do. 40 John Hallett, by do., dated 16 Jan. 1698, do. 20 Rich. March, by do., dated 6 Jan. 1710, do. 150 John BuRRiDGE,by do., dated 1710, do. 30 250

All given for the benefit of the poor; and with this money an estate was purchased, called *Wesiford,* in the parish of Thorncombe, co. *Devon;* vested in the Mayor and Bur.

DESCRIPTION of the CHARITY, bj vhom, when, and for what porpoi'

Timotht Hallett, by will, dated 20 Nov.

1728, gave £20

John Edwards, bydo. dated 1 Nov. 1/32,do 12 32

The profits for the poor, lent at 4 cent. in Lyme turnpike.

Crewkerne branch; vested in Parish Officers......

John Burridge, *merchant,* by will dated 11 Sept. 1732;

MAhy Burridge, his wife, by ditto, dated 2 Sept. 1736;

Robert Burridge, merchant, by ditto. dated 21 Jan.

1744, gave in money, £150:18s. 8d. the profits thereof to be distributed to the poor; vested in the heirs of Benjamin, John, and Benj. Follett, jun. gents, deceased...

Edw. Edwards, *mayor,* by will, da. 15 Jan. 1684, gave £10

Wal. Tucker, *mayor,* by do. da. 1 Nov. 1632, do. 10

Do. bydo. do, do. 40

The two first was given for the benefit of the poor, and the last, *£40,* was to be lent to decayed merchants and craftsmen; vested in the Mayor and Burgesses, and Churchwardens; but no account can now be given of this £60..

ALMSHOUSE.

John Tudbold, by will, dated 11 October, 1548, gave two almshouses for the use of the poor, now occupied by the poor; vested in the Mayor. Burgesses, and Parish Officers

Walter Tucker, by will. dated I Nov. 1632, gave two rooms, for two single poor women, occupied by them; vested in ditto 136-MAIDEN NEWTON.

George Browne, Esq. by deed, inrolled in Chancery, dated 24 Jan. 1774, gave an annuity of £5, payable out of Cruxton Farm, to be divided between 20 poor persons of this parish and *Frame Vauchurch,* not receiving alms; vested in John Whittle and his heirs....

G 1 10 4 12 10 2 10 147-MILBORNE ST. ANDREW.

Lady Elizabeth Morton, by deed, dated 8 June, 1709. gave an annuity of *J"* li annum, issuing out of land, at, to be disposed of in the following manner, viz. to the minister of this parish, for a dinner, 20s.; to the parish clerk, 10s.; and for cloathing four poor children, and four poor men and women, of this parish, £6:10s.; vested in E.M.Pley-deU,Esq

Wr. Edward Smith, by will, dated —, 1774,gave £50,1 Old S. 8. Ann. the interest to be paid for instructing six poor children of this parish to read, &c. ; vested in

Annual

Produce

Bernard Mitchell, by will, dated 22 March, 1646, gave a rent-charge issuing out of land called the *King Head Inn*, in Melcombe Regis, payable by the lessee to the poor of this parish; vested in the parish officers (see *Mel. combe Regis...*

Dewlish.

Samuel Adams, by witt, dated 9 July, 1699, gave,£120 in money, since laid out in the purchase of land, at, the profits thereof to be distributed weekly to the poor of this parish; vested in late W. Davis deceased...

i, (supposed an ancestor of Thomas Gnndrey,

Esq.) by, gave a sum of money, but what sum, or for what particular purpose, unknown; the sum of 10s. is paid in aid of the poor rate yearly; vested in the heirs of late Thomas Uundiey, Esq.

148-MILTON ABBAS.

William, the Abbot of Milton, or Middleton, by deed, dated 10 Feb. 1521, (12 Henry 8,) under the common seal of the Abbey, founded a free school in this town, and endowed the same with the manor farm and free chapel of Littlemayne, in this county, which he had about the same time purchased of Thomas Kirton; and the said manor, &c. was, a short time afterwards, (28 Hen. 8, 1536), granted and conveyed in trust to Giles Strangwayes, Knt-, Thomas

Arundell, Km. Matthew Arundell, his son and heir apparent, Thomas Trenchard, Knt., John Horsey, Knt., Geo. de la tiynde, John Rogers, Thomas Uussey, Robert Martin, Thomas Morton, Robert (Joker, Robert Strode, Henry

Ashley, John Frampton, Thomas Trenchard, John Wil

Hams, Walter (Jrcy, Esq. and others, for the purpose of maintaining a free grammar school in the said town of

Milton, and to employ t he profits of the said manor, &c. to the maintenance of the school, and of a schoolmaster; vested in Francis John Browne, Henry Bankes, Edmund

Morton Fleydell, Esqrs. and others

Sole.—In the year 1785 this school was removed tot

Blandford Forum, by Act (private) of the 25 O. III.

John Tregonwell, Esq. by will, dated, 1674, charged his estate called *Bagbore Farm*, in this parish, with the payment to six poor women,of Is. week each, three yards of cloth for a gown, a pair of shoes and stockings, and 20s. in money, to be given on St. Thomas's Day.The late Earl of Dorchester and Lady Caroline Damer have added Is. 6d. and the Parish Officers, 6d., making 3s. *V* week. *Note* There is an almshouse for the residence of the said women, the annual produce not ascertained;

but the whole is about...

149-MINTERNE MAGNA.

Sir William Napier, Bart. by will, dated 27 August, 1745, gave a rent-charge, payable out of his estate at Witchampton, to the poor of this parish; vested in the parish officers

Sir Nathaniel Napier, Bart. by deed, dated 2 Nov.; 1700, gave,£30 in money, the interest thereof to be distributed to the poor of this parish annually; vested in Henry Charles Sturt, Esq....

DESCRIPTION *at* the CHAKITY, by whom, when, given. and for what purpose gp 150-MORETON.

William Frampton, Esq. by will, dated 15 Nov. 1687, orders his executors to lay out the sum of *one* hundred pounds, upon and for the absolute purchase of lands of inheritance, to be settled to this intent—that the yearly pro fits thereof may be for ever used and bestowed in and for the binding and putting forth to be apprentices, such poor children as, are, or shall be born or otherwise settled in this parish —This money having accumulated, in 1742 the Court of Exchequer directed that an estate called *Culease,* in the parish of Bere Regis, in the co. of Dorset, should be purchased and conveyed to *nine* trustees, that the

yearly profits mifjht be applied according to the directions of the will. In 1758, it having been represented to the Court of Exchequer that there were not sufficient objects of the cha. rity in the parish of Moreton, an order was made that the rents and profits of the estate should be applied in the first place for apprenticing poor children of Moreton, and that when such children shall have diligently and faithfully served their apprenticeships, the trustees shall have liberty to advance, if they think proper, any sum not exceeding *twenty pounds* towards enabling such apprentice the better to follow his trade and occupation—and after placing out and advancing such children of Moreton as shall be deemed proper objects, the surplus of rents shall be applied in ap prenticing and in like manner advancing such poor children as shall be born or otherwise settled in the parishes of Affpuddle and Tonerspuddle. In 1800 the land-tax, and in 1824 the great tithes of Culease Farm were purchased by the trustees. Culease farm now letts for *eighty pounds W* annum, and there is a sum of.1450 3 *W* cent. consols applicable to the uses of the charity; vested in James Henry Arnold, James Frampton, Charlton Byam Wollaston, Edmund Morton Pleydell, William Charlton Frampton, Thomas Bowyer Bower, Henry Frampton, Esqrs. the Rev. Richard Waldy and Rev. James Shirley, trustees, &c...

Rev. Roger Coker, rector of Moreton, by will, dated' —, proved in Prerogative Court of Canterbury, 20 Aug 1813, gave £170, 3 Cent. Red. Ann. the interest, divi- DESCRIPTION of the CHARITY, by whom, when, and for what purpose) given.

dends, and produce thereof to be applied by the trustees towards teaching and instructing the poor children of this parish in reading, working, and the catechism of the Church of England, in the way they shall think most pro per; vested in James Frampton, Esq. and the Kector forj the time b sing 151-MORDEN EAST—None.-MOSTERTON—*see South Perrot—None.* -MOTCOMBE—*see Gillingham.* 152-MONKTON TARRANT— None. 153-LAUNCESTON TARRANT—

JVone. 154-MONKTON WINTERBORNE-AW. 155-NETHERBURY.

Mrs. Susanna Lake, by will, dated 9 Feb. 1691, gave 13 acres of land, lying at Combe, within the manor of liea minster *Secunda,* in Beaminster, in trust for such poor people of the parish of Netherbury, as the churchwardens for the time being shall think fit. These are customary copyhold lands; vested in Mr. John Clare, the present trustee

Robert Brodrepp, Esq. by will, dated 24 Sept. 1708, gave „£200 in money, to trustees, for cloathing and binding out apprentices the poor children of this parish; vestedj in Rennet Combe, of Lincoln's Inn, in the county of Mid dlesex, Esq. heir at law of the donor; it being directed by the deed, that the donor's heir should be always one of the trustees

James Gollop, a grocer of Bristol, by will, dated4 Sept. 1710, gave all his lands, tenements, and hereditaments, in the parish of Siston, and two pasture grounds at Stowick, in the parish of Henbury, in the county of *Gloucester;* and also the house in which he lived in Horse.Street, in the parish of St. Augustin, in Bristol, unto trustees, that By a Decree in Chancery, dated 19 August, 2 G. t. this money was laid out in the purchase of lands, called Furseleaze, in this parish; the profits thereof are to be for ever employed for the above purpose.—No new trustees have been appointed sir.ce the original conveyance was made, in pursuance of the Decree and Order sf the Court of Chancery.

they would, out of the rents and profits thereof, (but it does not say what the amount is), place as many poor boys within the hospital, as the same would sufficiently keep and maintain for ever; one of which said boys to be had always out of this parish; vested in the Governors of the Hospital called Queen Elizabeth's Hospital, in Bristol, and their successors for ever *Note*—The boy is sent to the Hospital by the nominai tion and recommendation of the minister, churchwardens, and overseers of the parish, and the representa- tive or heir at law of the donor.

Mr. Ralph Gollop, of Lillington,by will,

dated 20 April, 172i, gave an annuity of 50s. out of his estate in Lilling. ton, for ever, to ten poor people of this parish, not receiving any relief, to be paid on *Easter* Sunday yearly. This estate belongs to the heir at law of Thomas Gollop, late of Sherborne, Esq. deceased; vested in George Tilley Gollop, Esq. his son

Mr. Richard Gollop, of Charmouth, by will, dated 12 Sept. 1725, gave an annuity of „£10, payable out of his lands at Hogbear and Bitlake, in this parish, towards binding out two poor boys of this parish apprentices yearly; Sir William Oglander, Bart. the present owner of the lands; vested in the Churchwardens and Overseers of the poor of Netherbury...

-, by an award, dated 3 January, 1558, 7 Eliz. certain copyhold lands of inheritance, called Broadnam and Paradise, lying within the manor of Slape, are to be for ever employed for the maintenance of a grammar-school within this parish, and for such other uses as the church wardens and the majority of the parishioners shall think most beneficial, and for the best advantage of the parish, and of the inhabitants thereof; vested in Mr. John Clare, the present trustee by .., dated, gave certain burgages1 and lands in *Dorchester, Bridport, Up Loder,* and this pa They consist of three houses at Dorchester, the tike number in Bridport, a dwelling-house and several small parcels of laid in Up-Loders, and divers small pieces of ground in this parish. The whole of this property seems to have belonged to the Fraternity or Brother wood of the Holy Crosi and St. Christopher, in the church of Netherbury. On the passing of the Act 1 Edw. 6, for the dissolution of the Chantries, *Stc.* there was much opposition in the House of Commons respecting that part of the bill which vested in the Crown the lands belonging to Guilds and Fraternities; bat those who managed that House for the Cour, took off the opposition by an assurance that the Guild lands should be restored: and Burnet informs us that that assurance was made good by the Protector.—Hist. Reform', v. 9, p.*46*. In all probability these lands,

now vested in feoffees, for the use of the parish, eccaped being seized in consequence of this assurance. There is express evidence that a part at least belonged to the fraternity, which would have been taken away by the said statute had not the favor of those in power interposed.

H DESCRIPTION of the CHARITY, by whom, when, and for what purpose given.

if fitted for it; such boys to be successively chosen by her executors:—Also,,£30 annum out of her said lands, to Susannah Hood, wife of Arthur Hood, for her life, and after her decease, so much of her land in yearly value as the said annuity of,£30, was supposed to arise out of (and not the annuity itself), free from charge, to be thus disposed of, viz. one-third of the said lands for the benefit of the said school for ever, for the binding out one or more boys ap prentices, unless only in such a year wherein a new trustee should be chosen; and the remaining two-thirds to her cousin Elizabeth Hood, the wife of Samuel Hood, clerk, for her life, if she outlived her husband, and not otherwise; and afterwards for such pious ues as her executors should appoint:—And she gave to her four executors and trustees, out of her said lands, „£10 each, to be paid them at their first entrance on it; and so to each of their successors £10 upon the decease or failure of any one of their number, upon his being chosen by a majority of the surviving executors and trustees.—The estate is let at,£100 annum, clear, except land-tax and repairs; vested in Sir William Oglander, Bart., and the late Bennet Combe, and Mr. Samuel Cox, merchant WORK-HOUSE, OR ALMSHOUSE.

Gilbert Adams, mercer, by will, dated 20 Feb. 1626, gave „£200 in moDey to the poor,,£40 for building a house for them, and,£20 for the maintenance of the same house. With part of these monies a workhouse was built for the poor in Beaminster, and with the residue, a tenement in *Allen's Loscombe,* in Poorstock, was purchased j the rent whereof is applied towards maintaining and repairing the said workhouse; vested in Sir William Oglander, Bart. Bennet Combe, Samuel Cox, sen. John Russell, Bishop Dunning, James Daniel, sen. Thomas Harris, John Banger Russell, Daniel Cox, Samuel Cox, jun. James Daniel, jun. and James Dunning, trustees

Sir John Strode, by deed, dated, 1627, (or there.

abouts) built and founded an almshouse in Beaminster, for six poor men and women, (but not confined to inhabitants of DE&CRIPTION of the CHARITY, by whom, given. when, and for what purpose Beaminster only,) and endowed the same with two-thirds ofj BUsliay Farm, in Loders, which is of the yearly value of,£32, let to one Stephen Symes, but subject to disburse, ments, and also to a charge upon the said farm of £6 a-year to the poor of Symondsbury. It is also endowed with a house in Beaminster, called God's House, formerly belonging to a chantry, now the almshouse, and, with the scite of another house, now a garden, let to Mr. John Brown at one guinea a-year; and also some quit-rents, called St. Helen's Rents, amounting to 2:15s. a-year; vested in Sir William Oglander, Bart, the donor's heir..

Thomas Keate, mercer, by a nomination in writing, dated 18 May, 1709, (according to the custom of the manor of Beaminster Secunda,) gave to one Bernard Newman, a close of arable land, called Wood's Water, containing one acre, (more or less,) with the appurtenances, lying near Wood's Water, and parcel of the said manor, in trust, that he should out of the profits of the said close, the first Sunday in every calendar month, for ever, buy eight sixpenny wheaten loaves for eight of the poorest persons in Bea. minster, who should have the greatest need thereof, that do not receive any relief or pay of the parish; and in case it should happen that the money raised out of the profits of the said close be not sufficient to pay for the said loaves, that then the said loaves are not to be given in time of harvest, in such or any of the said years. The said close lets for about £3:10s. annum, and is thrown into another close

belonging to the late Thomas Cook, Esq. the hedge between them being thrown down by John Cook, his late father, to whom Bernard Newman's wife surrendered this close; vested in the heirs of the late William Thomas Cook, Esq....

Rev. William Hillary, of Minstead, co. Hants, by will, dated 27 Oct. 1712, gave to Rodney Troath, a parcel of land, called Ernly Wood, containing 61 A. situate at Benville, in Corscombe, for 99 yrs,, to commence immediately from his death, and then devised the same to 12 of the poorest families of the parish of Beaminster, for ever; and nominated and appointed William Mills of Merehay, William Chllcott of the same, Launcelot Mills and Thomas Phelps alias Hitt, DESCRIPTION of Ihe CHARITY, by »bom, given.

when, aud for what purpose g of Beaminster, and their heirs Tor ever, overseers and as-J sistants, together with the churchwardens and overseers of Beaminster for the time being, or the major part of them, to receive the profits of the said estate, and yearly thereout equally to distribute the same to such twelve poorest fami lies as aforesaid, as to them should seem meet, and not receiving any benefit or relief of the parish; and upon the death of any of the said trustees, another is to be elected and chosen, so that four trustees be always appointed for collecting and distributing the profits as aforesaid. Krnly Wood was formerly in possession of J. Arundell Hanne, Esq. who held itfor the remainder of the said term of 99 yrs. , and is of the yearly value of,£30.— Launcelot Mills survived W. Mills, Chilcott, and Phelps; and the trust is now vested in Iiauncelot Mills's heirs, there never having been any new trustee elected in the room of those dead Francis Champion, alias Clark, butcher, by a nomination in writing, dated 19 Jan. 1741, (according to the custom of the manor of Beaminster Secunda,) gave to his nephew, Richard Dematt the younger, a close called Culver. hays, in Beaminster aforesaid, containing two acres, upon trust, and subject to the payment of 15s. at Christmas yearly; and

from and after his decease, the churchwardens of Beaminster for the time being, for ever, shall purchase 30 loaves, to be distributed by them to and among such poor of the said parish as have no relief, &c. The said close is let at jf4 V annum, clear of all deductions, and is in the occupation of Thomas Bozie, as tenant thereof vested in Richard Tizzard and Robert his son, who were nominated by the said Richard Dematt -NETHER CERNE_«e Cerne Nether.

John Rake, by will, dated, 1707, gave a rent-charge or annuity of £5 yearly, upon his estate in this parish, for This money was always placed in the hands of the overseer for the time being, one of whom failing, a moiety was last, so that now only £3 remains.

f This money was lent, and by that means £31 has been long since lost: there now only remaina £29. Three bonds dated in 1671,1699, and 1706, are in the church box for the remaining £su In the year 1741, this money was in the hands of Philip Thresher; since which no account of it time there is DESCRIPTION of the CHARITY, b; given. whom, when, and for what purpose. The Hon. Henry Dawney, D. D. by will, dated — 1753, gave in money, to be placed out at interest by the trustees, and to be distributed at Christmas yearly, to the poor of the said parish; vested in the heirs of Air. Robert Boswell, trustee to this charity...

Nute—In the parish register is this entry, made by Or

Dawney, vicar of Piddletown, dated Oct. 1725:

"Mr. Joseph Rawlins, grocer, in the Strand, London,

"bequeathed by will, „£100, in the year 1724, for the

"use of the poor of this parish, the interest of whichj

"was designed to be distributed in bread every Christ

"mas. This legacy continues unpaid, and I believe

"will continue so, either through a defect of money or

"honesty."

176-PIDDLETRENTHIDE.

John Harding, by will, dated 27 October, 1750, gave', £431:13s. in S. S. Annuities, for teaching poor children! of this parish reading, writing, arithmetic, and true reli gion; vested in the vicar, the late Fras. Newman, Esq. and Mr. Stephen Isles, the only surviving trustees

Frances Oxenbrigge, widow of William Collier, and afterwards wife of Robert Oxenbrigge, Esq. who died 1708.

by, dated, gave out of an estatej, (as supposed,) held by lease under the College of Winchester, by Wm.

Cox, Esq. for the benefit of the second poor of this parish;

vested in, (unknown)....

John Jennings, Esq. by will, dated 28 Feb. 1772. gave in

S. S. Stock, „£150, for placing out children of this parish to useful trades; vested in Henry €onstantine Jennings,

Esq. and his heirs—supposed annual produce...

177-PIDDLEHINTON.

Nicholas Kellaway, by will, dated, 1783, (or there abouts.) gave.£20 in money, the interest thereof to be an ually paid to poor widows of this parish; vested in thej rector and cuurchwardens Note—His effects producing no more than £12:6s. 6d. that sum only was received.

Owing to a disagreement among the trustees of this chariiy, there has been much irregularity in the payment of the schoolmaster's salary, who, by his own account, had, at Midsummer 1786. due to him Jc59:10s. 10d., of which he says he has received nothing. % Value unknownj not having been paid for some years. DESCRIPTION of the CHARITY, by whom, when, and for v given.

Annual Produce.

178-PULHAM.

Richard Camden, of London, Gent, by deed, dated, 1649, gave a rent-charge, issuing out of two closes of land, called *Mountwood Hill,* in the parish of Buckland Newton, the profits thereof to be distributed among the second poor of this parish; vested in the parish officers

179-PUNCKNOWLE.

William Napieb, Bsq. lord of the manor, by will, dated , about 1619, gave

£10, laid out in laud in this parish, the profits thereof for the relief of the poor of this parish; vested in the parish officers

R.

180-RADIPOLE—*see Melcombe Regit-None.* 181-RAMPISHAM.

Christopher Stickland & Petronella Byworth, his sister, by deed, dated 20 Nov. 1628, 4 Car. 1. gave £30 in money, the interest thereof to be distributed among the second poor of this parish; vested in 12 trustees, *(unknown)* Note— This sum is now reduced by lending to £15.

Francis Lawrence, by will, dated, gave some land, in, the profits thereof to be paid among poor, aged, and impotent persons of this parish; vested in the rector and

Rev. Richard Hele, rector, by will, dated, 1755, gave,£50 in money, the interest thereof to be paid annually to the poor of this parish; vested in ditto 132-RAWSON TARRANT—Atone.

183-RUSHTON TARRANT—*None.* 184-RYAIE INTRINSECA.

John Hunter, by will, dated, 1785, gave,£10 in money to the poor of this parish, which was distributed accordingly...

DESCRIPTION of ihe CHARITY, by whom, »hen, nl for nhat purpOK -ST. MARTIN'S WINT.1—sw MartintfeiTM. 185-SHAPWICK— *None.* 186-SHAFTON, *alias* SHAFTESBURY. SPILLER'S SPITTLE, OR HOSPITAL, OR SPILLER'S

Sir Henry Spiller, Knt. by deed, dated 17th March, 1042, conveyed a tenement and bakehouse, in the parish of St. Lawrence, near a place or street called Hocken Bench, now called the Bakehouse in Parson's Pool, with several closes of land in Alcester, containing 24 acres, with common of pasture there and in the parish of St. James, to W'm. Byerley, Esq. and others, and their heirs, to be conveyed unto the mayor and burgesses of Shafton for the time being, and their heirs and successors, for the erecting an almshouse for the habitation of ten poor people, and for the relief, clothing, and maintenance of them; and also, the said Sir Henry, on the 17th June, 1646, surrendered divers copyhold closes and lands, called Puck-

more and North, hayes, situate in Motcombe, containing 26 acres, and five acres of allotment land there, unto six burgesses of the said borough, and to their heirs, to such pious uses and intentions as he formerly declared, or should thereafter declare under his hand and seal. On the 25th June following, Sir Henry, by bargain and sale, enrolled in Chancery, stating, that being desirous to manifest some act of charity for the relief of ten poor msn, to be for ever elected out of the most aged and impotent persons within the said borough, granted all the above-mentioned premises in Shafton, Alcester, and the parish of St. James, to the said burgesses, the rents and profits to be employed towards building the said almshouse, for the said persons, in and near unto a street called Salisbury-street, within the said town of Shafton as might be, and in such manner as he should by deed, or writing, or by his last will direct or appoint, and in default thereof in such manner as the said mayor, and capital ALMSHOUSES.

DESCRIPTION of the CHARITY, by whom, when, and for what purpos burgesses, and feoffees, or the greater part of them should direct or appoint, according to the truat in them reposed; vested in the mayor, and capital burgesses, and others

Chubb's Almshouse.

Matthew Chubb, of Dorchester, Gent, by, dated , 1611, founded an almshouse in Shafton, for sixteen poor women of the said town, built on the site of part of the lands of the mayor and corporation of Shaftesbury, in Salisbury-street, which seems to have been conveyed by them to Mr. Chubb for this purpose. What the original endowment was cannot now be ascertained. A brass plate, stating Mr. Chubb to be the founder, appeared over the entrance from 1611 to 1768, and it is fair to presume that his name w.uld not have been suffered to appear as the founder for so many years, if he had not given any thing for its support; vested in the corporation and others

Margaret Chubb, *widow,* by, dated, 1630,!

gave £100 in money, afterwards laid out

in land at. (supposed in the town lands, whereon the workhouse after wards stood, which would now be worth £20 per annum, ifj then laid out.) towards the support of the said almshouse;! vested in the mayor and corporation

Jane Gbove, of Shaftesbury, *widow,* by deed, dated 1 Aug. 1625, in performance of the last will of John Boden, (Budden), deceased, her father, and of the last will of William Grove, deceased, her husband, granted unto John Grove, Thomas Bennett, John Foyle, and other feoffees, £26 rent annum, out of Gawen's Lands, Vile's Moor Mead, Thorne Mead, Shepherd's Close, and Goffe's House, lying part in Shafton and part in Alcester, to be distributed half-yearly, for the relief of the sixteen poor women as aforesaid; vested in the heirs of the above-named feoffees

Robert Jesse, of Melbury, by will, dated 26 Dec. 1614, charged his lands, called Wilkins's Hayes, in St. James's parish, with 20s. *V* ann. payable to the said almshouse, Sec.; vested in the mayor and corporation

Thomas Pett r, by will, dated, gave. £20 in money, to remain as a stock for ever, to be paid to the almswomen; I in the mayor and corporation DESCRIPTION of *the* CHARITY, bj

Ann Mbubeh, widow of Anthony Murrell, on the 12; Sept. 1707, gave £100 in money to the corporation, intrust, either to be deposited on security, in purchasing land, orj otherwise. This money has been lent to divers persons and lastly, (on 13 July, 1713,) to Mr. George West, on mort gage of the *King's Head lm* ; and the interest is to be paid yearly amongst the alms women aforesaid; vested in the mayor and corporation

Frances Wykes, of Shafton, *ipinster,* by will, dated 26 June, 1738, gave „£100 in money, to the corporation, to be laid out at interest for the benefit of the said alms women; vested in the mayor and corporation *Note*—This interest was continued to be paid till the year 175S.

John Bennett, by will, dated — Jan. 1778, gave £ 1001 in money, the interest thereof towards the support of

Chubb's almshouse; vested in the mayor and corporation FREE GRAMMAR SCHOOL.

William, Karl Of Pembroke, lord of the manor of Shaftesbury, by deed, dated 16 *t'eb.* 1625, gave, granted, enfeoffed, and confirmed unto Sir Francis Ashley, Sir Walter Erie, John Browne, Esq. John White, Clerk, Walter Newburgh, Clerk, Anthony Prowse, Clerk, (then rector), Edmund Cole, and Christopher Weare, Gents., their heirs and assigns, for the erection and perpetual continuance of a Grammar School in this town—All that messuage, tenement, and stone-built house, called *The Maudlin,* (Magdalen), in this town, with all gardens and plots of ground therewith used or enjoyed; and also, one little house or cottage, and a little garden plot adjoining, on the north part of the said Maudlin, in the whole one acre and half: and it is said (according to the account of the recorder, William Whittaker, Esq.) that by the same deed he granted a plot of ground leading from the church-yard of St. Trinity, by the Lord Arundell's stable over Sansom's Green, and through two little gardens between Sansom's Green and the Maudlin, for a way, &c. To Hold to the said feoffees and their heirs, to the intent that they should DESCRIPTION of the CHARITY, by «hom, when, and for what purpose given.

employ the said premises for ever as a school-bouse, and for the benefit of such a schoolmaster as the said feoffees should appoint, under the rent of 4d, with a letter of attorney to execute livery of seizin, *which were not endorsed, and probably not executed.*

It appears that the corporation bestowed above „£40 in the reparation of the Maudlin; but after the death of the said *William,* Earl of Pembroke, which happened on the 10 April, 1630, his successor, *Philip,* Karl of Pembroke, discovered that the indorsement of livery and seizin had been omitted, and again took possession of the property.

The said William Whittaker, recorder, not long after. 1630, purchased, for the sum of.40. of Hugh

Grove, Esq. of Chissenbury, co. Wilts, and Jane his wife, one messuage, tenement, garden, and offices, in that part of *Bimport,* nearly opposite the gate leading into the church-yard of the Holy Trinity; and by deed of feoffment, dated, 1646, the said William Whittaker and William Hurman, of Shafton, attorney-at law, did grant, enfeoff, and confirm unto Albinus Aluston and Nicholas Cooper, of the same place, gents, the aforesaid premises, which were late in the occupation of Thomas Garden, A. M. the schoolmaster of the said school, TO Hold to the said Albinus M us ton and Nichs. Cooper, their heirs and assigns for ever, to the only proper use of the mayor, recorder, and capital burgesses of the borough of Shafton aforesaid, for the time being, and their successors, and to be employed for the erecting a school-house or free-school within the said borough, and accommodation for the schoolmaster, according to the intention of the original purchase. ..

William Ltjsh, by will, dated 27 Feb. 1718, gave some land, situate at Motcombe, and three houses in the town, towards the cloathing, schooling, and apprenticing poor boys or girls of the borough, not exceeding *twenty* in one year; the residue of the income and yearly rents, if any BLUE SCHOOL.

Thii person is mentioned as a benefactor to Chubb's almshouse, in several accounts published. DESCRIPTION of the CHARITY, by given for the benefit of all such poor persons within the borough, as should stand most in need of charity; and likewise to allow yearly out of the rents, unto all persons whomsoever that should be related to the testator as near as cousin german, and should fall into poverty and real want, such annual sum for his, her, or their maintenance and support during his, her, or their lives, as to his trustees should seem fit; vested in John White, Esq. (since dead,) John WiU

kins, John Robert Kveritt, Charles Pinhorne, (since dead)

Gents, and the Rev. Wm. Topham

Note—The gross annual produce is

„£139:15s. out of which £5 *V* annum is paid to each of the trustees, ac cording to the will of the donor, and taxes paid there,

out, reduces it to the above sum.

GENERAL CHARITIES.

Peter Bennett, by will, dated, charged his estatej called *Holy Hood Mead,* in St. James's parish, with the payment thereout, to twelve poor persons *weekly* for ever,

of the said parish of St. James, twelve penny loaves;

vested in Benj. Lester Lester, Esq.

John Foyle, Esq. by deed, dated 20 May, 1647, gave some land, situate in St. James's parish, for the use and benefit of the poor of the Holy Trinity parish; vested in Gorges

Foyle, Esq....

Note—A charity, called Foyle's, of £100, which is said to have been formerly given by one Foyle to the corpo. ration, for which £6 cent. annum was to be paid,

viz. £4 to the overseers of the poor of the parish of

Holy Trinity, and £2 to the overseers of the poor of the parish of St. Peter, for the benefit of the poor; but no traces can be found of this,£100, or of the receipt of it, or whether given by Foyle or not.

Albinus Muston, by, dated, (after 1630) charged two houses in *Muston-Lane,* towards the support of1

the poor of the parish of the Holy Trinity; vested in the,

overseers of the said parish

Note— The two houses were bought some time ago by!

Mr. John Bennett of John and Joseph Matthews, who

It appears by an account published, that Sir Matthew Arundell deposited £100 in the hands of this gentleman, to which he added *iou* and purchased the said land m St. James's parish.

DESCRIPTION of the CHARITY, by whom, when, given.

Annual Produce.

allowed the same in the purchase money, and Mr.

Bennett took the houses with that incumbrance, and sold them afterwards to Mr. Mortimer.

William Williams—see *Blandford Forum.*

Simon Whetcombe, by will, dated 23 Aug. 1721, gave

.£50, to be lent to ten poor tradesmen, to each of them £5,

who are to give security for the repayment of the same,

without interest, at five equal yearly payments; and as often as there should be.£5 in the hands of the trustees, they, or the major part of them, should lend the same to some poor tradesman, to be repaid in manner as aforesaid; vested in the corporation and rectors of the Holy Trinity and St.

Peter for the time being

Note—No tradesman to have more than £5 at one time,

so that ths said,£50 may continue as a perpetual fund for the help and relief of ten poor tradesmen residing within the said borough.

William Lush, by bond, dated 22 April, 1713, gave £100

to the mayor and corporation, to purchase lands, the profits thereof to be disposed of yearly to such poor people as he by will or deed, under his hand and seal, should appoint;

for want of such appointment, to the use of such poor per.

sons within the borough, as the mayor and corporation in1

common council should think fit; and having made no such appointment, he gives by his said will to his trustees, (appointed by the will,) and their successors, full power to dispose of this charity with the rest, provided the mayor and corporation, for their own ease, would agree to it; but if that be refused, the said sum was to be paid by the trustees under the will, to discharge the bond, desiring the yearly interest of the said sum might be applied to such uses as are mentioned relating to the same; vested in the corporation, to whom the bond was given

187-SHERBORNE.

FREE SCHOOL.

King Edward VI. by patent, dated, 1550, (4 Edw.VI.) founded a free grammar school in this town, in which school DESCRIPTION of the CHARITY, by whom,

when, and for what purpose the plan of education is similar to that at Eton. This! school is richly endowed by lands in Martock,oo. Somerset, Bradford Bryan and Bamesley, in Wimborne Minster, Gillingham, Silton, Lytchett Matravers, Sturminster Marshall, Thorton in Mamhull, and Symondsbury, in this; county; vested in twenty governors, inhabitants of this town ALMSHOUSE, OH ST. ADOUSTIN's HOSPITAL.

Robert Neville, bishop of Sarum, by patent, dated 26 Jan. 1448, (26 U. 6), gave some land and houses in this town for the support of twelve poor men and four women, and one perpetual chaplain, of the town of Sherborne: and directed £10 to be paid to the poor of *Hereford* yearly; vested in the 20 governors 616 13 4; vested in the twenty governors. The governors, by principal savings of these charities, purchased an estate in 1692, at, for the above purposes, which produces the gross annual sum of..

Agnes Broughton, by deed, dated 1633, gave in land, at

—, towards binding out apprentices; vested in the said 20 governors

Richard Forster, by deed, dated, 1640, gave in land, at ———, for the education of ten boys and ten girls of Sherborne; and from the surplus of the rents *£b* yearly, towards maintaining one of the said boys at the *Univenity,* if any should be sent; and further, towards purchasing any necessary plate for the communion service DESCRIPTION of the CHARITY, by whom, when, trad lor what purpose of the church, and the residue for the almshouse; vested in the said *20* governors

Dorothy Uasi.hext, by gift,in 1685, gave £50 in money, for linen changes for old women of Sherborne; vested in the said 20 governors... ''V;Jt'

John, Earl Of Bristol, by will, dated, 1698, gave ,£200 in money, the interest thereof to be paid to the poor of Sherborne; vested in the said 20 governors...

Smith, by will, dated, 1705, gave,£100 in money, the interest thereof to be paid as above; vested in the said 20 governors...

Note—The governors, with these last two donations, pur-

chased an estate in 1757, at

Robert Avoke, by will, dated 1720, gave two houses, the profits thereof to be given in bread to the poor of Sherborne;

vested in the said 20 governors

Simon Whetcombe, by will, dated 23 Aug., 1721, gave £50 in money, to be lent without interest, in small sums, to poor tradesmen, inhabitants of Sherborne, £5 each vested in the said 20 governors......... '...

John Eastment, Esq. by verbal gift, in 1723, gave £100

in money, for clothing poor men of Sherborne; vested in'

the said 20 governors...

Note—The money remains in the hands of his repre-

sentative, but the interest is regularly paid.

William Lord Digby, by deed, dated, 1743, gave some land, at, the profits thereof to be applied in educating and clothing thirteen poor girls of the town of Sherborne; vested in the said twenty governors

John Gillett, by word, &c. in 1636, gave some land at, to the poor of Sherborne; vested in the churchwardens, &c.

George Connington, by will, dated, 1698, gave some land at ———, to the poor of Sherborne, the profits thereof to be given in bread; vested in the churchwardens DESCRIPTION of the CHARITY, bj whom, when, and for »h»t pmpne 111

John Woodman, of London, Gent, by will, dated 12

Dec. 1717, gave £250 in money, (since laid out in land at

,) towards educating poor boys of the town of

Sherborne; vested in the vicar and churchwardens .robert GoadbY, by will, dated 7 Aug., 1778, gave £200

3 ¥ cent. Consols, lodged in the Bank of England, the interest thereof to be paid to the poor of, Sherborne;

vested in the vicar and churchwardens...

Note— £2 annually is also paid to the vicar, for preach ing a sermon, the first Sunday in May, on a certain subject

specified in the will.

Charles Bull Hart, Gent, by, dated, 1805, gave „£50 to be laid out in government securities, and the interest to be applied yearly in providing dowlas shifts for poor deserving old women of this town; vested in the governors, master, and brethren of the almshouse

Giles Russell, by will, dated29th July, 1664, and proved 15th March, 1670, gave all and singular his messuages lands, tenements, and hereditaments, as well freehold as copyhold or charter hold, (which he had surrendered to the uses of his will), to his wife Miloah for her life, and then to certain trustees, who should permit and suffer the president, treasurer, and governors of Christ's Hospital, in London, to enjoy the rente and profits thereof, in order that they should educate, bring up, and maintain in Christ's Hospital aforesaid, nine poor children, to be taken out of the town of Sherborne, and the parishes of *Ann,* Blackfriars, and *St. James's,* Clerkenwell, co. Middlesex, viz. three out of the said town, and three out of each of the said parishes, until the ages of 16 years, and then others to be appointed in their place and stead; and if the rents and profits thereof shall be sufficient, to place them out appren tices; and when the said trustees shall die, then the election and nomination to be by the parish officers of the said pa rishes; vested in the mayor and commonalty and citizens of the city of London 188-SHAPWICK-JW -SHILLING OKEFORH-sce *Okeford Shilling.-None.* DESCAlPTION of the CHARITY, by whom, when, and for what purpose g « given.

John Crandon, John Bovett, and eight others, their heirs and assigns, for ever, 18 acres of land in this parish, called *Parish Land,* without mentioning any particular purpose: but in subsequent deeds, and in the last, dated 27 July, 1791, it was directed, " that the trustees, or the majority of "them, should from time to time hereafter dispose of the "rents and profits of the said premises, towards the repa"ration of the parish church of Stockland, or else towards ' the relief of the poor of the said parish, or else towards "the maintenance of the

common highways and bridges "within the said parish; or to any other purposes, or cha. "ritable use or uses, within the said parish, as the trus. "tees, or the majority of them, should think fit." The profits of these lands have usually been applied to the relief of the poor; vested in the late W. T. Cox, T. Knott, Thomas Newcomen, Edward Broughton, William Pratt, James Reed, Matthew Davy, Robert Davy, John Cooke, and three other feoffees -dalwood.

Richard Downing, by will, dated 8 March, 1621, gave,£10 in money, laid out in an annuity, charged on certain lands, for the use of the poor of this parish for ever, by the discretion of John Downing, William Downing, Bartholomew Palmer, and Richard Gill, with the best help and aid of the constable, churchwardens, and overseers, and more of the better sort of parishioners of this parish; and the profits thereof to be distributed at the feast of *Easter,* by the said trustees and their heirs for ever, unto such poor people as they in their discretion should think fit; vested in Bartholomew Palmer, as heir at law to the last surviving trustee 202-STOKE ABBOT—*Hone.* -STOBOROUGH—*see Wareham, Sf Stoke E None.* 20a-STOKK EAST—*None.* DESCRIPTION of the CHARITY, by whom, when, and for what purpose s given. *a* 205-STOKE WAKE-AW 206-STOWERPAINE—None.

207-STOWER PROVOST.

Rebecca Stonestreet, by, dated 21 Nov. 1785, gave „£200, O. S. S. Stock, for teaching poor children of this parish to read; vested in the rector and churchwardens 208-STRATTON—«e *Charminster—None.* 209-STUDLAND.

———, by, dated, gave two cottages and gardens, about 30 perches each, for a poor-house and the use of the poor; vested in the parish officers 210-STURMINSTER MARSHALL.

Gen. Sir Walter Erle, by will, dated 12 Aug. 1605, gave £!1 in money, for the use of the poor of this parish, the interest thereof to be paid annually; vested in the heirs of T. Erie Drax, esq.

Note—This charity is withheld.

Thomas Lyne, Gent. by will, dated 7 May, 1621, gave a rent charge, payable out of Bradford Bryan Farm, in W'imborne Minster, to the use of the poor annually for ever; vested in the heirs of Henry William Fitch, esq. deceased

William Mackerill, of Spettisbury, Gent. by deed, dated 10 June, 1799, gave £1200,3 cent. Cons, the in terest, profits, and produce thereof to be applied towards the instruction of 52 poor children belonging to the said parish; vested in the vicar and parish officers of the said parish

William Churchill, Esq. by deed enrolled, dated IS) Jan. 1825, gave a piece of ground as a site for a schoolhouse for the use of the said children; vested in ditto -corfe Mullen.

Thomas Phillips, Esq. by will, dated, 1660, gave some money, now vested in land, at ——, in co. *Somers* the interest thereof to be distributed to the poor of this parish in bread; vested in the late Lewis Cockram

Philip Baker, *rector,* (inst. in 169i), died in 1714), and James Kennel, (whose sister Klizabeth married Lewis

Cockram, in 1683,) by, dated, gave 50s. for the like purpose; vested in William Smith 214-SWYRE.

, (supposed one of the Gollop family,) by, dated, gave £ 24 in money, tor the use of the poor of this parish, the interest to be paid them annually; vested in the heirs of late Francis Steward, esq. 215-SYDLING ST. NICHOLAS.

John Barber, of Chale, in the Isle of Wight, by will, dated 12 May, 1795, gave „£S00, which was afterwards vested in the funds in the name of the minister and churchwardens, and a house has been erected for the accommodation of a master and scholars; but owing to an improper person being appointed master, the parish has not reaped that benefit from the institution-which might have been expected. The schoolmaster was to be chosen by the minister and churchwardens, to teach children to read and write, and instruct them in the catechism of the church of England, and until such a schoolmaster be procured, the interest and profits arising from the said sum shall be applied in acts of charity; vested in the minister and church wardens -HILFIELD.

Thomas Sturmey built and occupied a cottage in this parish, which cottage was built by leave of the Lord, DESCRIPTION of the CHARITY, by whom, whtn, and for what purpoaej giren.

Annual

Produce.

(Thomas Trenchard, Esq.) as appears by an agreement dated, 1697, for erecting the said cottage, entered in the Records of this County, the 31 October, 1775. This cottage has been used for the benefit of the poor, as a poorhouse, and is vested in the parish officers 10 gave one close of meadow, lying in the parish of Bothen hampton, for the use and benefit of those honest and welldisposed people, *which should live* by the relief and alms of the parishioners. This close was rented, in 1786, by Mr. Jos. Hayter, at,,£10 a year, which is annually distributed by the minister and churchwardens of this parish; vested in Seymour Gulston, *Clerk,* Robert Chilcott, Richard Battis combe, John Alford, Anthony Stevens, John Symes, John Hounsell, Arthur Oliver, William Colmer, and Joseph JMorey, the younger, and the heirs and assigns of the survivor of them Walter Nswbtjkoh, B. *D.* Clerk, Thos. Barnes, Gent. and Others, principal inhabitants of this parish, by subscription, dated 1632, (or thereabouts,) purchased an annuity or rent-charge of £6 a year, aut of an estate called *Biishay,* in Loders, for the putting out apprentices the children of such honest poor people of this parish, who are not able to place them out. The owner of Bilshay Estate is Sir William Oglander, bart.; vested in the trustees aforesaid

Giles Stranqways, Wm. Strode, John StranoWats, Humphry Bishop, and John Bishop, by indentures of lease and release, dated 12 and 13 April, 1675, purchased a piece of land, called *Thortteombe,* in this parish, containing about 46 acres, of Peter Gailham, esq. William Stanley, merchant, and

Fowke, gent. for., »» vested in Giles Strangways, William Strode, John Strangwaye, Humphry

Bishop, John Bishop, their heirs or assigns...... .f g

430 of the consideration money be-

longed to Charle Pitfield, ofHoxton, in the countr of Mid. diner, eotnmonly called PlrneWe Charity. ' DESCRIPTION of the CHARITY, hv whom, when, and for what purport wardens of the several parishes above mentioned; vested! in the heirs of the late Francis John Browne. esq.

Ditto, by deed. dated 24 Jan. 1774, gave a rent charge, is. suing out of lands in Toller F'ratrum, for the benefit of 60 poor persons, settled parishioners of this parish and Toller Fratrum, who shall not receive alms, and to such poor persons only as the vicar for the time being shall think proper objects of this charity; vested in the heirs of John Whittle 224-TURN WOO D—*None.* -TONERSPIDDLE_. ee *Moreton.* 225-TYNEHAM—*None. V.* 826-UPWAY.

Mrs. Payne, by will, dated, (sometime in the last century,) gave a sum of money to the poor of this parish, the produce thereof to be distributed annually; vested in the heirs of George Gould, esq.

W.

227-WALDITCH—iVone. 22a-WAMBROKE—None. 229-WARM WELL— *None.* 230-WAREHAM. FREE SCHOOL.

George Pitt, of Stratfieldsay, co. *Hants,* Esq. by will,! dated 28 Nov. 1693, founded a free school here, and gave the sinecures of *St. Peter's* and *St. Michael,* in this town, and all tithes belonging thereto, and a messuage, called *Chafin's,* likewise,£20 in money for this town, and £5 for Stoborough, towards the support of a *schoolmaster,* to in There is no more than £28:17t.6d. remaining, which ii placed in the hands of Mr. Gould, who pays interest for it— There is also a piece of ground on Mr. Gould's farm, called Kitchen Plot, which, report says, was a gift by one of his ancestors to the poor of this parish, to cut Furze:— '" another place on Elwell Down, called "the Poor's Lot," an i used for the same purpose:— ther lands, called "the Feoffee Lands," in Upway, belonging to the poor of Blandiord Fen the write. and eaat accounts. and other good learning; and a fit person was to be nominated by the mayor and corporation to the said churches when vacant, who was to be the school master; but finding it difficult to procure a clergyman to accept it, it was agreed with the son of the donor, that hel should present and allow £25 f annum in lieu thereof but this agreement was not reduced to writing, or if so it was lost, and the witness thereof dead. The affairs were litigated some years in Chancery, till, in 1754, the will was declared void, the donor being only tenant for life, therefore it was settled that the school should be established at a salary of „£25; the appointment of the master to belong solely to the descendants of the donor and his successorst...

Henry Harbin, of London, merchant, by will, dated 19 July, 1703, gave £200, afterwards laid out in land, situate at or near Wimborne Minster, which produces „£10 ann paid to a person to instruct the poor children of this town in the English tongue, and the interest of „£50 to be added if the principal was not sufficient; vested in H. Bankes, esq.

ALMSHOUSE.

Jomf SrHECHEs.of Exeter, Esq. by will, dated, (soon!

after 1435,) founded an almshouse for the lodging, cloth' ing, and maintaining six poor men and five poor women decayed housekeepers of this borough, and endowed the same with land at Baileyridge Farm, in the parish of Lillington, Ulwell Farm, and a Mill in Swanwich and Eangton Matravers, 16 messuages and gardens in Wareham, the foreshare of two acres of meadow in H'estport Farm, three pieces of arable and pasture on the north and south sides of Broadway in Worgrett, and a chief rent of 5s. yearly out of North Bestwall Farm; vested in the mayor and corporation

Bernard Mitchell, by will, dated 22 March, 1646. charged some lands with the payment of 20s. yearly, to the industrious poor of Wareham; vested in the minister and churchwardens—see Melcombe Regis

Lady Elizabeth Holford, relict of Sir William, by will, dated 19 November, 1717, charged her lands, called *Marsh Farm*, in Bloxworth, and a messuage

and three closes of land, called Green Closes, and pasture land called Parson's Close, and a moor called Soutbbrook, in Beer Regis, devised to John Harbin, of Portsmouth, in 1786, belonging to *Mr. Shirley*, with the payment of,£10 ann. J the profits thereof to be given to the industrious poor of thisl town who received no parish relief; vested in the minister) and churchwardens................

Mr.Stephen BiitD.lateof Wareham, cordwainer, by will dated 27 June, 1806, gave the interest of all his monies and effects, to be distributed amongst the poor inhabitants of this borough and town, yearly, on the 26 November, and directed that his will should be read in the parish church of *Lady St. Mary*, Wareham, once in every three years, at the time of distributing such interest, or in default thereof, that it should be idistributed in like manner amongst the poor inhabitants residing on Portsmouth Common; vested in the executors of deceased, and the minister and church wardens 231-WESTON, BUCKHORN.

Extracted from the Poor Book, dated June 5, 1720.

"The interest of,£18 principal money, heretofore bequeathed to the second poor of this parish, by the piety of cert well disposed persons, was distributed this day." MEMORANDUM.

"With the approbation and consent of the parish, We, the churchwardens and overseers, that we might secure the *above-mentioned legacies*, for the use to which they were designed, (some part of the principal money being, for want of good security, lost already) have, with the residue of the said money, purchased the land of an house and backside, adjoining to the common, on the north side of New Gate; which house and backside is to be applied to sush uses, as the officers and principal inhabitants of our parish shall at any time think most convenient:—And we do hereby oblige ourselves and successors, to pay lawful interest for the abovesaid „£18 once every year, to the second BESCRlrTlON of die CHARITY, by i fi.en. when, and for what purpose c!"2 si J poor of our parish for ever; which money is to be distributed at the discretion

of the minister, churchwardens, and overseers, to poor persons not receiving monthly pay." 232-WEYMOUTH And MELCOMBE REGIS. WEYMOUTH.

Lady Browne, by will, dated, 1632, gave £50 in money, the interest to be paid yearly to the poor of Wey. mouth; vested in the corporation

Note—This was Mary, the daughter of Lewis Williams of Shitterton, esq. who was the wife of Thos. Browne, of Frampton, esq.

Arnold De Sei.lanova, M. D. of Weymouth, by will, dated, 10H4, gave j5 in money, the interest to be, paid yearly to the poor of Weymouth; vested in ditto...

Ditto, by ditto, gave a leasehold shop in Weymouth, which1 lease is supposed to have expired; vested in the church wardens

Jonathan Taylor, Esq. of Lyme Regis, by will, dated 24 Aug. 1753, gave i7j in money, since laid out in the purchase of stock,.£235, Navy 5 cent., now reduced to 3.J cent. for the maintenance of eight poor boys at school, to be instructed in the art of navigation, forever; vested! in the corporation, minister, and churchwardens...

Ditto, by ditto, gave a sum of money to be distributed to 50 poor persons not receiving alms; vested in ditto, and duly distributed

Bernard Mitchell, by will, dated22 March. 1646, gave: a rent charge issuing out of his freehold lands, for the poor of this parish, one moiety of ten bushels of sea coals yearly, to be paid in money; vested in the parish officers— see *Melcombe Regis*...

John Carswell, by deed, dated 16 April, 1741, gave some land, situate at Weymouth, the rents and profits thereof to be paid to four poor widows, upon a supposition that the toleration act should cease, or there should be no dissenting meeting or minister in Melcombe or Weymouth; vested in the dissenting minister for the time being : Thii will was litigated in Chancery, and about the year 1768, the principal, with ten jeart interest, was paid to the treasurer of the corporation, viz. *£28*, and because the purposes of this legacy have been but lately fully known, it hath been hitherto unapplied, but the trust me t» apply it as soon as they can procure a sufficient master.

Jonathan Edwards and Rebecca his wife, by deed, dated 14 Jan. 1716, (in trust, after the death of Thomas Dyer, who was buried 28 Dec. 1748,) gave in land, called the *Brickfield,* in Weymouth, on which four cottages have been lately built for four poor widows of Weymouth side only; vested in the corporation, minister, and parish officers of Weymouth MELCOMBE REGIS.

Lady Browne, by will, dated, 1(132, gave „£50 in1 money, the interest to be paid yearly to the poor of Mel combe; vested in the corporation

Ditto, by ditto, gave, in money, the interest to be paid to the repairs of Me!combe Regis church; vested in ditto

Arxoid De Sellanova, M. D. of Weymouth, by will dated, 1684, gave £5 in money, the interest to be paid1 yearly to the poor of Melcombe; vested in ditto...

William Hodder, by will, dated, 1688, gave „£10 in money, the interest thereof to be applied yearly to the poor of Melcombe Regis; vested in ditto

Jonathan Taylor, Esq. of Lyme Regis, by will, dated 24 August, 1753, gave a sum of money to purchase bread for fifty poor men and women who do not receive alms, which was distributed accordingly; vested in ditto

Sir Samuel Mico, Knt. citizen and merchant in London, by will, dated 25 Sept. 1665, proved 26 May, 1666, gave £500 in money, since laid out in the purchase of land at *Usmingtou,* the rents of which (after deducting 20s. for a sermon), to be distributed to ten poor decayed seamen in the borough and town; vested in the corporation

Ditto, by ditto, gave certain lands, viz. the *George Inn* which lets for £55:13s.; also a cellar for 10, and a shop for £13, the profits and produce to be employed to bind out poor boys apprentices; vested in the corporation...

Robert Middleton, by, dated, ., gave,£100 to be divided and lent to four young merchants in this town, for three years, at £5 cent *V* annum, which was to be given weekly in bread, for the use of the poor; and at the! end of three

years the monoy to be paid, and lent to four other young merchants on their bond. Id the year ltilri this was lent to Henry Knight, Owen Molman, William Pitt, and William Williams, and seems to have been regularly lent to one set of young people, till the civil wars, when the papers and records of this town were burnt or destroyed; and about the year 1664, this money was reduced to A'50, and then lent to *two* merchants. How it was lessened does not appear. In 16H5, one Swetman was prose, cuted for his part of the money, and £ 25 seems then to have been lost; and from that period no other circum stances occur, than paying annually £1: 5s. to the over seers for the use of the poor, which continues to this day; vested in the treasurer of the corporation, &c....

Madame Elizabeth Haysom, by deed, dated, 1704,! gave,£30 in money, to bind out three poor boys appren tices, viz. S. Holmead, E. Harvey, and H. Chick; which was done accordingly...

Bernard Mitchell, by will, dated 22 March, 1646' gave a rent charge, issuing out of his freehold lands called the *King's Head Inn,* in this parish and town, for the poor thereof, one moiety of ten bushels of sea coals yearly, to be paid in money; vested in the parish officers...

Note—The whole of this charity is paid by the *Lessee* of the King's Head Inn, viz.—Abbotsbury, £ 1; Beer Regis, £; Bridport, £1; Fleet 13s. 4d.; Langton Herring, 13s. 4d, Milborne St. Andrew, £; Milborne Stileham, £; Weymouth, £1:13s. 4d.; Melcombe Regis, 12s.; Ware, ham,,£1; Wimborne Minster,,£1; Wyke Regis £ : 13s. 4d.

N. B.—There is a sum of money paid in charity arising out of the Town Marsh, viz.,£1:2s. 8d. to Melcombe, and £1:10s. to Weymouth.

233-WH1TECHURCH CANON1CORUM
Rorert Salter, by will, dated, 1642, gave,£300 in money, since laid out in lands called *Cattlebury,* or *Cat tlt-borotigh,* in this parish, for the benefit of the poor of this DESCRIPTION of the CHARITY, by whom, when, and for what purpoie parish and Charmouth, and the

hospital at Allington, (belonging to Bridport). The share to this parish is *(see Bridport Charities* -mabshwood— *None.* 234-WHITECHURCH W1NTER-BORNE.

-mr. Jonx Hutchinson, by will, dated, 1780, orl thereabouts, gave „£100 in money, which was distributed among the poor of this parish at *three* payments James Duke, by will, dated, 1781, or thereabouts, gave

'10 in money, to be distributed as above; vested in his executors...

Note—This money has not been paid, and an action has! been commenced against Duke, the executor. 235-WHIT-COMBE—*None.* (236-W1MBORNE MINSTER. ST. Marqaret's Hospital. some land in this parish, (about 34 acres), and founded an almshouse, called St. Margaret's, for the support of ruw almswomen, and *five* almsmen; vested in H. Bankes, esq.

Thomas Boxley, hy will, dated 5 October, 1561, gave some land, called *Rowlands,* in this parish, for the benefit of St. Margaret's Hospital; vested in John Tory, Samuel Bugden, Matthew Raindle, and Thomas Raindle

William Stone, Clerk, by will, dated 12 May, 1685, gave some land in this parish for the benefit of this hospital; vested in the Rev. Sir James Hanham, ban.

THE HOSPITAL OR ALMSHOUSE OF GERTRUDE,

MARCHIONESS OF EXETER.

Gertrude Courtney, *Marchioness of* Enter, by will, dated 27 May, 1557, gave some land, situate at Canford BBSCRIF-TION of the CHARITY, by whom, when, and for what purpose given.

M;igna. for the support of six poor men and women, and for building them six houses to dwell in; vested in the heirs of the late Sir John Webb, bart.

SCHOOL AND ALMSHOUSE AT PAMPHILL.
Koger Gillingham, of the Middle Temple, London. Esq. by will, dated 2 July, 1695, gave some lands at Little Shalford, co. *Cambridge,* for the support of a schoolmaster, and four men and four women; vested in the governers of Queen Elizabeth's free grammar school *ote*—No account was returned of the

free grammar school in this town, founded by Queen Elizabeth in the 5th year of her reign, 1562, the particulars of which may be seen in *Hutchint's JIUt. of Dorset, vol. 2, p. 540.*

GENERAL CHARITIES.

Thomas Boxley, by will, dated 5 October, 1561, gave a moiety of a meadow, called *Rushly,* for the benefit of the poor, at the discretion of tbf trustees; vested in John Tory. Samuel Bugden, Matthew Raindle, and Thomas Kaindle

Joseph Collett, by deed, dated 5 Dec. 1622, gave some lands, situate at Corfe Castle, for the relief of five poor men and five poor women; vested in late Henry YVm. Fitch, Esq. and William Russell

Alice Brown, *widow,* by will, dated 2 June, 1637, gavel some land in this parish for the use of the poor, viz. to six poor unmarried women; vested in lata Henry Wm. Fitch, esq. William Russell, gent. Thomas Fitch, clerk, Wm Leer, gent, and Thomas Basket, surgeon, trustees—

Richard Hapgood, by will, dated 1 Dec. 1642, gave two messuages and gardens in this parish, for the above purpose; vested in the said trustees—

Edith Hall, *widow,* daughter of the said Richard Hapgood, by deed, dated 24 October, 1683, gave some land at , for the above purpose; vested in the said trustees.— *Tlie three preceding donations amount to ...*

Mart Gundry, *widow* of John Gundry, by will, dated 23 Feb. 1617, gave a yearly rent, issuing out of a farm at Walford, in this parish, for the use of the poor; vested in the overseers DESCRIPTION of the CHARITY, by whom, when, and for what purpose, given.

IS a mentof a charity school, for the instruction of twenty poor boys, viz. ten from this parish, six from Leigh, and four from Chetnole, in reading, writing, and arithmetic. By a decree in Chancery, this money was laid out in the purchase of lands lying at *Knighton,* two miles.from Yetminster vested in the Earl of Ilchester, Earl of Digby, Arthurj Cosens, esq. Wm. Jenkins, clerk, and Bartho. Watts, gent

Dame Dorothy Gorges, by will, dated,

gave pounds in money, for the relief of poor persons and decayed tradesmen, inhabitants of this parish, and for bind ing apprentice the children of poor persons of the same parish, as the trustees should think proper: with this money, Woolley Miller, esq. the brother and executor of the will of the donor, purchased lands in the parish of Byme Intrinseca, as he was impowered; vested in the late Kev Wm. Jenkins, John Jenkins, William Warry, gent. and Arthur Cosens, esq....

John Dowkion, *Clerk,* by will, dated, 1625, gave 20s. a year, payable out of land, lying at Beer Hackett, to the intent that the curfew bell might be rung at this parish church, at four in the morning, and eight at night constantly

10s. for each; vested in...

bote—This custom is continued during the winter season only.

John Ball, Gent, by deed, dated, 1716, or thereabouts, gave some land, purchased of Mr. Henry Bishop, lying at' *Wootton Glanville,* to trustees, for the purpose of paying, an assistant curate for this parish church, and to the intent that divine service should be performed there every Sunday morning throughout the year. The estate nets about *,£25* annum; 50s. is paid thereout yearly in bread, distributed every six weeks to the second poor of this parish; 20s. for a sermon to be preached by the assisting minister on *Shrove Tuesday,* at this parish church; and 20s. for a sermon to be preached on *Holy Thursday,* by the minister of Cerne Abbas. the remainder to the assisting minister or curate of the vicar of this parish; vested in the late Warren Lisle and Bar tholomew Watts, gents.

Annual Produce.

£. s. d. 40- DESCRIPTION of the CHARITY, by whom, given.

I for what purpoMrg

Thomas Ring, Gent, by will, dated, 173(5, gave 10s a year, to be issuing and payable for ever, out of his lands lying at, in trust, to be given to the poor of this parish, annually on *St. 'Ihomas's Day*; vested in...

Lady Gorges, by, dated, 1739, or thereabouts gave,£200 in money, for

augmenting the vicarage-house of this parish; „£200 more, as is usual, was paid out of! Queen Anne's bounty; with part of which monies an estate) in the adjacent parish of Thornford was purchased, which produces £13:13s. clear 1 annum; and there now remains; *J_* 98:18s. 4d. in the treasurer's hands, to be laid out for the same purpose; vested in ditto

John Reynolds, by will, dated, gave the sum of 20s.

V annum, charged on his lands called *Whettles,* in this parish, to be distributed to the poor in bread; vested in —

Mrs. Bowring, of Kingston, by deed, dated 12 March. 1811, gave.£145:14s. 6d., 3 ? cent. Consols, the dividends arising therefrom to be distributed f.t *Christmas* annually, amongst six poor old widows of this parish; vested in the vicar and churchwardens

Leigh. 11R. Read, of Upway, by deed, dated, gave „£50 Navy 5 Cents. , the dividends arising therefrom to be distributed in bread at *Christmas* annually, to the poor of this parish; vested in the vicar and other trustees...

John Bridle, Gent, by deed, dated, 1779, gave an annuity of,£'5, issuing and payable for ever, out of his lands at Leigh, to be laid out in bread at *Christmas,* yearly, and to be distributed to the poor of Leigh, not receiving pay of the parish. The present owner of the estate is ; vested in the vicar of Yetminster, and the church wardens of Leigh for the time being

Robert Bridle, by will, dated 20 April, 1779, gave out of land in this tithing, to the poor of this place not receiving alms, £5 yearly; vested in Mr. Bartholomew

Watts, of Sherborne...

Note—In this place was also formerly given, on a *Good.*

Friday, 24 penny loaves of bread. This has been

DESCRIPTION of the CHARITY, by whom, when, given.

and for what purpose: 5 J many years discontinued, nor is it known who was thej donor. *Query* if not Sir John Hele— *see Bradford*

Abbas.

COUNTYPAUPER LUNATIC ASYLUM, at Forston, in the Parish of Charminstek.

In the year 1827, Francis John Browne, Esquire, or Frampton, offered to make over to the County, as a voluntary Donation, his Mansion-house, Garden, and Lands" amounting to about seven acres, at Forston, for the Establishment of a Lunatic Asylum, for the benefit of Pauper Lunatics belonging to the several Parishes within the County; and also the sum of £4000, 3 Cent. Consol Ann. towards the endowment thereof.

This munificent offer was gratefully accepted at the Epiphany Sessions, 1828, and steps were immediately taken, under statute 48 Geo. 3, c. 96, then in force, and afterwards under statute 9 Geo. 4, c. 40, which repealed the former statute, for carrying Mr. Browne's intentions into effect.

A private Act of Parliament was afterwards procured, at the further expense of Mr. Browne, which received the Royal Assent on the 21st of March, 1828, for the purpose of securing this donation to the uses proposed; and to avoid any difficulties which might arise from the statutes of mortmain.

It was found necessary to make considerable additions to the house and premises at Forston, in order to render tbem suitable for the reception of patients: and these additions, and the enclosures for the separation and accommodation of the patients, together with the necessary furniture and fittings of %

These four Pages to be pasted in at the end of the Donations, p. 94, and pp. 95 and 96 to be cancelled. DESCRIPTION of the CHARITY, by whom, when, and for what purpose given.

all kinds, have cost something less than £14,000, of which sum above £3000 sterling was raised by voluntary subscrip. tions, and the rest by *special* County Rates, ordered fron: time to time, and by loans payable by instalments, undei the provisions of the above-mentioned statutes. All the expenses attending the maintenance, care, and clothing, of the patients, and the wages and subsistence of the officers and servants, are borne by the *weekly rate* charged on the respective parishes

to which the paupers belong, aided, as to the salaries of the officers, by the dividends arising from the donation of Mr. Browne towards the endowment of the asylum. Repairs and other expenses are borr.e by the county. A fund has also been created, by legacies and voluntary donations, which is applied towards extraordinary and contingent expences. The asylum was opened for the reception of patients on the 1st August, 1832. It is calculated to contain about 35 male, and 30 female patients. It is superintended and governed by visitors appointed by the Justices in Sessions, who must themselves be acting justices of the peace, and who have framed a set of Rules and Regulations for its management. The officers and servants, consisting of a *Medical Siiperintendant,* a *Matren,* and as many Keepers and Nurses as may be thought necessary from time to time, are appointed by the visitors.

The present *Medical Superintendani* is Mr. Geo. Wallett, whose salary, fixed by the visitors, is, £140 annum.

The present *Matron* is Mrs. Fran Ces White Parsons.

Her salary is annum.

The superintendant and matron reside constantly at the asylum.

The Treasurer, Rorert Pattisojt, Esq. is also appointed by the visitors.

The Chaplain is appointed by the Justices in Sessions. The present Chaplain is the Rev. Dacre Clemetsojt. His salary of £50 *V* annum is paid by the county.

The present Clerk to the Visitors is Mr. Thomas Fooks,

the Clerk of the Peace for the county, who receives an additional salary of £25, for his trouble, which is paid by the county.

DESCRIPTION" of the CHARITY, by whom, when, and for what purpose giyen.

-KINSON, in CANKORD MAGNA, *seep.* 17.

John Weare, by will, dated, 1667, gave in land at , the profits thereof to be given to the poor of Kinson

Cudnell and Knsbury, in Canford Magna parish; vested in the heirs of the late Isaac Gulliver DORCHESTER, see p.

28.

Matthew Chubb—*for* £1000 *read* £500.

Henry Edwards, by, dated, (hedied 1610.) gave an annuity, payable out of his lands in Pease-Lane, heretofore the lands of Thomas Channing, and now of the Rev. J. Davis, to be divided in support of the poof of the threej parishes; vested in —— -FIFEHEAD MAGDALEN, *see p.* 35., by, dated, (since the year 1679,)

Annual Produce!

gave £30 in money, the interest thereof to be distributed to the second poor of this parish; vested in the parish officers -JJTTON CHENEY, see p. 46,

Thomas Hollis, Esq. by deed, dated, (about the year 1771,) gave a schoolhouse and two acres of land, for the residence and further support of the master; vested in the late.Brand Hollis, Esq. and others...

Hippolet Mocket, by will, dated 20 Sept. 1653, gave £25 in money, the interest thereof to be distributed yearly to the poor of this parish; vested in the heirs of the late J. Richards, *Clerk...* , by, dated, gave out of an estate late *Turner's,* for the relief of poor widows, 6s. 8d. yearly; vested in Turner...........

-LYTCHET MATRAVERS—*None-seep.* 49. -STOKE EAST and HOLME EAST-see*p.* 77.

The Right Hon. Nathaniel Bond, by will, dated 7th October, 1823, gave the sum of „£l00, to be laid out under sufficient securities, by his executors in trust, and the interest thereof to be paid to the officiating minister for the time leing, in support of a *Sunday School* in the parish o

East Stoke. The sum of money above mentioned, minus the legacy duty, was invested in the savings' bank; but in consequence of a regulation enforced in that establishment it was withdrawn. In 1837. at the request of the surviving, trustees, the sum of 90 was received by the Rev. Nath. Bond, on the above account, and a bond was given by him to pay the interest, amounting to „£3:4s. 6d. annum, as the will directs; vested in the Rev. Wm. Bond and Charlton Byam Wollaston, esq. the surviving trustees.

...., *Note*—Besides the above legacy, there were several sums of money given to the poor of Holme East, Stoke *East,* and Steeple parishes, which werB distributed immediately after the death of the donor, as he directed by his will.
-MARTINSTOWN—*seep.* 50.

Blanchars, by will, dated the day of — gave, in money, £ , for the use of the second poor, not receiving alms in this parish; vested in Thomas Balston, esq. and his heirs THE END.

Holnest
Holt
Holton
Holworth N. S. and B.... Holy Trinity...
Trinity...
Trinity...
Honybrook
Honey com be...
PACES.
Netherbury
Hilton
Whitechurch Cann'
Worth Matravers
Charminster
Lydlinch
Wareham
Okeford Child...
Gussage St. Michael
Cattistock
Askerswell
Ditto
Shapwick
Witchampton...
Sturminster Marshall
Ditto Buckland Newton
Charminster
Swanwich
Stoke East
Cattistock
Canford Magna...
Bothenhampton...
Bere Regis
Wimborne
Minterne Magna
Sydling St. Nicholas
Netherbury
Whitechurch Cann
lwerne Minster...
Melcombe Regis
Whitechurch Cann'.
Lydlinch
Alton Pancras...
Cattistock
Ditto
Ditto Buckland Ripers Cranborne
Stoke East
Longburton
Wimbome
Wareham
Milton Abbas...
Dorchester
Shafton *alias* Shaftesbury
Wareham
Wimborne

Broad winsor...
113 82 100 103 82-118-123-140-155 75
85 99-113-120 90 81-112-123-134-146
81 81-117-123-139-154 74 69 6« 93
102 97 97 72 82-113-123-135-148 82-
110-123-132-144 75 97-114-124-128
96 73 73 71 70-114-120 101 88 98-113-
123-135-149 82-115-123-136-150 89
101 82-115-123-138-152 82-115-123-
138-151 83-117-123-139-154 82-115-
123-137-150 100 101 84 69 73 73 73
72 78-115-122 82-114-123-135-149 96-
114-127 73-118-123-140-155 102 100
88-114-125 78-111-122-132-144 93-
117-127-139-153 99-114-136-129-150
m 71 PLACES.
Hooke... ...
Hookeswood
HonJiill
Horsych 11 or ton
Houndstreet
Houg.ton Wintetborne... Huisn lluish
Uuish
Hull or Hill...
Hull or Boyswood
HuNDREDSBARROW H".
Hungerhill North
————South
Huntleford
Hur lands
Hurst
Hurstoneshay...
Hussey's or Browne's
Husey
Hyde
Hyde or Stoke Hyde
Hyde
Hyde
Hyde
Hyde / PARISHES.
Farnham
Stoke Abbas
Cranborne
Sherborne
Milton Abbas... Zelston Wintetborne
Sydling St. Nicholas Iwetne Minster...
Mappowder
Wareham Stoke East Gillingharo
Netherbury Moreton
Whitechurch L'ann' BJandford St.
Mary
Burstock
Frampton
Tarrant Hinton...
Lydlinch l'iddletown

Stalbridge
Steeple
Kingston Winterborne...
, Maurward
Russel
Kingswood
Kingcouibe Over
Nether
Kir son or Kingston
Kinson
Knapshill
Knaveswell
Knighton West...
Knighton
Knighton
Knighton East...
Knighton West...
Knighton
Knight Street...
Knitson or A il wood
Knolle
Knowle Church...
Knowle
Knowle *alias* Knoll
Knowxton Hukd1 or Knowlhill
Beer Reiris
Stinsford l.ongbredy
Langton 'Matravers
Toller Porcorum
Ditto
Canford Magna
Haselbury Bryan
Buckland Newton
Corfe Castle
Beer Hackett...
Durweston
Winfrith Newburgh
Ditto
Canford Magna
Marnhull
Ijangton Matraverse
Netherbury
Buckland Newton
Lulworth East...
Horton 70-113-124-136-149 95 85-
110-124-132-144 84 98-111-128 98-
112-128-130 73-115-124-138-152 HI *n*
76 83-110-124-132-144 70 79-115-122
102 102 73 86 84 90 84-113-124-135-
149 72-113-121 85 116 82-116-129
Lady St. Mary...
Lake...
Lane House
Langley
Langdon

Gussage All Saints
  Ahner, West,...
Netherbury
  Poorstock
  Iwerne Minster...
  Bloxworth
Ibberton
  Whitechurch Cann'
  Ditto Steepleton Wint.'
  Stock Gay lard...
  Loders...
  Horton
  Cattistock
  Netherbury
  Melbury Abbas
Do.
  Melcombe Horsey
  Regis
  Bingham Melplaish, East
  West
  Merley
Merryiield
Michaels tone...
Michels
  Middleborough, E. & W.
Middlemarsh...
M iddlestreet
Milborne St. Andrew
  Churchstone...
  Stileham
  Milton Abbas...
onStour...
  West...
  Minchington
Minterne Magna
  Parva...
  Modbury
Monkwood Hill...
Monkwooi Hill
  Monkton-up Wimbokne Hundred
  Melcombe Horsey
Netherbury
Do.
  Canford Magna...
Cattistock
  Milborne St. Andrew
Dewlish
Wareham
Minterne Magna
Spettisbury
  Milborne St. Andrew
Bere Regis
  Gillingham
Poorstock
Handley

Buckland Newton
  Swyre...
  Buckland Newton
Mappowder
... 07 ... 101 ... 89 ... 78 ... 81 ...86-117-124-139-154 ... 09-116 ... 90 86-111-120-122-124-134-147 ... 91 ... 06-113-124-135-149 ... 03-116-125-139-153 ... 06-117-125-139-154 ... 71 ... 83 .. 101 101-112-125-126-129-134-147 ... 95 .. . 87-110-125-133-145 ... 96 ... 85-112-124 ... 82 ... 74 ... 90 ... 07-125-139-153 ... 07-116-125 ... 07-116-125 ... 07-113-125-135-149 ... 87-118-125-140-155 . .. 87-110-125-132-144 ... 87-113-125-135-149 ... 100-111-129-133-145 ... 07 ... 89-111-125 73 74 07 87 99 88-113-125 94 07-115-125-137-150 07-115-125 70-114-125-137-150 87-115-125-137-150 80-117-123 91-112-126 03-116-123 8M13-125-135-149 72-113-121 97 72 86 115-116 78-116-122. 08-115-125-137-150 88-110-125-132-144 81 91 100
  Nailers
Nash-
Nash...
  Court
  Netherbury *in terra* in *ecclesia*
  Netherhay
Nethercombe...
Netherstoke
Nettlecombe
  Tout
  Newburgh
  Newland or Newton Mont' Newland
  Newland Borough
  Newmill...
  Newnbam
  Newton Peverell
  Newton
  Newton
  Newton
  Newton
  Newton
  Netherbrook
  Noke
  Norbrook
Nordon
Northport
Northover
  Northaven Point or Coles
North Mills
  Cary
  Nottington

Notton
Nutford
Nyland Upper and Lower.
  Whitechurch Cann'
  Morden, East...
Sturminster Marshall
Marnhull
  Perrot, South...
Gillingham
Swanwich
Bradford Peverell
Piddlehinton...
Kingston Wint'
  Askerswell
Broadwinsor
Marsh wood
Marnhull
  Netherbury Do.
Broadwinsor
Sherborne
Halstock
Poorstock
Melcombe Horsey
Mappowder
Wootton Glanville
Batcombe
Sherborne
Corfe Caslle
Stalbridge
  Sturminster Marshall
Coombe Keynes...
Sturminster Newton
Studland
Swanwich
Hilton...
  Buckland Newton Ditto
Swanwich
Corfe Castle
Wareham
Frampton
Canford Magna
Wareham
Ditto
Broadway
Maiden Newton
Blandford Forum
Keinton Magna...
  Corscombe   Canford   Magna..
Coombe Keynes
  Marsh wood 100 88-116-125-138-152 88-116-125 96 8b' 88-114-125-136-149 91-1!1-125-134-147 80-117-125-139-153 97 71-110 92 70-114-124 71 100 86 88-111-125-134-147 71 94-117-127 81 91-112-126 87 86 103 70-

113-120 94-117-127 76 94 96 76 97 96 97 82 72 72 97 76 100 80 78 100 100 71 86 70-91 83 77 73 76 90-118-125-140-156 101

Okeford, Child

Shilling t'itzpaine

Okerswood

Ola Hill

Orchard

West

Bast...

East and West...

Organford

Organford

Oschill

Osmington

Otterhay or Dotterhay... Overcoombe

Owermoigne Liberty

Owermoigne

Ower

P,

Pain's Place...

Pallington......

Pamphill

Paradise

Park

Park

Parkpale

Parkmead

Parkston

Parley West...

Parnharn

Pelsham

Pegges

Pentridge

Perrot South

Perry Court

Petersham

Phillips

Philliholds

Phillipson

Phillyholme

Picket...

Piddletrenthide L. Piddletrenthide...

PIDDLEHINTON LIB'...

Piddlehinton

PIDDLETOWN HUND'...

Piddletown

Pierston and Milton

Pilsdon

Pimperne Hundred...

Pimperne

—— Warnership

Pinford

Pipsford

Plumber

Plush

Pollingston

Pomise

Affpiddle

Coombe Keynes

Whitechurch Cann'.

Fontmell Magna

Iwerae Minster...

Knowle

Wareham

Lytchett Minster

Wootton Glanville

Loders

Sherborne

Corfe Castle

Motcombe

Affpiddle

Wimborne Minster

Netherbury

St. Martin Winterborne..

Broadwinsor

Tollpiddle

Wyke Regis...

Canford Magna...

Netherbury

Buckhorn Weston lwerne Minster...

Sturminster Newton

Wimborne Minster

Corfe Castle

Bere Regis

Wimborne St. Giles

Hawkchurch

Perrot South

Gillingham

Blandford Forum

Sherborne

Corscombe & Mapperton..

Lydlinch

Buckland Newton

Charminster

Netherbury 90-117-125-140-154 90-117-125-140-154 90-117-125-140-154 69 76 100 79-116-125-139-153 83-116-125-139-153 84 100 97 103 90-110-125-132-144 85 94-117-127 111 90-111-125-133-145 77-114-122 80 69 102 89 87 71 98 103 73-115-124-126-138-152 90-116-126-138-152 90 100 83 91-116-126-138-152 91-112-126-134-147 97 102-116-129 77 70 101-116-129 82-112-123 91 113 92-113-126-135-149 111 92-111-126-133-145 110-115 92-110-126-133-145 80 91-112-126-134-147 115-117 91-115-126-

137-150 70-115-120 94-118-127 77 85 72-113-121 75 PLACES.

P0OR8TOCJC LIBERTY..

Poorstock

Poorton North...

—— South...

Portisham

Portland Liberty..

Portland

Potwell

Povington Poxwell Poynings Preston or Peason

Tarrant...

Preston

Primesly

Priors Down

Pulham

West

East

Grove...

Puncknowle

Putton

Pymore

Q.

Quarr...

Quarleston Winterborne..

Poorstock

Broadwinsor

Tyneham

Lulworth West...

Iwerne Minster...

Gillingham

Crawford Tarrant

S!-erborne

Stalbridge

Pulham

Ditto

Ditto

Chicke'ri'll West

Loders

Worth Matravers Stickland Wint' 112 91-112-126-134-147 91-111-126-134-147 91-111-126 92-110-126-133-145 HI 91-111-126-133-146 72 99-114 92-110-126-133-145 102 83 80-117 78-115-126 92-111-426-133-145 94 94 92-135-149 92-113-126 92-113-126 92-113-126 92-110-126-133-145 75-111-121 85 103 95-115-127

Ray ton or Reforne

Racedown

Radipole

Ratnsbury *alias* Ridge

Rampishatn

Ranston